THE PALACE GATES HAGGADAH

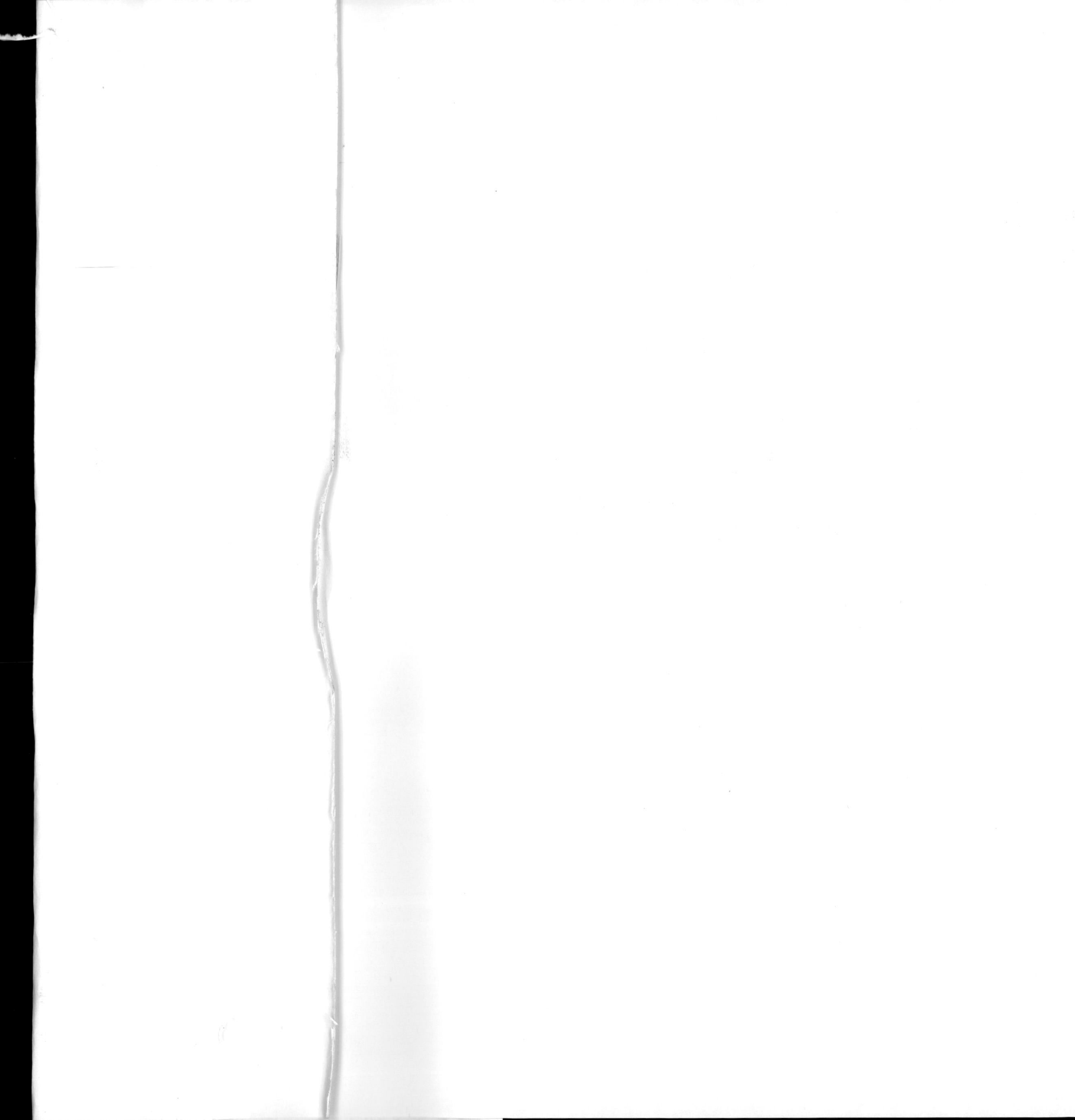

הגדה של פסח

THE PALACE GATES HAGGADAH

Parables for the Pesach Seder

compiled by
Rabbi Shalom Wallach

Translated by
Avraham Sutton

With an interpretative translation of
Shir Hashirim

FELDHEIM PUBLISHERS
Jerusalem/New York

Originally published in 1995 in Hebrew as
Sha'arei Armon, Meshalim La-Haggadah Shel Pesach
by Tevunah Publishers

First published 1995
ISBN 0-87306-703-7

Copyright © 1995 by
Shalom Wallach and Feldheim Publishers

All rights reserved.
No part of this publication may be translated, reproduced, stored in a retrieval system or transmitted, in any form or by any means, electronic, mechanical, photocopying, recording, or otherwise, without permission in writing from the publishers.

FELDHEIM PUBLISHERS
200 Airport Executive Park
Nanuet, NY 10954
POB 35002 / Jerusalem, Israel

Printed in Israel

10 9 8 7 6 5 4 3 2 1

Translator's Introduction

The annual recurrence of Pesach is one of the highlights of the Jewish calendar year. Pesach is all-encompassing. Every facet of our lives undergoes transformation during the seven days of this Festival. For the essence of Pesach is not only to remember, but to relive the Exodus from Egypt. By speaking about the Exodus, delving into the meaning of its miracles, and performing the commandments specifically associated with it, we come to know and feel what our ancestors experienced. Most importantly, we internalize the Exodus in our own lives. We come to believe and know that Hashem's providence is never inoperative in the history of our people and in our personal lives.

There are many laws and commandments that are unique to Pesach. By the time Seder night arrives, everyone has surely participated in clearing the house of bread and all chametz (leavening substances). Some have even had the opportunity of baking matzos. Eating matzos and not eating or even seeing chametz are both a fulfillment of the commandment, "[Since] unleavened bread must be eaten for seven days, no leaven or leavening substance may be seen anywhere in your territories [during this time]" (*Shemos* 13:6-7). Since these commandments are performed only once a year, they are a constant source of renewal for the entire Jewish People.

By far the most exciting part of Pesach is the Seder night. Traditionally, it is on this night that Jewish fathers and mothers transmit the essence of Judaism to their children, dating back to the original Exodus thirty-three hundred years ago. By hearing and telling the miracles of the Exodus, and performing the commandments associated with this night, our children develop a deep faith in Hashem. They learn that the Exodus was not a one-time affair, but rather a sign of Hashem's ongoing providence that has accompanied Yisrael throughout its long and difficult history. They learn that Yisrael's special relationship with Hashem only *began* thirty-three hundred years ago, and that He will ultimately direct history to culminate with the Final Redemption, when He will bring all

His people back to their beloved land and build the Third Beis Ha-Mikdash.

The commandment to tell and retell the Exodus is based on the verse, "And you shall relate to your child on that day, saying: 'It is because of this that Hashem acted for me when I came forth out of Egypt'" (*Shemos* 13:8). "V'higadeta — You must relate," herein is the source for the term *Haggadah shel Pesach*. Actually, Hashem commanded us, "Remember the day you came forth out of the land of Egypt all the days of your life!" (*Devarim* 6:3). It is for this reason that we constantly refer to the Exodus in our prayers during the entire year. However, the night of Pesach was specially set aside for *reliving* the Exodus. On Pesach night, it is not enough to remember the Exodus. We must actually taste and feel what it was like and know that our very lives are extensions of those awesome miracles. This is the meaning of what we say in the Haggadah, "In every single generation one is obligated to look upon himself as if he had gone forth out of Egypt personally. Not only our fathers did the Holy One, Blessed be He, redeem, but us, too, He redeemed together with them." It is also for this reason that we begin the Seder by saying, "We were slaves unto Pharaoh in Egypt," and not, "Our ancestors were slaves." As the Haggadah makes abundantly clear, if Hashem had not taken our ancestors out of Egypt, we would still be slaves.

Reliving the Exodus is vital to the survival of the Jewish People, since it was at the Exodus that we learned the essentials of our faith. We saw that there exists an Omnipotent God, and that He is concerned with Yisrael. We saw that He has the power to change the course of nature and to produce miracles that violate its laws. The Exodus also helps us understand that the world and its laws of nature were actually created by God. This is what Ramban (Rabbi Moshe ben Nachman) writes in his commentary to the Torah (*Shemos* 13:16):

> And now I will declare to you a general principle with regard to the reasons for many commandments. Beginning in the days of Enosh, when idolatry came into existence, people began to err in their beliefs about God. Some denied the root of faith by saying that the world is eternal. They denied the existence of the Eternal God and said it was not He who called the world into existence. Others denied His knowledge of the details of Creation.... [To this day] some admit His knowledge but deny the principle of providence....
>
> When God is pleased to bring about a change in the natural order of the world for the sake of a people or an individual, however, the fallacy of these beliefs becomes known to all, since a supernatural miracle demonstrates that the world has a God Who created it, Who knows it and supervises it, and Who has the power to change it. And when that miracle is decreed beforehand by a prophet, another principle is strengthened, namely, the truth of prophecy, that God speaks to man, that He reveals

His secrets to His servants, the Prophets. In this way, the truth of the entire Torah is confirmed....

And it is through the great miracles that one acknowledges the hidden miracles that constitute the foundation of the whole Torah. For a person does not have a portion in the Torah of our teacher Moshe unless he believes that everything we [are commanded to] do, as well as everything that befalls us, is totally miraculous, beyond any natural law or probability. This principle applies to the community as well as to individuals.

As mentioned, we are not only instructed to tell and speak about the Exodus but to relive it. And what better way to do this than through the medium of parables? The parables of the masters breathe life into us, imbue us with a deeper understanding of what we are doing and saying, and inspire us to break through what is for many a mere rote repetition of religious ritual to the living experience of leaving Egypt and receiving the Torah. Parables help us do exactly what the Haggadah was meant to do: relive the Exodus of our people in order to open our eyes to an entirely new dimension of Divine Providence operating in our own lives. On Pesach, we not only recount the story of liberation from slavery and exodus toward freedom, but we also imbibe it with the wine, the matzos and the bitter herbs. We internalize it. We take it with us and become bearers of its truths.

It is in this spirit that we present *The Palace Gates Haggadah* with its breathtaking array of parables compiled and edited by Rabbi Shalom Wallach of Bnei Brak. Each parable is a jewel, and each nimshal—interpretation a masterfully crafted crown. It is our sincere hope that many will draw inspiration, strength, and conviction for our own day from the deep wellsprings of truth and faith that permeate the *Palace Gates Haggadah* and from the treasure house of parables that accompanies it from beginning to end. In recognizing Hashem's constant providence over the Jewish People, may we all merit His promise of Final Redemption, "As in the days of your exodus from Egypt, I will show them wonders" (*Michah* 7:15).

THE PALACE GATES HAGGADAH

בְּדִיקַת חָמֵץ, בִּטּוּלוֹ וּבִעוּרוֹ

The Search for Chametz Annulling and Destroying Chametz

On the evening of the 14th of Nissan (or, if this falls on Friday night, on the evening of the 13th), every corner of the house must be searched for chametz. Although some families have the custom of putting out ten (well-wrapped) pieces of bread to be found during the search, this is by no means a substitute for making a thorough search for all *chametz present. The search is made by the light of a candle. However, in places where it is more convenient, a flashlight may be used.*

Before starting the search, one is required to make the appropriate berachah. All those who will help in the search should be present and attentive when the berachah is recited by the head of the household or whoever is leading the search, having in mind that it is being said for them, too. Immediately after the recitation of the berachah, one may not speak or delay before beginning the search, and it is preferable not to speak at all until the search has been completed, except when necessary for the performance of the search. One should have the intention that this berachah is not only for the search but also for the annulling of the chametz immediately afterward, the burning of the chametz the next morning and the final annulling after that. The berachah is as follows:

בָּרוּךְ אַתָּה יהוה אֱלֹהֵינוּ מֶלֶךְ הָעוֹלָם אֲשֶׁר קִדְּשָׁנוּ בְּמִצְוֹתָיו וְצִוָּנוּ עַל בִּעוּר חָמֵץ:

Blessed be You, Hashem our God, King of the universe, Who has sanctified us by His commandments and commanded us concerning the removal of chametz.

At this point, all remaining chametz which is unknown to the head of the household is to be annulled. The following declaration is not a prayer *but an act which, in order to be valid, must be understood. Therefore, it should be said in a language understood by the one reciting it.*

כָּל חֲמִירָא וַחֲמִיעָא דְּאִכָּא בִרְשׁוּתִי. דְּלָא חֲמִיתֵּהּ וּדְלָא בִעַרְתֵּהּ וּדְלָא יָדַעְנָא לֵיהּ. לִבָּטֵל וְלֶהֱוֵי הֶפְקֵר כְּעַפְרָא דְאַרְעָא:

All leaven and leavened products in my possession, which I have neither seen nor removed nor know about, shall be deemed of no value and ownerless like the dust of the earth.

On the morning of the 14th of Nissan (if it is not Shabbos) during the fifth hour of the day (see tables on pages 286-9 for local times), all chametz previously put aside or left over from breakfast is to be burned. After it has been burned, a declaration annulling all remaining chametz must be said in a language understood by the one reciting it. If erev Pesach is on Shabbos, then the chametz from the search is burned on Friday morning, and the declaration is said on Shabbos morning, at the regular time, after disposing of any leftover chametz from the meal by flushing it down the drain. The declaration is as follows:

כָּל חֲמִירָא וַחֲמִיעָא דְּאִכָּא בִרְשׁוּתִי. דַּחֲזִתֵּהּ וּדְלָא חֲזִתֵּהּ דַּחֲמִתֵּהּ וּדְלָא חֲמִיתֵּהּ דְּבִעַרְתֵּהּ וּדְלָא בִעַרְתֵּהּ. לִבָּטֵל וְלֶהֱוֵי הֶפְקֵר כְּעַפְרָא דְאַרְעָא:

All leaven and leavened products in my possession, whether I have seen them or not, whether I removed them or not, shall be deemed of no value and ownerless like the dust of the earth.

On the evening of the 14th of Nissan...every corner of the house must be searched for chametz.

Our Sages (*Berachos* 17a) have informed us that in addition to chametz referring to any physical substance which causes fermentation or leavening, it is a symbol representing the yetzer ha-ra (evil inclination). What candle must we use to search for this second kind of chametz? How should we search with it? What will we find in the process? The answers to these questions are found in the following penetrating parable by Rabbi Yehudah Leb Chasman.

A villager once visited the big city for the first time in his life. Understandably, he was awestruck by everything he saw — the tall buildings, the traffic, and all the people — all these fascinated him and made his head swim. Being a man of action, however, he focused his attention on finding something to buy so that he could take it home with him. He saw exquisite suits made of the finest silk. They were not suitable wear for a village where clothes had to be sturdy and warm. He saw valuable ceramics. These too were not practical or useful in a place where everyone used simple earthenware vessels. He saw electric lamps. His village had no electricity. Finally he spotted a pocket flashlight. What a wonderful invention! He could use it to find his way in the dark. The entire village would envy him!

He purchased the flashlight, slipped it into his pocket, and happily continued on his way. As he walked, he noticed a crowd of people gathered on the opposite sidewalk.

"What are they selling?" he asked.

"Tickets for the moving picture," people answered him.

"A moving picture," he wondered out loud, "what's that?"

Everybody there mocked the villager's ignorance, and didn't even bother to explain. Being a man of action, he decided to find out for himself. He stood in line and purchased a ticket. He entered the theater along with all the other moviegoers. They went into a large, dark hall. He followed them in, found a seat, and sat down. He stared in wonder at the huge blank screen at the front of the theater. Suddenly, the screen came to life. People, scenes, action, breathtaking vistas, a wondrous magical world! He thought: What a pity the room is so dark. If this "moving picture" is so special in the dark, think how much better it would be if it were lit up! The villager remembered the little flashlight in his pocket. He took it out, aimed it at the screen and flicked the switch to "on." Suddenly, something very curious happened. The entire spectacle began to fade away until it disappeared altogether!

Shouts and protests could be heard from all sides, "Stop that! Put out the light!"

But the villager defended himself, saying, "What's the big deal? I just wanted to see better!"

"But don't you understand?" they shouted. "Here you can only see in the darkness!"

All the desirable things in this world, all the lures of the yetzer ha-ra...all of them are illusory. Unreal and deceptive, they can only be seen in the absence of light and truth. With just a little bit of light, on the other hand, nighttime comes to an end and the shadows of darkness begin to flee. Their illusory nature revealed, their falsehood is exposed for all to see.

This is the meaning of searching for chametz by the light of a candle, the light of the Torah — of untarnished truth. When this light shines, the evil inclination flies away like a dream.

Or Yahel 63

Every corner of the house must be searched for chametz.

The holy Rabbi Yehoshua of Belz pointed out that the words "bodkin es ha-chametz" literally mean, "search the leaven." This is more than a directive merely to "search the house for leaven." As pointed out before, chametz symbolizes the yetzer ha-ra. It is obviously not sufficient to search for and locate all the various kinds of chametz within. Rather, after we locate them, we must examine the chametz itself! With the light of truth, we must determine its origin, identify the weak spots in our personality through which the yetzer ha-ra gained its unwelcomed entry, and fortify them with extra safeguards. We must cease looking at our lives superficially, and learn to identify the roots of our problems. Then we must learn to uproot these problems and begin anew.

With this penetrating insight, we can understand the following parable that was told by Rabbi Yehoshua's son, Rabbi Yissachar Dov of Belz, to a group of Chassidim one day between Minchah and Ma'ariv.

Once there were two merchants who took their wares to the fair in the neighboring township. They each sold everything at a decent profit and were about to return home. As the hour was still quite early, their destination so close, and the weather so pleasant, they decided to travel by foot.

They walked and walked until they grew tired. The noonday sun beat mercilessly upon their heads, and their legs began to feel heavier than lead. Spying in the distance a tree that offered plenty of shade, they agreed to lie down for a short while and renew their strength. Wanting nothing more than to rest their weary bones, they were ready to take their naps, but one problem prevented them. What to do with the money bag they were carrying which was overflowing with coins? Where could they put it while they rested? Looking around, they were glad to confirm that there was not another human being in sight, just some cows grazing in the adjacent field. Without further ado, they hung the money bag on one of the stronger branches of their shade tree, and peacefully fell asleep.

Where there are cows, a herdsman is usually not far away. And this particular one had been sitting there the entire time, peering through the bushes at our twosome as they made themselves comfortable. When he was sure they were sound asleep, he tiptoed into their little encampment and made a beeline straight for the money bag. It was heavy, all right — full of coins. He lifted it gently off its branch and carried it silently away.

Returning to his place behind the bushes, he thought: This is a real fortune. What shall I do with it? If I herd away all the cows now with loud screams and whacks on their hindquarters, those men are sure to wake up and realize that their bag is gone. If I run away by myself, the owner of the cows will get angry and whip me to death. What should I do?

He thought and thought and finally came up with a plan. He would empty the coins out of the sack and bury them under the bushes. Then, he would fill the bag back up with cow dung and return it to its original place. And so, he stuffed the bag as full as he could until it bulged. He then stole back to the scene of the crime and silently suspended the bag from the same branch. He returned to his place behind the bushes and waited.

The merchants awoke from their nap. With great relief, they noted that the bag was still hanging suspended from the branch. They got up and lifted it off the branch and immediately realized that it was ten times lighter than before. They also felt it. It was soft. Terrified, they hurried and opened it. Heavens, it was filled with cow dung! They turned around and looked everywhere. There was still no one in sight. Not a soul could be seen except those cows grazing in the adjacent field.

They sighed and shrugged their shoulders in an attempt to make peace with the situation. "Those cows," they commented, "look what they have gone and done! Without a doubt, they did it. After all, it is their dung we found in place of our coins. Of course, who has ever heard of cows climbing up a tree,

untying a bag, stealing coins — what do they need money for? — gathering dung, and filling a bag with it?! It seems that they are guilty, yet, how can we try them for their crime?"

The rabbi ended his story. All the Chassidim laughed. All, that is, except one — the rabbi's son, Rabbi Aharon. He stood up and began to tremble.

There is certainly something eerie about this parable. And although the rabbi did not explain its moral, we shall attempt to unravel it. First, however, let us examine the parable again.

The merchants were foolish. They saw the dung and the cows, and they came to their absurd conclusion. Strange, but they didn't even take the trouble to register just how absurd their conclusion was. With just a little thought, they would have realized that their questions were, in actuality, answers. No, cows do not climb trees; they do not untie bags which are suspended from branches; they do not need money. They would have concluded that somebody had fooled them, that somebody was close at hand, near the cows, perhaps the herdsman. They would have gone out and searched for the culprit. They would have found him and retrieved their money and not made themselves into a laughingstock.

Doesn't it begin to sound familiar? Our hearts could be filled with precious "coins" of knowledge, good deeds, and refined character traits for which we have worked and struggled. But no one can remain awake at all times. It is bound to happen that we fall asleep and lose consciousness. And it is for such opportune times that our old friend, the yetzer ha-ra, waits. We may be asleep, but he is fully awake. Before we know it, something is missing. The yetzer has stealthily crept in, taken from us what is real and enduring, and exchanged it for... chametz. When we finally come to our senses and take stock of ourselves, we find that we are full of chametzdik delusions and illusions, worthless ideas, unrefined impulses, unwanted merchandise. Without realizing it, however, we shrug our shoulders in an attempt to make peace with the situation.

"That is how life is," we say. "The world is full of such things, and somehow a little of it rubbed off on me. I thought I had something good, but it seems to be lost now, while these other things have entered into my heart and mind and sullied my soul. That's the situation and there's hardly anything I can do about it."

But such acquiescence is a grave mistake! We mustn't give up and admit defeat and think that we can just go on without correcting ourselves. We must go a little deeper and contemplate: How did this happen? Who penetrated our fortress? Who stole our riches? We would then discover the culprit, the yetzer

ha-ra. We would realize that nothing just happens; there is always a cause. We would chase after our precious belongings, reclaim and retrieve what is rightfully ours, and seal the breaches in our walls!

In other words, it is not sufficient to search our houses or our selves for chametz and to find that it is indeed there. We must search the chametz itself, find out how it came to be there, and pull it out by its roots.

Imrei Kodesh; Admorei Belz

Arrangement of the Matzos and the Seder Plate

Three shemurah matzos are placed on the table, one above the other, in front of the leader of the Seder (according to the custom of the Gaon of Vilna, only two matzos are used). They are separated by napkins or the like. Some place the Seder plate over the matzos, while some put the matzos on the Seder plate.

A sampling of the items which will be used during the Seder should be arranged on the Seder plate.

In most homes, it is common to arrange the Seder plate according to the custom of the Arizal, Rabbi Yitzchak Luria. Some follow the custom of the Gaon of Vilna, while others follow the instructions of the Rama.

As mentioned previously, these are only samplings. The proper amount of matzah, maror, etc. for all assembled at the Seder must be prepared separately.

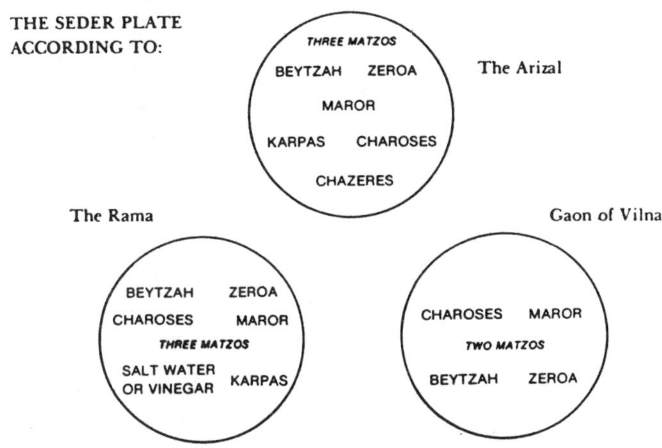

The egg on the Seder plate.

Why do we place an egg on the Seder Plate? The holy Rabbi Leibele Eiger of Lublin saw the egg as a parable for the effect the Passover Seder has on us.

In the writings of our holy teachers, we learn that on this sacred night the gates of holiness are opened above, just as they were opened on that first Pesach night, and Hashem's light shines down without restriction, irrespective of how worthy we may or may not be. On this night, each and every Jew can bask in the light of the Exodus and actually leave Mitzrayim (a double form of the noun "metzarim" — the narrow straits and double-bind constrictions which have hitherto held him back from growing to his full potential). On this night we can all depart servitude and darkness and attain freedom in the great revelation of Hashem's light.

Believing in these precious teachings of our teachers is one thing, and actually feeling them is another. It is no simple thing to experience real change and lasting transformation. But it is for this reason that our Sages instructed us to place an egg on our Seder Plate.

When a mother hen lays an egg, it is completely round and hard, enclosed on all sides. It certainly gives no indication of containing a chick. Even when we open it, all we see is white and yolk and no more. Still, we know that the egg contains all that is necessary for a chick to take form within its shell and finally emerge. All that is required is incubation in a warm environment.

The same is true of the wondrous illumination that shines down on us on this sacred night. Seeing family and friends gathered around the Seder table, and proceeding together through all the steps of the Seder, we share the experience of the Exodus. Before we realize it, however, the night is over and the excitement seems to disappear. We leave the Seder table feeling that we would like to bask in the warmth of Hashem's Exodus-light forever. The truth is that on a deeper level, this light has not been snatched away from us. It has simply gone straight into our hearts and become hidden and inaccessible. All that is required is the proper incubation and warmth, the yearning to serve Hashem with consistency during the coming days of the Omer. If we truly nurture this little "egg," then fifty days later, on Shavuos night, it will have developed into a full-fledged chick. The egg will hatch and Hashem's light, the Torah, will be born in our hearts in all its glory.

Toras Emes

הַדְלָקַת הַנֵּרוֹת

Kindling of the Candles

The lady of the house kindles the yom tov lights. She then extends her hands, placing them between her eyes and the lights, and recites the following berachah:

בָּרוּךְ אַתָּה יהוה אֱלֹהֵינוּ מֶלֶךְ הָעוֹלָם אֲשֶׁר קִדְּשָׁנוּ בְּמִצְוֹתָיו וְצִוָּנוּ לְהַדְלִיק נֵר שֶׁל (שַׁבָּת וְשֶׁל) יוֹם טוֹב:

Blessed be You, Hashem our God, King of the universe, Who has sanctified us by His commandments and commanded us to kindle the (Shabbos and) yom tov light.

In many communities the women also say:

בָּרוּךְ אַתָּה יהוה אֱלֹהֵינוּ מֶלֶךְ הָעוֹלָם שֶׁהֶחֱיָנוּ וְקִיְּמָנוּ וְהִגִּיעָנוּ לַזְּמַן הַזֶּה:

Blessed be You, Hashem our God, King of the universe, Who has kept us alive and preserved us, and enabled us to attain this season.

סֵדֶר לֵיל פֶּסַח

The Traditional Order of the Seder

Kaddesh קַדֵּשׁ

Kiddush, the sanctification of the Festival

Urechatz וּרְחַץ

Washing the hands in preparation for karpas

Karpas כַּרְפַּס

Eating a bit of vegetable dipped in salt water or vinegar

Yachatz יַחַץ

Dividing the middle matzah and hiding the larger part

Maggid מַגִּיד

Reciting the Haggadah, the story of our Exodus and liberation

Rochtzah רָחְצָה

Washing the hands before the meal

Motzi מוֹצִיא

Blessing over the matzah

Matzah מַצָּה

Special blessing before performing the mitzvah of eating matzah at the Seder, and eating it

Maror מָרוֹר

Special blessing before performing the mitzvah of eating the bitter herbs, and eating them

Korech כּוֹרֵךְ

Combining the maror with matzah and eating them together

Shulchan Orech שֻׁלְחָן עוֹרֵךְ

Eating the yom tov meal

Tzafun צָפוּן

Eating the afikoman, that part of the matzah which was hidden

Barech בָּרֵךְ

Birkas hamazon, grace after meals

Hallel הַלֵּל

Chanting psalms of praise and affirmation of faith in God

Nirtzah נִרְצָה

Concluding the Seder with the hope and prayer that it was properly observed and was acceptable to God

Kaddesh

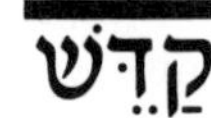

The matzos are covered and the first cup of wine is poured. Everyone should have in mind that, with this cup, it is his intention to fulfill the requirement of reciting kiddush on (Shabbos and on) yom tov over wine and also of drinking the first of the four cups of wine.

On Shabbos add:

בלחש: וַיְהִי־עֶרֶב וַיְהִי־בֹקֶר

יוֹם הַשִּׁשִּׁי: וַיְכֻלּוּ הַשָּׁמַיִם וְהָאָרֶץ וְכָל צְבָאָם: וַיְכַל אֱלֹהִים בַּיּוֹם הַשְּׁבִיעִי מְלַאכְתּוֹ אֲשֶׁר עָשָׂה וַיִּשְׁבֹּת בַּיּוֹם הַשְּׁבִיעִי מִכָּל מְלַאכְתּוֹ אֲשֶׁר עָשָׂה: וַיְבָרֶךְ אֱלֹהִים אֶת יוֹם הַשְּׁבִיעִי וַיְקַדֵּשׁ אֹתוֹ כִּי בוֹ שָׁבַת מִכָּל מְלַאכְתּוֹ אֲשֶׁר בָּרָא אֱלֹהִים לַעֲשׂוֹת:

Quietly: And it was evening and it was morning,

The sixth day: Thus the heaven and the earth and their whole host were brought to their destined completion. Then God completed with the seventh day His work that He had made, and with the seventh day He ceased from all of His work that He had made. And God blessed the seventh day and made it holy, for with it He had ceased from all of His work which He, God, had created in order to continue shaping it.

סַבְרִי מָרָנָן וְרַבָּנָן וְרַבּוֹתַי:

By your leave, my masters and teachers:

בָּרוּךְ אַתָּה יהוה אֱלֹהֵינוּ מֶלֶךְ הָעוֹלָם בּוֹרֵא פְּרִי הַגָּפֶן:

BLESSED be You, Hashem our God, King of the universe, Who creates the fruit of the vine.

Kaddesh — the Four Cups of Wine.

What is the meaning of these four cups? the *Midrash* (*Bereishis Rabbah* 88:5) states: They correspond to the four different expressions of redemption used in the Torah, as it is written, "I will *bring* you out from under the burden of Egyptian forced labor, *deliver* you from servitude to them, and *redeem* you with an outstretched arm and powerful judgments. I will *take* you to Me for a nation, and I will be your God..." (*Shemos* 6:6-7).

Rabbi Moshe Shimon Zivitz of Pittsburgh asked: Why are there four expressions of redemption here? The truth is that they are really four in one. At one and the same moment, Hashem redeemed His people and took them to Himself for His own! He illustrated his answer with a parable.

A wealthy industrialist who owned a textile firm employed hundreds of workers. He also had one child, a bright and intelligent boy named Moishe, who refused to take his lessons seriously. Moishe was only interested in eating sweet foods and drinking sweet beverages, playing games, amusing himself with all kinds of distractions, and lying around doing nothing! Moishe's father hired the best tutors in town to educate him. They used every trick in the book, from promising sweets to threatening punishments, but all for naught. Moishe's father also tried explaining to him that if he wished to be associated with the company and continue benefiting from its profits, he would have to learn how to operate the machinery in the factory as well as recognize different

Blessed be You, Hashem our God, King of the universe, Who has chosen us from among all peoples, exalted us above all tongues, and has sanctified us by His commandments. And You have given us, Hashem our Lord, in love, (Sabbaths for rest and) festivals of assembly for rejoicing, feasts of rallying and seasons for delight, (this Shabbos day and) the

בָּרוּךְ אַתָּה יהוה אֱלֹהֵינוּ מֶלֶךְ הָעוֹלָם אֲשֶׁר בָּחַר
בָּנוּ מִכָּל־עָם וְרוֹמְמָנוּ מִכָּל־לָשׁוֹן וְקִדְּשָׁנוּ בְּמִצְוֹתָיו.
וַתִּתֶּן לָנוּ יהוה אֱלֹהֵינוּ בְּאַהֲבָה (שַׁבָּתוֹת לִמְנוּחָה
וּ)מוֹעֲדִים לְשִׂמְחָה חַגִּים וּזְמַנִּים לְשָׂשׂוֹן אֶת יוֹם

types and qualities of textiles. His words fell on deaf ears. Moishe thought only of his foolish pastimes.

"I am responsible for your future," Moishe's father announced one day. "As things are now, Moishe, if you continue to act like this, refusing to take anything seriously, you will surely dissipate the entire family fortune in no time at all. I cannot allow this to happen. By refusing to familiarize yourself with the secrets of the textile trade, you are dissociating yourself from the wealth that accompanies it. Still, I shall not leave you to your own devices. If you want to behave like a shoemaker's son, I will take you to live with a shoemaker. One way or the other, you will learn to support yourself!"

He took Moishe to Yankele the shoemaker who lived in a hovel at the edge of town. Moishe was to live with Yankele and become his apprentice. Moishe was quite confused. Was his father disowning him? He didn't quite know what to think.

In the evening, Yankele's family sat down to eat stale bread and cooked onions. Although they ate with relish, Moishe couldn't stomach a thing. No one paid attention, and before he knew it, the candles were blown out and everyone went to sleep. Everyone, that is, except Moishe. He couldn't sleep because the straw that stuck out of the mattress kept stabbing into his flesh. If this wasn't enough, bedbugs crawled all over him and dined on his blood. Moishe's stomach gnawed with hunger pangs.

In the morning, Moishe accompanied his mentor to shul. On the way, he caught sight of his father, "Father, Father, save me!" he called out in tears. "I cannot eat there and I cannot sleep!" But his father ignored his pleas and continued on his way.

After davening, he returned to the shoemaker's hut. For breakfast he was served a dish of warm yogurt. He couldn't bring himself to touch it. Now it was time to work. Under Yankele's strong hand, he was forced to cut thick and brittle swatches of leather and punch holes along straight lines drawn by the shoemaker. He hands ached and his fingers bled. When the holes deviated from the pattern, Yankele hit him with a switch. The pain was excruciating. He

day of this Festival of Unleavened Bread, the season of our freedom, (in love), a convocation to the Sanctuary, a remembrance of the departure from Egypt. For You have chosen us and You have sanctified us from among all peoples; and (Shabbos and) Your holy festivals of assembly (in love and in favor) in joy and delight have You given us as an inheritance. Blessed be You, Hashem, who sanctifies (Shabbos,) Yisrael and the festive seasons.	(הַשַּׁבָּת הַזֶּה וְאֶת־יוֹם) חַג הַמַּצּוֹת הַזֶּה זְמַן חֵרוּתֵנוּ (בְּאַהֲבָה) מִקְרָא קֹדֶשׁ זֵכֶר לִיצִיאַת מִצְרָיִם. כִּי בָנוּ בָחַרְתָּ וְאוֹתָנוּ קִדַּשְׁתָּ מִכָּל־הָעַמִּים (וְשַׁבָּת) וּמוֹעֲדֵי קָדְשֶׁךָ (בְּאַהֲבָה וּבְרָצוֹן) בְּשִׂמְחָה וּבְשָׂשׂוֹן הִנְחַלְתָּנוּ. בָּרוּךְ אַתָּה יהוה מְקַדֵּשׁ (הַשַּׁבָּת וְ)יִשְׂרָאֵל וְהַזְּמַנִּים:

shrieked and cried out, but Yankele told him to shut up and continue working. Totally humiliated, Moishe finished his job. Lunch time arrived. Reluctantly, he ate the cooked lentils that the shoemaker's wife served him, almost vomiting and gagging on every spoonful. When he went to daven Minchah and Ma'ariv, he saw his father again and pleaded with him, his tears flowing down his cheeks, "Please, Father! Save me! I can't take it anymore. The shoemaker beats me!" His father ignored him this time as well.

Following prayers, his former friends surrounded him and mocked him, saying, "Moishe, Moishe, your father has rejected you and sold you to the shoemaker! Spoiled little rich Moishe is now the shoemaker's apprentice!"

Moishe stood still as they surrounded him to taunt him. He was confused. They kept shouting at him, but he no longer heard.

Again he caught sight of his father on his way home. He ran to him and cried out, "Father! Look how they are taunting me! They say you have rejected me."

His father continued walking. He didn't even turn around to acknowledge Moishe's presence.

The other children were all shouting together now, taunting him, "We told you so! We told you so!" Tears flowed down Moishe's cheeks as he returned home with Yankele's steel hand pressing down on his neck.

Brokenhearted, Moishe couldn't bring himself to eat that night. Lying on his bed in the dark, tears flowing from his eyes, Moishe wondered about all that was happening to him. The next morning at dawn he accompanied Yankele to shul. Seeing his father, Moishe broke loose from Yankele's hands. He ran to his father and fell at his feet. "Abba, Abba, I am ready to learn and obey everything you tell me. I promise that you will be pleased with me. Just please take me back home, Abba, take me back home!"

Moishe's father took the boy and hugged him. He encouraged him and did not reject him.

At the close of Shabbos add the following two berachos:

בָּרוּךְ אַתָּה יהוה אֱלֹהֵינוּ מֶלֶךְ הָעוֹלָם בּוֹרֵא מְאוֹרֵי הָאֵשׁ:

Blessed be You, Hashem our God, King of the universe, Who creates the flames of the fire.

בָּרוּךְ אַתָּה יהוה אֱלֹהֵינוּ מֶלֶךְ הָעוֹלָם הַמַּבְדִּיל בֵּין קֹדֶשׁ לְחוֹל בֵּין אוֹר לְחֹשֶׁךְ בֵּין יִשְׂרָאֵל לָעַמִּים בֵּין יוֹם הַשְּׁבִיעִי לְשֵׁשֶׁת יְמֵי הַמַּעֲשֶׂה. בֵּין קְדֻשַּׁת שַׁבָּת לִקְדֻשַּׁת יוֹם טוֹב הִבְדַּלְתָּ וְאֶת יוֹם הַשְּׁבִיעִי מִשֵּׁשֶׁת יְמֵי הַמַּעֲשֶׂה קִדַּשְׁתָּ. הִבְדַּלְתָּ וְקִדַּשְׁתָּ אֶת עַמְּךָ יִשְׂרָאֵל בִּקְדֻשָּׁתֶךָ. בָּרוּךְ אַתָּה יהוה הַמַּבְדִּיל בֵּין קֹדֶשׁ לְקֹדֶשׁ:

Blessed be You, Hashem our God, King of the universe, Who has made a distinction between holy and profane, between light and darkness, between Yisrael and the nations, between the seventh day and the six days of toil. You have made a distinction between the sanctity of Shabbos and the sanctity of the festival, and You have sanctified the seventh day above the six working days. You have set apart Your people Yisrael and sanctified them by Your holiness. Blessed be You, Hashem, Who has made a distinction between holy and holy.

One should have in mind that the following berachah pertains to the yom tov as well as all the mitzvos of the evening.

בָּרוּךְ אַתָּה יהוה אֱלֹהֵינוּ מֶלֶךְ הָעוֹלָם שֶׁהֶחֱיָנוּ וְקִיְּמָנוּ וְהִגִּיעָנוּ לַזְּמַן הַזֶּה:

Blessed be You, Hashem our God, King of the universe, Who has kept us alive and preserved us, and enabled us to attain this season.

The required amount of the first cup should be drunk within the required period of time, while reclining to the left.

Hashem wanted the Children of Yisrael to receive the Torah of their own free will. With the Torah, we would elevate ourselves and attain, through our own efforts, the ultimate reward of closeness to Hashem in this world and throughout eternity. With the Torah, we would overcome and transform our base desires. The Torah would instruct us on how to rule justly and create a perfect society for all mankind to emulate. The problem was how to make us appreciate such an exalted mission and destiny to the point that we would call out, "We will do and obey all that Hashem has commanded" (*Shemos* 24:7). He decided to accompany us down to Mitzrayim. This is what the Sages mean when they tell us that the Shechinah accompanied Yisrael throughout the Egyptian exile (*Megillah* 29a). In Hebrew, Egypt is "Mitzrayim" from the root "metzar," meaning narrow and confined. The country was like a prison camp, with every precaution taken so that no slave would be able to escape. As time went on, our situation worsened. The entire nation groaned under the oppressive conditions. Although Hashem was with us in our anguish, He did not redeem us immediately.

As the author of the Haggadah recounts, the Egyptians ill-treated us. They afflicted us...they appointed slave drivers over us to oppress us with back-breaking work. Oh, how we groaned and cried out to Hashem.

"God of our ancestors," we cried out in our misery, "save us!" He seemed to turn a deaf ear to us, however, and did not answer us.

The Egyptians mocked us. They taunted us, saying, "Where is your God?" And all the while, we begged Hashem, the Holy One of Yisrael, to reveal His presence among us, to redeem us with a strong hand and an outstretched arm. During the day, while doing backbreaking work, and at night, on our beds, drenched with tears, we cried out to Him to save us. Still He restrained Himself and did not answer us.

At the last moment, when we could no longer withstand the test of His concealment, Hashem decided that we were finally ready to become a nation wholly dedicated to Him and His Torah. Only then did He redeem us! At that moment, our Father let us know that He had heard our every groan and counted our every tear. He had seen all our suffering and our subjugation. At that moment, He announced all four expressions of redemption to us at once: "I will *bring* you out from under the burden of Egyptian forced labor, *deliver* you from servitude to them, and *redeem* you with an outstretched arm and powerful judgments. I will *take* you to Me for a nation, and I will be your God. You will then know that I am Hashem your God who brings you out from Egyptian subjugation" (*Shemos* 6:6-7).

Cheker Da'as 2:2-8

The season of our freedom.

Shelomo Ha-Melech said: "There is a season for everything, and a time to every purpose under the heaven" (*Koheles* 3:1). The Maggid of Dubno explained: When a great event occurs on a certain day, each year the anniversary of that day becomes fit for reexperiencing that same event. For instance, when Adam was judged on Rosh Hashanah, that day became established as The Day of Judgment for all future generations. When Hashem pardoned Yisrael for having worshipped the Golden Calf on Yom Kippur, that day became established as The Day of Atonement and Pardon for all future generations. When Hashem redeemed Avraham from the four kings on Pesach, that day became established as The Day of Redemption for all future generations. This is what the prophet meant when he declared: "Thus says Hashem: I have answered you at a favorable time; I have therefore come to your aid on a day of salvation" (*Yeshayahu* 49:8). Hashem is saying to us: The times I have answered you were not accidental. Pay attention and realize that if I have saved you once on a particular day, I have established that day as a favorable time to save you in the future!

This can be likened to a king who was traveling with his retinue. At one point in their journey, the water supply ran out. One of the king's soldiers became so dehydrated that he fainted. The king ordered another soldier to race to the closest river to bring water to revive him. The second soldier dashed off at lightning speed. While he was gone, however, the first soldier's condition worsened. Seeing this, the king said, "Who knows when he will return and whether he will be too late. Dig a well right here by the side of the road. Perhaps we shall come upon an underground spring!"

All the king's soldiers began working together to dig a well. When they had reached a certain depth, one of the soldiers called out, "Water!" They immediately brought water to the first soldier and revived him. A few minutes later, the second soldier came galloping back with a skin-bag full of water. There was no longer any need for this water, however, so the king's retinue continued on its journey.

The next day, a lone traveler passed by that same spot. The powerful rays of the noonday sun beat down upon his head, and he too was sorely in need of some water. Imagine for a moment what his reaction would have been if someone had told him that just the day before one of the king's soldiers fainted from dehydration and water was brought to him from a distant river. "Pretty stories don't satisfy a dying man's thirst," he might reply.

But arriving at the very spot where the king's men had dug to find water, seeing the water and bending down to drink his fill...that is a different story! How happy he would be. He would praise the king no end for having saved his life!

Pesach and all the other holidays that are sprinkled throughout the Jewish calendar year are not only commemorations of events that happened long ago in the distant past. They are like wells that were dug in the past, whose living waters continue to flow in the present so that we may draw life-giving inspiration from them. This is the meaning of the blessing we say on Chanukah and Purim, "Blessed be You, Hashem our God, King of the universe, Who performed miracles for our ancestors in those days, at this very time." As we have said, the salvation light that shone in "those days" continues to illuminate "at this very time." This is also the meaning of the verse: "You must carefully observe this [Pesach] day for all generations; it is an eternal law" (*Shemos* 12:17). We experience the true power of the holiday when we understand that a unique, never-before revealed light from the first Pesach shines each and every year on Pesach! This is the meaning of "the appointed

Urechatz ורחץ

A washbasin is brought to the leader of the Seder who proceeds to wash his hands without reciting a berachah. In some communities, the one who brings the water also pours it over the leader's hands, and in many homes, all the participants of the Seder wash their hands, too.

Karpas

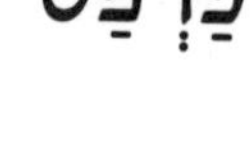

The leader of the Seder takes a piece of karpas (less than a kezayis so as not to incur the obligation of saying a berachah acharonah), dips it in vinegar or salt water, and distributes similar pieces to all assembled at the Seder. Then the following berachah is recited with the intention that it refers also to the maror which will be eaten later on:

אַתָּה יהוה אֱלֹהֵינוּ מֶלֶךְ הָעוֹלָם בּוֹרֵא פְּרִי הָאֲדָמָה:

BLESSED be You, Hashem our God, King of the universe, Who creates the fruit of the earth.

In some communities, the custom is to eat the karpas while reclining, while in some communities they do not recline.

time of our freedom." This is the eternal law that Hashem established. And this is why our Sages stated emphatically (*Rosh Hashanah* 11a): "Since we were once redeemed in Nissan, we will surely be redeemed in Nissan!"

This is similar to a man who becomes ill and visits a doctor. The doctor writes out a prescription with directions for how and when to take the required medication. Instead of going straight to the pharmacy, however, the man visits the home of a tzaddik who writes a Kabbalistic amulet specially suited for healing his illness and places it around his neck. Clearly, the first piece of paper on which the doctor wrote his prescription is worthless in and of itself. It can be effective only when taken to a pharmacist to fill the prescription and give the man the medicines he requires. The amulet, on the other hand, because of the holiness of the Divine Names written upon it, has special properties.

In the same way, the holidays have special properties. These special properties arouse the same power of salvation that was demonstrated on those days long ago. This is what Mordechai and Esther meant when they wrote, "These days will be remembered and kept in each generation, in every family, land, and city. These days...will never pass away from the Jewish People, nor shall their memory die out among their children" (*Esther* 9:28).

Kol Rinah Vi'Yeshuah 59b

Yachatz

יַחֵץ

The leader of the Seder then takes the middle matzah and breaks it in two. The larger portion is hidden away for the afikoman, while the smaller portion is to be replaced between the two whole matzos.

Maggid

מַגִּיד

Before beginning the narrative part of the Haggadah, everyone should have in mind that it is his intention to fulfill his obligation to recount the Exodus from Egypt. The narrative should be read or explained in a language that is understood by all those assembled at the Seder, including the women and the children. Upon beginning the narrative, the leader of the Seder displays the broken piece of matzah to those assembled and recites the following (many lift the entire Seder plate in order to display the uncovered matzos thereon and some first remove the zeroa and the egg):

הָא לַחְמָא עַנְיָא דִּי אֲכָלוּ אַבְהָתָנָא בְּאַרְעָא דְמִצְרָיִם. כָּל דִּכְפִין יֵיתֵי וְיֵכֻל. כָּל דִּצְרִיךְ יֵיתֵי וְיִפְסַח. הָשַׁתָּא הָכָא לַשָּׁנָה הַבָּאָה בְּאַרְעָא דְיִשְׂרָאֵל. הָשַׁתָּא עַבְדֵי לַשָּׁנָה הַבָּאָה בְּנֵי חוֹרִין:

THIS is the bread of dependence which our fathers ate in the land of Egypt. Whoever is hungry, let him come and eat; whoever is in need, let him come and celebrate the Pesach. This year we are here; next year may we be in the Land of Yisrael. This year we are in bondage; next year may we be free men.

This is the bread of dependence.

In some versions of the Haggadah, two variations of this statement which introduces the Pesach Seder are given. One version reads: "Ha lachma anya" (This is the bread of dependence that our ancestors ate in the land of Egypt). the other reads: "K'ha lachma anya" (This is *like* the bread of dependence our ancestors ate). What is the difference between these two versions, and which one is more correct? The Maggid of Dubno answered with a parable.

A poor peddler used to travel with his backpack and staff from town to town, selling his wares. He always had difficulty supporting his family, but when he came to one city, he was very successful there. He began saving money until he was able to open a store, and he eventually became very wealthy. Still, he never forgot his humble beginnings. He remained as modest and unassuming as he had been all his life. Every year, on the anniversary of the day he arrived in town, he would take his backpack and staff from the

days of his poverty, gather his family around him, and tell them the story of how he became prosperous. He would admonish them to never become smug and conceited, but always to be grateful to Hashem for their present good fortune. The family came to look forward to the anniversary celebration when the father would show them what their days of affliction had been like long ago, for he would mark the occasion by presenting all of them with costly gifts which he took out of his backpack.

Unfortunately, this man's prosperity did not last. He suffered serious business setbacks and he was forced to sell his store and many of his possessions.

As he sat in his home, despondent and brokenhearted, his wife said to him, "Why are you sad? Hashem gave and Hashem took away. Let us be thankful to Him for the time He blessed us with plenty. Now we must return to our former poverty. Take up your backpack and begin traveling from town to town again with your staff."

He listened to his wife's advice, and took up his backpack and his staff. When his children saw him dressed thus, they shouted for joy, for they had come to associate such attire with feasting, games and expensive toys.

But this time their father looked at them with tears in his eyes and said, "No, my children. In years gone by I would dress this way only to show you how poor I had been long ago. I would put on my backpack and take my staff in hand in order to act like a poor man, and then I would shower you all with gifts. This time it is no longer an act. I am afraid that we have truly become poor again. Today I must wear the backpack in order to earn my living."

What happened to this family, said the Maggid of Dubno, may be compared to what happened to the Jewish People. When the Beis Ha-Mikdash stood and we prospered in our own land, we sat down to celebrate the Seder and joyously lifted up our matzos to proclaim, "This is *like* the bread of dependence we were forced to eat long ago when our ancestors were slaves in the land of Egypt ('k'ha lachma anya')!" We then would offer thanks to Hashem for the many miracles which saved us from sharing the same misery our ancestors had to endure. But now that the Beis Ha-Mikdash is destroyed, we are in exile, and many of our brethren the world over are suffering. Today the matzah is more than just a symbol recalling an unhappy past. Hence, unfortunately, at our Seder service today, when we raise aloft our matzos we must say, "This is the *very* bread of dependence our ancestors ate long ago in the land of Egypt ('ha lachma anya')!"

Thus we understand the two readings.

Emes L'Yaakov

Whoever is hungry, let him come and eat; whoever is in need, let him come and celebrate the Pesach.

Why do we invite everyone to join us for the Seder and share in our rejoicing? The Maggid of Dubno answered with a parable.

A number of beggars formed a union. Instead of each beggar going from door to door to collect for himself, they agreed to gather together every evening to divide the day's earnings equally among all the members of the union.

Of course, they knew from experience that relying on people's generosity alone could not guarantee a decent income. They decided to supplement their earnings by carrying a small stock of cheap merchandise: strings for tzitzis, gartles for davening, benchers, needles, thread, a large assortment of buttons, etc. The more established among them contributed a gold or silver dinar, while the poorer beggars contributed whatever pennies they could afford. With this money they purchased merchandise, divided it among themselves, and left prepared to peddle their wares the following day.

Out on the street, donations were still welcome, and every contributor was blessed. Those who hestitated parting with their savings were shown whatever merchandise the beggars had in stock that day. One way or the other, the beggars ended up with a few pennies. At the end of the day, they all gathered together.

First they divided all contributions equally among every member of the union. For dividing the money from the sales, however, a different procedure was followed. Those who contributed larger sums felt it was only right that they should be given a larger cut of the earnings. It did not seem fair that the profit of someone who had contributed a dinar should equal that of someone who had only given up a penny. This claim was voted on and ratified by all present. It was decided that the allocation of profits would be proportionate to the amount of money invested.

If the Jewish People had been redeemed individually from Egyptian bondage solely on the basis of each one's merits, there might have been weight to the claim that some were more worthy than others. Our Sages have informed us, however, that we were not redeemed on the basis of merit. We had no merits to speak of, as the prophet described: "You were naked and bare [of mitzvos]" (*Yechezkel* 16:7). The redemption was thus an act of complete charity on Hashem's part. As such, we all have a right to share in it equally. We are therefore obligated to open our doors and invite all Jews who wish to rejoce together with us on this night!

Ohel Yaakov, Bo

This year we are here; next year may we be in the Land of Yisrael. This year we are in bondage; next year may we be free men.

A poor beggar, through a change in fortune, became extremely wealthy. He purchased a mansion and lived in the lap of luxury. Still, in order not to let his appreciation for all his good fortune wane, he always ended each meal with a portion of dry bread and salt. In this way, he kept fresh his memory of his former destitute days and enjoyed his present good fortune all the more.

Time passed and his luck changed again. He lost his entire fortune and had no choice but to return to a life of poverty. Once, as he went from door to door collecting charity, he came to the door of a wealthy man who recognized him from his former good days. The latter's mercy was aroused, and he invited his old friend in to dine with him at his table. They sat down to a delicious meal, after which the poor man requested a piece of dry bread and salt. The wealthy man was taken aback, but the poor man explained that it had always been his custom to end each meal with such a dessert in order never to forget his former days of poverty.

The wealthy man laughed. "This custom of yours was fine when you were well-off. Now that you have resumed wearing the mantle of poverty, however, you do not require any reminder of poverty."

The guest answered and said, "You are mistaken. I have certainly lost a large part of my fortune, but while I was still wealthy I loaned ten thousand gold pieces to a merchant for a fixed period of time. At the end of this period, we have agreed to divide the profits. That merchant has been very successful in his business dealings, and he has already earned a fortune. Indeed, I am a very rich man, and my poverty is merely temporary. I await the day when my wealth will be evident to everyone around me. I am a wealthy man, and it is very fitting that I continue eating dry bread and salt at the end of my meals."

Once we were slaves in Egypt. The Holy One redeemed us from bondage, and brought us to the Land of Yisrael. While we enjoyed freedom in our own land, we were still supposed to look back and remember our former bondage by eating matzos and bitter herbs each year. This would pevent us fom becoming smug and conceited, and keep us grateful to Hashem for all the good He had bestowed upon us.

But those days are gone. Our Beis Ha-Mikdash was destroyed and we were exiled. Many of our brethren the world over are suffering. If someone asks, therefore, why we need to recall our bondage of long ago now when things look so bleak, what shall we answer?

Our answer is, "This bread of dependence which our fathers ate in the land of Egypt," we eat it now as well. And if they should ask further: "How can we invite everyone who is hungry to come and join us? Are those of us who are hungry also obligated to commemorate our ancestors' hunger? Isn't the entire reason for eating matzos to prevent us from becoming smug and conceited during times of good fortune and economic plenty?"

Our answer again is, "This year we are in bondage; next year may we be free men." That is, despite all outward appearances, we still have not given up hope in the return of our true fortune, when Hashem will redeem us again and for all time! It is this hope that makes us truly wealthy. And it is for this reason that we are still commanded to eat the bread of dependence. It is in anticipation of the time when our wealth will be evident to all!

Emes L'Yaakov 6

This year we are in bondage.

In Egypt we were slaves to the Egyptians, and now we are slaves to the nations. Thus Rambam wrote in his *Iggeres Teiman*: "Since our exodus from Egypt, our oppressors have not stopped afflicting us, as David Ha-Melech lamented (*Tehillim* 129:1): 'They have tormented me greatly since my youth!'"

True, said the Maggid of Dretshin, but in certain ways our situation is even worse than it was back in Egypt! We are like a young lad with nothing to eat who once entered a large city. Hungry for a morsel of bread, he walked through the streets begging and offering to hire himself out to anyone who needed a job done.

As time went on, and with great effort, he was able to amass a small fortune. Fortune continued smiling on him, and he became extremely wealthy. He married the daughter of a wealthy merchant and brought his children up as aristocrats.

Many years passed and unfortunately the wheel of fortune turned full circle. He lost his fortune, his merchandise, his store, and his home. In the end, he was left with no choice but to assume his former occupation, namely, going door to door begging for bread.

Broken and crushed, he approached his next-door neighbor's house and knocked. A wealthy man opened the door and beheld the pathetic sight. Bent down, the poor man's hand was extended to receive charity. Suddenly the dam burst, and he began to sob bitterly and uncontrollably. The owner of the house was taken aback. He immediately took him by the hand, brought him into his home, and sat him down at his table.

"Don't worry," he assured him, "the wheel will turn again and things will look brighter. When you arrived here a number of years ago, you were poor and bereft of friends. You knocked on this very door, you stretched forth your hand...and somehow you made it. You became extremely wealthy for a number of years, and now you have returned to your former poverty. So why cry? Why take it so hard? You haven't lost anything. On the contrary, you've gained a number of good years!"

The poor man dried his eyes and looked at his benefactor. "You are right. I first arrived here in wretched condition and now I have returned to being wretched again. Still, there is no comparison between then and now. Then, I was alone. When I received a morsel of bread, I ate it and was satisfied. When I found a corner to lie down in, I slept like a baby. When someone was kind enough to give me an old piece of clothing, I was grateful for having something to wear. Now, however, I carry a millstone around my neck. I have a wife and young children. I must feed and clothe them, and provide them with proper living conditions." At the thought of his family suffering privation, he broke down again and began to cry.

It is true that we suffered bitterly in Egypt. At that time, however, we were still not obligated to keep the Torah and its commandments. Our suffering was our own. Now, in our present exile, we are obligated to keep all the commandments. But in subtle or overt ways, the pressures that the nations employ against us to manipulate us makes it impossible for us to fulfill our obligations properly. Our Sages alluded to this when they said: "Master of the world, it is clearly revealed before You that our sole desire is to fulfill Your Will! What prevents us? The chametz in the dough (the evil inclination within us) and our subjugation to foreign governments" (*Berachos* 17a).

Our prayer is that Hashem will save us and redeem us for His own sake, so that we can truly fulfill our exalted task, the perfection of the world through the fulfillment of His Torah. For this we never tire pleading, "This year we are in bondage; next year may we be free men!"

Toldos Adam 2:11b

The second cup is then poured. Some have the custom to cover the matzos, some move the Seder plate to the other end of the table, and some remove it from the table completely, while others do none of these. And now the youngest child (or, if there are no children present, the wife or some other adult present) asks the Four Questions:

מַה נִּשְׁתַּנָּה הַלַּיְלָה הַזֶּה מִכָּל־הַלֵּילוֹת. שֶׁבְּכָל הַלֵּילוֹת אָנוּ אוֹכְלִין חָמֵץ וּמַצָּה הַלַּיְלָה הַזֶּה כֻּלּוֹ מַצָּה. שֶׁבְּכָל הַלֵּילוֹת אָנוּ אוֹכְלִין שְׁאָר יְרָקוֹת הַלַּיְלָה הַזֶּה מָרוֹר. שֶׁבְּכָל הַלֵּילוֹת אֵין אָנוּ מַטְבִּילִין אֲפִילוּ פַּעַם אֶחָת הַלַּיְלָה הַזֶּה שְׁתֵּי פְעָמִים. שֶׁבְּכָל הַלֵּילוֹת אָנוּ אוֹכְלִין בֵּין יוֹשְׁבִין וּבֵין מְסֻבִּין הַלַּיְלָה הַזֶּה כֻּלָּנוּ מְסֻבִּין:

WHY is this night different from all other nights? On all other nights, we may eat leavened or unleavened bread; tonight we must eat only matzah.
On all other nights, we may eat all kinds of vegetables; tonight we must eat bitter herbs. On all other nights, we are not required to dip even once; tonight we are required to dip twice. On all other nights, we may eat either sitting or reclining; tonight we must all recline.

In some communities, the leader of the Seder repeats the Four Questions.
If the matzos were covered or removed, they are now returned and/or uncovered and are to remain so throughout the narration of the Hagaddah, except when the cups of wine are lifted.

The narration of the Hagaddah is not said reclining, but rather in a spirit of awe and fear of the Almighty.

עֲבָדִים הָיִינוּ לְפַרְעֹה בְּמִצְרָיִם. וַיּוֹצִיאֵנוּ יהוה אֱלֹהֵינוּ מִשָּׁם בְּיָד חֲזָקָה וּבִזְרוֹעַ נְטוּיָה. וְאִלּוּ לֹא הוֹצִיא הַקָּדוֹשׁ בָּרוּךְ הוּא אֶת אֲבוֹתֵינוּ מִמִּצְרַיִם. הֲרֵי אָנוּ וּבָנֵינוּ וּבְנֵי בָנֵינוּ. מְשֻׁעְבָּדִים הָיִינוּ לְפַרְעֹה בְּמִצְרָיִם. וַאֲפִילוּ כֻּלָּנוּ חֲכָמִים. כֻּלָּנוּ נְבוֹנִים. כֻּלָּנוּ זְקֵנִים. כֻּלָּנוּ יוֹדְעִים אֶת הַתּוֹרָה. מִצְוָה עָלֵינוּ לְסַפֵּר בִּיצִיאַת מִצְרָיִם. וְכָל הַמַּרְבֶּה לְסַפֵּר בִּיצִיאַת מִצְרַיִם הֲרֵי זֶה מְשֻׁבָּח:

WE were slaves unto Pharaoh in Egypt, and Hashem our God took us out from there with a strong hand and an outstretched arm. And if the Holy One, Blessed be He, had not taken our fathers out of Egypt, then we, our children, and our children's children would still have been enslaved to Pharaoh in Egypt. Therefore, even if we were all wise, all understanding, all experienced, and all versed in the Torah, we would nevertheless be obligated to recount the story of the departure from Egypt; and he who elaborates upon the story of the departure from Egypt is worthy of praise.

מַעֲשֶׂה בְּרַבִּי אֱלִיעֶזֶר וְרַבִּי יְהוֹשֻׁעַ וְרַבִּי אֶלְעָזָר בֶּן־עֲזַרְיָה וְרַבִּי עֲקִיבָא וְרַבִּי טַרְפוֹן שֶׁהָיוּ מְסֻבִּין בִּבְנֵי־בְרַק וְהָיוּ מְסַפְּרִים בִּיצִיאַת מִצְרַיִם כָּל־אוֹתוֹ הַלַּיְלָה עַד שֶׁבָּאוּ תַלְמִידֵיהֶם וְאָמְרוּ לָהֶם. רַבּוֹתֵינוּ הִגִּיעַ זְמַן קְרִיאַת שְׁמַע שֶׁל שַׁחֲרִית:

It happened that Rabbi Eliezer, Rabbi Yehoshua, Rabbi Elazar ben Azaryah, Rabbi Akiva and Rabbi Tarfon were reclining [at the Seder table] in Bnei Berak, and were recounting the story of the departure from Egypt. They continued the entire night until their pupils came and said to them: "Our teachers! The time for the recital of the morning Shema has arrived."

Said Rabbi Elazar ben Azaryah: "Behold! I am like a man of seventy years old, and I did not succeed in proving that the Departure must be mentioned at night, until ben Zoma explained that the Torah states... 'so that you may remember the day when you came forth out of the land of Egypt *all* the days of your life' (*Devarim* 16:3). 'The days of your life' refers to the daytime. '*All* the days of your life' — includes nighttime as well. But the Sages say 'the days of your life' indicates your life in the present; '*all* the days of your life' refers to the time of the Mashiach as well."

אָמַר רַבִּי אֶלְעָזָר בֶּן־עֲזַרְיָה. הֲרֵי אֲנִי כְּבֶן שִׁבְעִים שָׁנָה. וְלֹא זָכִיתִי שֶׁתֵּאָמֵר יְצִיאַת מִצְרַיִם בַּלֵּילוֹת. עַד שֶׁדְּרָשָׁהּ בֶּן זוֹמָא. שֶׁנֶּאֱמַר לְמַעַן תִּזְכֹּר אֶת יוֹם צֵאתְךָ מֵאֶרֶץ מִצְרַיִם כֹּל יְמֵי חַיֶּיךָ. יְמֵי חַיֶּיךָ הַיָּמִים. כֹּל יְמֵי חַיֶּיךָ הַלֵּילוֹת. וַחֲכָמִים אוֹמְרִים. יְמֵי חַיֶּיךָ הָעוֹלָם הַזֶּה. כֹּל יְמֵי חַיֶּיךָ לְהָבִיא לִימוֹת הַמָּשִׁיחַ:

"All the days of your life" refers to the time of the Mashiach as well.

In the Talmud (*Berachos* 12b), Ben Zoma replies to the Sages by questioning whether there will be any need to mention the Egyptian exodus after the arrival of the Mashiach. Doesn't the verse say: "Behold, days are coming, says Hashem, when they shall no longer swear [in the name of], 'The living God who brought the Children of Yisrael out of Egypt,' but 'The living God who raised up and brought the seed of Yisrael out of the northern country and from all the countries to which He had driven them,' for I shall bring them back to dwell on their own land which I allotted to their ancestors" (*Yirmeyahu* 23:7-8; 16:14-15). This would seem to indicate clearly that after the Mashiach comes and gathers in the exiles, the Exodus will no longer be mentioned! The Sages replied, however, that the prophet did not intend to say that the Egyptian Exodus will be completely forgotten. He was merely informing us that its memory will become secondary to that of the Final Redemption, for then, unlike after the Exodus, the Jewish People will no longer suffer exile or subjugation.

The Maggid of Vilkomir asked: Recalling the Exodus from Egypt is surely an obligatory positive commandment, while mentioning the benefits of the Final Redemption would seem to be optional. How can a primary obligation become secondary to something which is voluntary? He answered with a parable.

A poor man fell ill with a stomach virus. He lost his appetite completely, to the point that all food became repulsive to him. As he grew weaker and

weaker, he felt his time was approaching. But a local physician found out about the poor man's condition and treated him without charge until he was able to restore his health and get him back on his feet. From that time onwards the poor man would salute the physician whenever he saw him on the street. Without the least trace of genuine enthusiasm, however, he would mutter what seemed to be an obligatory thank-you and continue on his way. This was certainly a strange way to act after having his life saved!

One day the man unexpectedly showed up at the physician's home. He began thanking the physician with tremendous enthusiasm and heartfelt sincerity, blessing him a million times over for the great kindness he performed in reviving him and restoring his health.

"What makes today different from all other days?" the physician inquired. "Ever since I cured you, you have acted like you preferred not to see me. Now, after all this time, you come to me to thank me! Why?"

"I will tell you the truth," the man answered. "When you healed me and restored my appetite, I was still poor. I was only able to satisfy my hunger with dry bread and salty fish. For this reason, I did not feel that much gratitude to you for what you had done. Recently, however, I received a large inheritance, and my table is now filled with the finest foods. Now, for the first time, I can enjoy all of these foods. Therefore I finally appreciate the tremendous favor you did for me. So I have come to your home to express my heartfelt gratitude to you for your great kindness."

Hashem redeemed us from Egypt, and we are certainly obligated to thank Him for this "all the days of our lives." This idea is so much a part of the Haggadah that we say, "In every single generation one is obligated to look upon himself as if he personally had gone forth out of Egypt." The way we fulfill this obligation, however, is similar to this poor man who was unable to truly appreciate the gift he was given. And the reason is clear: The initial exodus was eventually succeeded by exile from our land and subjugation to foreign nations. The time will come, however, when Hashem will usher in the Final Redemption, and we will be privileged to live in a world of unending bliss and happiness. At that time, we will recognize and appreciate retroactively the tremendous favor that Hashem did for us when He redeemed us from Egyptian bondage.

Haggadah Chachmei Yerushalayim 36

BLESSED be the Omnipresent, Blessed be He! Blessed be He Who has given the Torah to His people Yisrael, Blessed be He.

The Torah spoke about four sons: one wise, one wicked, one simple, and one who does not know how to ask.

The wise son — what does he say? "What are the testimonies, the statutes, and the social ordinances which Hashem our God has commanded you?" (see *Devarim* 6:20). As for you, instruct him regarding the laws of the Pesach: "After the Pesach offering, no dessert is to be eaten!"

בָּרוּךְ הַמָּקוֹם. בָּרוּךְ הוּא. בָּרוּךְ שֶׁנָּתַן תּוֹרָה לְעַמּוֹ יִשְׂרָאֵל. בָּרוּךְ הוּא.

כְּנֶגֶד אַרְבָּעָה בָנִים דִּבְּרָה תּוֹרָה. אֶחָד חָכָם. וְאֶחָד רָשָׁע. וְאֶחָד תָּם. וְאֶחָד שֶׁאֵינוֹ יוֹדֵעַ לִשְׁאוֹל:

חָכָם מַה הוּא אוֹמֵר. מָה הָעֵדוֹת וְהַחֻקִּים וְהַמִּשְׁפָּטִים אֲשֶׁר צִוָּה יהוה אֱלֹהֵינוּ אֶתְכֶם. וְאַף אַתָּה אֱמָר־לוֹ כְּהִלְכוֹת הַפֶּסַח. אֵין מַפְטִירִין אַחַר הַפֶּסַח אֲפִיקוֹמָן:

"What are the testimonies, the statutes, and the social ordinances which Hashem our God has commanded you?"

Based on the text of the Torah, the Haggadah speaks of four children, one wise, one wicked, one simple, and one who does not know how to ask questions. The wise child asks: "What are the testimonies, the statutes, and the social ordinances which Hashem our God has commanded you?" (*Devarim* 6:20). The wicked child asks: "What is this service to you?" (*Shemos* 12:26). The difference between the two is immediately apparent. The wise son asks with the intention of understanding, while the wicked child speaks with arrogance, intending to denigrate our serving Hashem. The Gaon, Rav Aryeh Leib Tzintz of Platzk, illustrated this difference with two complementary parables.

One way to understand the difference between an unlearned village farmer and a sophisticated aristocrat is to present them each with two goblets, one of glass and one of crystal, or two rings, one with a shiny glass inset and one with a real diamond. Since each of the two shine, the farmer will probably not note much difference between them. The aristocrat will discern the difference but may not be familiar enough with the details of crystal and diamond cutting to know how much these particular items are worth. Only an expert would know exactly how much to appraise each item for and how to explain all their differences.

Shelomo Ha-Melech referred to such a skill when he wrote: "A cauldron to [assess the quality of] silver, and a furnace to [assess the quality of] gold; a man [is assessed] by the things he values" (*Mishlei* 27:21). We usually recognize somebody according to their expertise. A merchant must know his merchandise, a carpenter must know which types of woods are best for different jobs, a builder must know his materials, an architect must know which type of construction is suited for different buildings, a physician must

recognize every type of symptom and know its treatment; and so the Sages of Yisrael must know all the intricacies of the Torah and the service of God.

A prince once arranged a gala banquet for his friends and acquaintances. Among the people invited were two merchants. One was an ignorant villager who was invited because he sold the prince all his fruits and vegetables. The other was a city-dweller who manufactured and sold fine fabrics, but who had never been invited to such a gathering of aristocrats.

Both merchants entered the banquet hall together. The tables were already set. Each guest was given three plates, three drinking glasses, and a selection of knives, forks, and spoons, all of different sizes. The villager smiled and said sarcastically, "What is all this for? All I need is one plate filled with potatoes and onions fried in fat and one mug of beer."

The other merchant cringed. He understood that this was not the place for a village guzzler, but he was completely in the dark as to the reason for all the different plates and silverware.

He went up to one of the waiters and asked in a whisper, "Why three plates?"

The waiter answered, "The first is for appetizers; the second is for fish and assorted salads; the third is for meat and cooked vegetables."

"And the three glasses, what are they for?" he continued.

"The large glass is for water, the medium-sized glass is for white wine to drink with the fish and red wine to drink with the meat, and the small glass is for whiskey or cognac," the waiter answered matter-of-factly.

"But why are there different-sized forks, knives and spoons?" the merchant pursued.

Pointing to each thing as he spoke, the waiter replied, "This fork and this knife are for the fish. This fork and this knife are for the meat. This set is for the cake. The large spoon is for the soup, and this tiny spoon is for the coffee that comes with the dessert."

In the meantime, the prince and his honored guests arrived. The merchant from the city, who had taken the trouble to ask and had received detailed answers to all his queries, ate in a very elegant fashion, and did not feel out of place among all the high society guests, whose company he shared and enjoyed. The villager, who did not understand a thing about his surroundings, went about eating his meal like an animal at its feeding trough. And this is exactly how the other guests related to him.

What is the difference between the wise son and the wicked one? The wise son understands that there are different types of mitzvos in the Torah, both

on Pesach night and in general. He therefore asks for a detailed explanation of what these differences are and how they affect him. His question clearly indicates that he has some knowledge, but wishes to increase it. He therefore willingly listens to the answers, until the very last one, where we tell him, "After the Pesach offering, no dessert is to be eaten!" The wicked son, on the other hand, resembles our village farmer. He doesn't want to know any details. None of it interests him. For him, all this "service" is superfluous, God forbid. He would prefer his feeding trough.

Birkas Ha-Shir

The wise son... "What are the testimonies, the statutes, and the social ordinances which Hashem our God has commanded you?"...The wicked son... "What is this service to you?"

As the Haggadah goes on to say, when the wicked son uses the expression "to you," he is making it very clear that he is not including himself in the Pesach ritual and is thereby dissociating himself from the Jewish People. The Haggadah therefore urges that you "blunt his teeth," that is, silence his biting criticism of our tradition and say to him curtly, "It is because of this [service] that Hashem acted for me when I came forth out of Egypt"....For me — but not for him! Had he been there, he would not have been redeemed. He would have died during the three days of darkness.

But the Maggid of Dubno asked: Did not the wise son also inquire about the laws which "Hashem our God has commanded you" instead of saying "that Hashem our God commanded us"? Why should this be less reprehensible than what the wicked son said?

The answer to this is really quite simple. Imagine a situation where a stranger is watching a servant engaged in strenuous labor for his master. He might ask him, "Why did your master ask you to do this job? What is its purpose?" This would be a courteous question, motivated by a genuine desire for information. The stranger is interested in learning more about the master and about his plan which the servant is implementing.

But if the stranger were to ask, "Why must you wear yourself out? What is this drudgery to you?" he is showing how little respect he has for the master's authority and seems to be implying, "Why do you need to do this work in the first place? If I were you, I would refuse to do it."

The wicked son — what does he say? "What is this service to you?" (see *Shemos* 12:26) To *you* — but not to *him*! Since he has excluded himself from the community, he has denied the essentials of our faith. Therefore, you should blunt his teeth, and say to him: "It is because of this [service] that Hashem acted for me when I came forth out of Egypt" (see *Shemos* 13:8). For *me* — but not for *him*! Had he been there, he would not have been redeemed.

רָשָׁע מַה הוּא אוֹמֵר. מָה הָעֲבוֹדָה הַזֹּאת לָכֶם. לָכֶם וְלֹא לוֹ. וּלְפִי שֶׁהוֹצִיא אֶת־עַצְמוֹ מִן הַכְּלָל כָּפַר בְּעִקָּר. וְאַף אַתָּה הַקְהֵה אֶת־שִׁנָּיו וֶאֱמָר לוֹ בַּעֲבוּר זֶה עָשָׂה יהוה לִי בְּצֵאתִי מִמִּצְרָיִם. לִי וְלֹא לוֹ. אִלּוּ הָיָה שָׁם לֹא הָיָה נִגְאָל:

Such is the attitude of the wicked son. We must not imagine him as a little boy, but as a full-grown man who has abandoned his parents' Judaism and holds it in disdain. Although he is seated at his father's table, his present ideas and ideologies are antithetical to our beliefs. What he wants, therefore, is not to ask for an explanation, but to criticize. The wise son, on the other hand, has asked a courteous, sensible question and is anxious to learn the meaning of the mitzvos that Hashem commanded his ancestors before he was born.

This is the difference between the questions asked by the two classic sons in the Pesach Haggadah.

Dr. Benno Heinemann, *The Maggid of Dubno and His Parables,*
[Feldheim Publishers, 1967] 209

"What is this service to you?"

Why is the father commanded to answer the wicked son abruptly rather than to explain in detail? The Maggid of Dubno answered with a parable.

In a small town, just before the Pesach holiday, there was a fair where holiday clothing could be purchased at almost wholesale prices. Now, in this town lived a Jew who was so poor that he and his family had little more than the clothes on their backs. In preparation for the holiday, he and his wife had saved up just enough money to buy wine and matzos for the Seder, but when the man heard of the bargains his friends were getting at the fair, he hastened there to see what he could afford. According to one version of the story, he bought a small bolt of cloth, intending to have his wife make from it some new holiday clothes for the two of them. According to another version, he found a suit of clothes that fit him perfectly. According to both versions, he was so excited by the prospect of exchanging his normal rags for real clothing that he forgot his financial straits and spent almost all of his Pesach money!

When his wife saw the cloth (or the suit), she wrung her hands and cried out, "Fool! What have you done? You have spent everything on clothing.

Where will we find the money now for wine and matzos? How could you be so thoughtless?"

Realizing his mistake, the poor man asked, "What should I do now?"

"Go back to the fair at once and return the cloth to the merchant who sold it to you," his wife replied.

"And what if he refuses to refund my money?" he interrupted.

His wife picked up the cloth and began examining it. She found a small defect. Pointing to it, she said, "Show him this, and he will refund the money."

The man quickly did as his wife had told him. He waited for the merchant to turn to him, and said, "Refund my money! Look at what you sold me!" Then, as he held up the cloth for the merchant to see the tiny defect, he added, "Look at the defect I found here!"

To his surprise, the merchant did not try to argue with him or even show him some of the other merchandise he had to sell. Instead, he took the cloth and refunded the money to the poor man without a word.

Afterwards, a customer who had overheard the brief conversation, asked the merchant, "Why did you give in so easily? You should have proven to him that the defect was tiny and unnoticeable. And besides, if he had really wanted something so perfect, you could have shown him another bolt of material without any defect whatsoever."

But the merchant smiled and replied, "If you would have paid attention to what he said, you would have understood why I did what I did. If he had really intended to buy this cloth, or any other, for that matter, he would have said, 'Look at the defect in this cloth. I request that you exchange it for another!' He did not speak thus, however, but began by demanding, 'Refund my money!' Only afterwards did he attempt to justify his request by saying, 'Look at this defect I found.' Upon hearing this, it became clear to me that his complaint was nothing more than an excuse for demanding his money back. What could I have gained by arguing with him and attempting to persuade him otherwise? If I had shown him another piece of cloth, he would have examined that too in order to find another defect. It is better for me to refund his money and have nothing to do with him!"

Shelomo Ha-Melech wrote two seemingly contradictory statements: "Do not answer a fool according to his folly" (*Mishlei* 26:4), and "Answer a fool according to his folly" (ibid. 26:5). How are we to make sense of this? The answer lies in the fact that there are three different kinds of people who ask about the reasons behind the mitzvos. One is wise, or wishes to be so. He has already accepted the yoke of the Torah upon himself. He believes in the Torah wholeheartedly. In asking about the mitzvos, he merely wishes to understand

them better so that he can perform them with greater alacrity and appreciation. Such a person is described by the verse, "The foremost wisdom is the fear of God; refined intelligence [is granted] to all who perform them [the mitzvos]" (*Tehillim* 111:10). That is, it is good and appropriate to wish for wisdom and knowledge, but only when the reason for such a wish is the desire to draw closer to Hashem. This is the real motive behind the wise son's query: "What are the testimonies, the statutes, and the social ordinances which Hashem our God has commanded you?" (*Devarim* 6:20). Since his question stems from a true desire to accept the yoke of Heaven, he deserves an answer which will help him in serving Hashem.

Acceptance of the Heavenly yoke is not foremost in the mind of a fool. Of course, some foolishness stems from ignorance. One kind of fool will therefore ask with the intention of adding to his present understanding, and when he does, he will actually want to observe the mitzvos. It is of such a person that Shelomo Ha-Melech spoke when he said, "Answer a fool according to his folly, lest he be wise in his own eyes" (*Mishlei* 26:5). He will come to perceive the wisdom of the Torah and wish to draw near its light, instead of thinking he knows everything already.

There is another kind of fool who has no intention of believing in or taking the Torah seriously. Instead, like the villager at the fair, who wanted to rid himself of the cloth, he devises many shallow excuses for finding fault and rejecting it. Therefore his questions are not sincere and honest, but malicious and impertinent, and no amount of reasoning or instruction can persuade him that he is wrong. He even tries to make us doubt our own answers. Therefore, since he is really begging for an argument, do not answer him, lest you be drawn into his web. Rather, "blunt his teeth" so that he will be too stunned to corrupt others with his wicked ways. Of such a person, Shelomo Ha-Melech said, "Do not answer a fool according to his folly, lest you also become like him" (ibid. 26:4). Look at him sternly and say forcefully, "What I observe here is in gratitude for what Hashem did for me. As for you, you have rejected His Torah and therefore have no part in our inheritance. Had you been in Egypt, you would not have been saved."

Emes L'Yaakov

Blunt his teeth.

Why blunt his teeth? Why not just correct him with kind words? The answer can be found in the words of Rabbi Chayim ben Attar, the holy Or Ha-Chayim.

A person who has allowed the yetzer ha-ra (evil inclination) to rule him becomes impervious to moral correction. The yetzer stands at the door of his

The simple son — what does he say? "What is this?" (see *Shemos* 13:14). And you shall say to him: "By strength of Hand did Hashem bring us out from Egypt, from the house of bondage" (*ibid.*).

תָּם מַה הוּא אוֹמֵר. מַה זֹּאת. וְאָמַרְתָּ אֵלָיו בְּחֹזֶק יָד הוֹצִיאָנוּ יהוה מִמִּצְרַיִם מִבֵּית־עֲבָדִים.

heart, blocking words of truth from entering his soul. He is like the "ben sorer u'moreh," the son whom the Torah describes as refusing "to hearken to his father's and mother's voice. They have corrected him, but he refuses to listen to them" (*Devarim* 21:18).

This is similar to a king who stationed guards outside his palace. Unknown to the king, these guards robbed everyone who came to visit him. Understandably, the victims wished to protest their treatment to the king. Knowing that they would immediately be found guilty, however, the guards would not allow them to enter. Unless something could be done, the king would never hear their cries and correct the situation.

What is the solution? First of all, the guards must be removed. "Blunt their teeth" and break their pride. Then we will be able to come before the King and voice our pleas.

Or Ha-Chayim, *Ki Tetze 21:18*

The simple son.

The simple son ("tam"), what does he say? [He merely asks,] "What is this?" (*Shemos* 13:14). You shall answer him, "By strength of Hand did Hashem bring us out from Egypt, from the house of bondage" (ibid.).

The Torah praises our father Yaakov as an "ish tam" (man of integrity and wholesomeness). It is a mitzvah to "Be 'tamim' (wholly devoted) to Hashem your God" (*Devarim* 18:13). Only in the Haggadah does "temimus" (innocence, naivete, simplicity) appear to be a less than desirable trait.

Rabbi Chayim Elazar, the holy Munkatcher Rebbe, explained this anomaly. According to his interpretation, the "tam" in the Haggadah is not asking a question to which he expects an answer. His words are not to be read as: "What is this?" but "What, this? [It is nothing to get excited about]." In his seeming acceptance of things lies his mistake. He illustrated this with a true story.

The holy Ba'al Shem Tov of blessed memory had a disciple whose name was Reb David Porkash. Reb David was a great ba'al emunah. He would always accept whatever happened to him with tremendous faith, saying, "God is our Father!" Once, Reb David came to his master as he was about to travel.

The Ba'al Shem Tov admonished him, "Be careful about what you say!"

Reb David did not understand what the Ba'al Shem Tov was referring to. He departed. Many months later, he returned.

The first thing the Ba'al Shem Tov said to him was, "Didn't I tell you to be careful about what you said?"

Reb David was dumbfounded by his master's harsh words. But he still did not understand what his rebbe was referring to.

To remind him, the Ba'al Shem Tov said, "Do you remember when you went ashore?"

At that, Reb David began to recall what had happened. On route, his ship had dropped anchor at a deserted island shore. He had gone ashore to explore, and ended up losing his way. When he finally found his way back, the ship had already set sail without him, and was no more than a tiny speck on the horizon. Initially, he felt frightened and depressed, but he immediately took heart and accepted his lot with faith in Hashem's Providence.

Our Father is great, he thought to himself, and whatever He does is for the good.

He resumed exploring the island, hoping to come upon one of its inhabitants.

Before long, he spotted a small cottage. In the cottage there was an ancient Jew whose countenance shone like the midday sun. The old man was completely absorbed in reading a Torah scroll. When he looked up, he smiled at Reb David and asked him about the condition of the Jewish People where he lived. He had heard that the Polish government had decreed a series of extremely harsh edicts, that the Jews were being forced to pay high taxes, and that the gentile villagers were mercilessly taking advantage of their sorry plight.

"Hashem is our Father!" Reb David replied with his usual temimus.

The old man accompanied Reb David to the beach where another ship had dropped anchor. He boarded the ship and set off for his destination.

Now, standing with his master, he understood that the Ba'al Shem Tov had seen all this with his ruach ha-kodesh (Divine inspiration).

The Ba'al Shem Tov asked Reb David, "Do you know who that old Jew was? I'll tell you. It was Avraham Avinu who was busy crying and pleading before the Heavenly Throne over the tragic plight of his children. In heaven he was told that, for various reasons, it was not as bad as he claimed. In order to settle the matter, it was decreed that you would be left stranded on that island so that Avraham Avinu could ask about the condition of our people. When you replied in your normal manner that our Father is great in heaven and that

everything He does is for our good, Avraham's complaints were dismissed and permission was given to the Accuser to carry out his evil schemes. Didn't I tell you to be careful about what you said?"

In a similar vein, it is well-known that another great disciple of the Ba'al Shem Tov, Rabbi Nachman of Horodenka, used to say, "This is also for the good!" about everything that happened to him. Once, an extremely serious decree was pronounced against the Jewish People and the Ba'al Shem Tov prayed and pleaded that the decree be rescinded. Rabbi Nachman said to him, "But this is also for the good!"

The Ba'al Shem Tov answered him thus: "It is a great miracle that you were not alive when Haman made a decree to destroy and annihilate our people. If you would have been there, you might have said, 'This is also for the good!' But thank God Mordechai stood in the breach and shook heaven and earth! Only thus was the decree rescinded. A Jew is obligated at all times to feel the pain of his fellows and to plead for mercy before the Heavenly Throne!"

This is the explanation for placing the "tam's" question in a negative light. For who is this "tam"? On the verse: "Be 'tamim' (wholly devoted) to Hashem your God," Rashi tells us in his commentary: "Accept all that passes over you with 'temimus.'" Certainly it is a good trait and a positive mitzvah to be a "tam," to believe with perfect faith that everything Hashem does is for the good. This is how we should accept any Heavenly decree that affects us personally. When tragedy strikes others, however, that is a different story. We must feel their pain and storm the Heavenly gates in order to nullify any and all evil decrees.

When witnessing some great tragedy, comparable to the suffering and bondage of the Jewish People in Egypt, the "tam" is liable to misinterpret it and say, "What, this? It isn't so bad. In fact, it is probably for the good!"

You must answer him very clearly, however, and say, "It is a fact that the generation of the Exodus suffered under the strain of Egyptian bondage and cried out to be saved. As a result of their cries, Hashem saved them from their servitude and redeemed them through the use of powerful miracles. If they had mistakenly concluded that it was all for the good and not worth bothering Hashem about — if they that had not cried out because of the pain of all their brethren who were dying daily before their very eyes — they would not have been saved!"

Sha'ar Yissachar, *Aggadeta D'Pischa 45*

The wise son — what does he say?... The simple son — what does he say?...

Rabbi Simcha Bunim of Peshischa used a parable to explain the difference between the wise son's and simple son's questions.

A king once sentenced three men to life imprisonment in a dark dungeon. Two of them were extremely wise, and the third was an ignorant simpleton. Every day the king's guards would lower their food down to them in a pail. Due to the extreme darkness in the dungeon, the fool could never figure out what food they were getting to eat. He was so disoriented that he mistook a spoon for a plate. His frustration knew no end when he tried eating a bowl of soup with a fork.

One of the wise men took pity on him. He sat by his side in the darkness and taught him how to feel and identify things using his hands. With extraordinary patience, he guided him, repeating what he had taught him many times over until the simpleton appeared to have mastered it.

All his work was for naught, however, for the very next day the king's guards would lower different vessels down to them, and the wise man was forced to sit with the simpleton for hours teaching him again how to use the different utensils they had been given.

The first wise man became annoyed at the second wise man for not assisting him in his efforts to educate their mutual charge. Instead of taking on his part of the workload, he was always busy over in the corner of the dungeon.

The second wise man answered him, saying, "You are occupied in trying to teach him anew every day. You are sapping your strength for naught on a labor which has no end. Meanwhile, I am busy trying to bore a hole through the wall so that a ray of sunlight can filter in. Then we shall all be able to see and eventually escape!"

"The fool walks in darkness" (*Koheles* 2:14). As a result, he bumps into and trips over every object that gets in his way. This is exactly how most of us learn Torah as well. We haphazardly bump into a mitzvah which we have trouble understanding, and we ask, "What's this?" But even when we learn enough about it, we fail to connect it with other things we have learned. Everything always remains fuzzy and disconnected. This is the meaning of the tam's question and the reason the Haggadah does not praise him for his temimus.

On the other hand, there are two kinds of wise men. Both are praiseworthy. Both are guided by the light of Torah that illuminates their minds and hearts. One of them attempts to share this light with others by entering deeply into

As for the son who does not know how to ask — you must begin the conversation with him, as it is stated in the Torah: "And you shall relate to your child on that day, saying: 'It is because of this that Hashem acted for me when I came forth out of Egypt'" (*Shemos* 13:8).

וְשֶׁאֵינוֹ יוֹדֵעַ לִשְׁאוֹל אַתְּ פְּתַח לוֹ. שֶׁנֶּאֱמַר וְהִגַּדְתָּ לְבִנְךָ בַּיּוֹם הַהוּא לֵאמֹר בַּעֲבוּר זֶה עָשָׂה יהוה לִי בְּצֵאתִי מִמִּצְרָיִם:

the intricacies of Torah with them, showing how everything is connected, not one thing without its place in the total scheme. The other is not satisfied with this. He seeks to cast greater and greater light into the darkness of this world by boring a hole in the wall that keeps us from Hashem. He knows that once he does this, once he allows the light to dispel the darkness completely, there will be no more need to teach the simpleton. He will see for himself. This is the meaning of our answer to the tam, "Hashem brought us out of Egypt, out of the dungeon of prisoners, by revealing His great light to us." When that light shone, we immediately knew that the time had come to leave Egypt.

Ma'amarei Simchah 43

"And you shall relate to your child on that day, saying: 'It is because of this that Hashem acted for me when I came forth out of Egypt.'"

Rabbi Shelomo Kluger of Brodi asked: According to the Haggadah, we see that the words, "It is because of this" refer to both matzah and maror. If this is the case, however, shouldn't the verse have been stated in the plural, "Because of these"?

He answered: The Torah gave preference to the matzah, as another verse states: "With unleavened bread and bitter herbs shall they eat it" (*Bemidbar* 9:11). The reason for it being in this order is that matzah symbolizes redemption, while maror symbolizes the bitterness of exile and subjugation. On Pesach night, the darkness and bitterness of the exile pale to insignificance in the light of Hashem's miraculous redemption.

Moreover, in the light of redemption, we look back on the bitterness of exile and perceive it differently. We realize that is was a necessary means to refine and purify us in preparation for receiving the Torah. This follows the statement by the Sages (*Berachos* 5a) that the Torah is one of three gifts which are only attained through suffering.

Moreover, the greater the subjugation, the greater the miracle of the exodus that follows it. So the suffering and subjugation of Egypt must be seen as a necessary cause and prerequisite for redemption.

יָכוֹל מֵרֹאשׁ חֹדֶשׁ. תַּלְמוּד לוֹמַר בַּיּוֹם הַהוּא. אִי בַּיּוֹם הַהוּא יָכוֹל מִבְּעוֹד יוֹם. תַּלְמוּד לוֹמַר בַּעֲבוּר זֶה. בַּעֲבוּר זֶה לֹא אָמַרְתִּי אֶלָּא בְּשָׁעָה שֶׁיֵּשׁ מַצָּה וּמָרוֹר מֻנָּחִים לְפָנֶיךָ:

מִתְּחִלָּה עוֹבְדֵי עֲבוֹדָה זָרָה הָיוּ אֲבוֹתֵינוּ. וְעַכְשָׁו קֵרְבָנוּ הַמָּקוֹם לַעֲבוֹדָתוֹ. שֶׁנֶּאֱמַר וַיֹּאמֶר יְהוֹשֻׁעַ אֶל־כָּל־הָעָם כֹּה־אָמַר יהוה אֱלֹהֵי יִשְׂרָאֵל בְּעֵבֶר הַנָּהָר יָשְׁבוּ אֲבוֹתֵיכֶם מֵעוֹלָם תֶּרַח אֲבִי אַבְרָהָם וַאֲבִי נָחוֹר וַיַּעַבְדוּ אֱלֹהִים אֲחֵרִים: וָאֶקַּח אֶת־אֲבִיכֶם אֶת־אַבְרָהָם מֵעֵבֶר הַנָּהָר וָאוֹלֵךְ אוֹתוֹ בְּכָל־אֶרֶץ כְּנָעַן וָאַרְבֶּה אֶת זַרְעוֹ וָאֶתֶּן לוֹ אֶת־

One might think that the obligation to recount the story of the departure from Egypt begins from the first day of the month of Nissan. However, the Torah states: "on that day."* "On that *day*" might be understood to mean *while it is still day*. Therefore, the text specifies "it is because of *this*." I can say "it is because of this" only at such time when the matzah and the maror are in front of you.

At first our fathers were idol worshipers, but now the Omnipresent has brought us near to His service, as it is said: "And Yehoshua said to all the people: 'Thus said Hashem, the God of Yisrael: "On the other side of the river, your fathers dwelt of old, Terach, father of Avraham and father of Nachor, and they served other gods. And I took your father Avraham from the other side of the river and led him through the whole land of Canaan, and I multiplied

This is similar to Shabbos. Shabbos is called "First in thought and last in deed." In other words, even though Shabbos does not actually begin until after six days of work, the idea of Shabbos preceded these days. So also, redemption is always first in Hashem's mind, even though it cannot become manifest until after we have suffered the tribulations of exile.

We can now savor the deeper meaning of the statement in the Haggadah: "He who elaborates upon the story of the departure from Egypt is worthy of praise." Of course, it is possible to speak about the Exodus quickly and concisely, without the slightest elaboration, i.e., without including in it the entire exile and subjugation that preceded it. But one is only deserving of praise when one includes the story of the exile in the story of the redemption.

This is similar to two artisans who were hired to fashion an exquisite vessel. The first artisan requested the finest and most expensive materials available. The second promised to make a stunning vessel from simpler materials. Which is more praiseworthy? The second! In the same way, one who praises Hashem for His miracles and His great kindnesses is fulfilling his basic obligations. One who praises Him even for the suffering he has undergone, transforming his grievances to praise — he is truly praiseworthy!

Ma'asei Yedei Yotzer 14b

At first our fathers were idol worshipers.

Rabbi Avlei, the Gaon of Minsk, asked the obvious question: Why must our retelling the story of the Exodus from Egypt start with our lowly beginnings?

his descendants and gave him Yitzchak. And to Yitzchak I gave Yaakov and Esav; to Esav I gave Mount Seir for an inheritance, and Yaakov and his children went down to Egypt'''' (*Yehoshua* 24:2-4).	יִצְחָק: וָאֶתֵּן לְיִצְחָק אֶת־יַעֲקֹב וְאֶת עֵשָׂו וָאֶתֵּן לְעֵשָׂו אֶת־הַר שֵׂעִיר לָרֶשֶׁת אוֹתוֹ וְיַעֲקֹב וּבָנָיו יָרְדוּ מִצְרָיִם:

Why must we start by recalling that our ancestors worshiped idols? He answered with a parable:

Two friends, Yaakov and Chayim, lived in tiny village. One day, both unexpectedly fell ill with the same symptoms. The local doctor, the elderly Dr. Rophe, was both a surgeon and a pharmacist, as was common in those days when doctors were called upon to act like traveling hospitals. He examined both men and prepared their respective medications. He then told Yaakov to pay him five gold pieces, while Chayim was to pay twenty.

Chayim protested. "What's the meaning of this? We both came down with the same ailment. Why should I pay four times more than Yaakov?"

Dr. Rophe looked at Chayim and answered, "True, your ailments are identical, but your medications and treatments, including the amount of time needed to recuperate, are totally different."

Chayim was shocked. "How do you know all this? What are you basing your diagnosis on?"

Old Dr. Rophe smiled. "You know that I am well-advanced in years," he said. "I have been the doctor in this area for many decades. I remember when your grandmother came down with this same condition. You see, you are congenitally predisposed by your heredity to this disease. Unlike Yaakov, who is relatively healthy and whose condition is therefore far easier to treat, yours is more serious. Your medications are more expensive, and your treatment will take longer."

When recounting the story of the Egyptian exile and our redemption from it, we find it difficult to comprehend how our ancestors, the grandchildren of Avraham, Yitzchak and Yaakov, the tribes of Yisrael, sank so low, in such a short time, to the point that they became immersed in forty-nine levels of impurity. Why was such an intense degree of Divine revelation needed to extricate them from that impurity before it was too late? Why did Hashem literally have to overturn all of nature, exposing all its constant, stable laws as nothing more than facades for His overriding providence? How did they sink so low and why did they require so much proof of Hashem's mastery over all the forces of nature in order to believe in Him and in His servant Moshe?

When we look back in time, however, to an era long before the Egyptian exile, it all begins to make sense. We need only recall Terach, the idol worshiper. True, Avraham, Yitzchak, and Yaakov had worked hard to purify themselves of that ancient sickness of idolatry. But a dormant gene was left in them from Avraham's father. When our ancestors were confronted with the overwhelming power of Egyptian culture and its belief in many deities, this gene reemerged as a dominant hereditary factor.

The expensive medications and treatment we required were given to us in the form of the ten plagues visited upon the Egyptians. Each plague cleared away a little bit more of the disease, until we were finally able to believe that there is only One Ultimate Power behind all that happens in this world. We then grew stronger and stronger as we left Egypt and approached Sinai. When we received the Torah, we became completely cured.

Zichron Avraham 30

An alternative explanation for this parable, which explains the difference between Yaakov and Chayim according to the teachings of Rabbi Yitzchak Luria Ashkenazi, the holy Ari, might go as follows:

When we look back in time, to an era long before the Egyptian exile, it all begins to make sense. We know that seventy souls came to Egypt with Yaakov Avinu. These were the pure seed of the Patriarchs and Matriarchs, exalted souls who purified themselves and merited to become embodiments of the Shechinah, Hashem's presence in this world. These souls are represented in the character of Yaakov in our story.

But, as the Ari explains in a number of places (see *Sha'ar Ha-Pesukim, Shemos Alef*), there were Egyptians who attached themselves to our people during the period of Yosef's ascendancy (these were the Egyptians whom Yosef had circumcised). They were followed, during the eighty final years of unbearable subjugation, by other souls who were actually born to Jewish mothers in Egypt. These souls had undergone numerous transmigrations since the time of Adam, and were in need of rectification. These were the children who were born six at a time. In both of these groups of souls much of that original defilement that had infected Adam and Chava remained dormant, waiting to activate at some point. These souls are represented in the character of Chayim. They were the ones who were more prone to idol worship.

By the time of the Exodus, the Jewish People as a whole was made up of a combination of Yaakovs and Chayims.

This explains why, even after the Patriarchs had succeeded in totally purifying themselves from the ancient sickness of idolatry, some of their descendants

remained pure, while in others the old hereditary sickness reemerged in full force. This also explains why the chain of miracles was so long and drawn out. These were the special medications and treatments needed to cure the Chayim-souls who had attached themselves to the Jewish People.

"To Esav I gave Mount Seir for an inheritance, and Yaakov and his children went down to Egypt."

The Maggid of Kaminetz commented: Esav certainly knew about the Covenant between the Portions. He was not interested in going to Egypt, however, even if the promised reward would be "great wealth." It just did not seem worth all the trouble of "going down" to Egypt in order to "come up" to Eretz Yisrael! He chose, rather, to inherit Mount Seir immediately, letting his twin brother Yaakov suffer in Egypt.

And so it was. The descent into Egypt was for the sake of a far greater ascent than Esav ever could have imagined. The "great wealth" was not just the gold and diamonds Yaakov's children took with them when they left their Egyptian hosts. It was the Torah itself, and the privilege of being the People of Hashem for all eternity!

But one thing remains unclear. Why did the process of becoming Hashem's people require living in Egypt and being subjected to its afflictions? The Maggid answered this profound question with an equally profound parable.

The lord of a large estate decided to make a big, gala celebration for his subjects in honor of his birthday. Long before the scheduled date, he summoned all of his chief ministers and butlers to provide them with detailed instructions for the upcoming occasion. He also summoned his tailor, to whom he gave meters of the finest and most expensive silk brought specially from the Far East, in order to sew him an elegant new suit of clothing. He also provided him with inexpensive wool material to sew new clothes for all his servants in honor of the celebration.

The tailor decided to get the servants' clothes out of the way first. He began by quickly cutting and basting each suit together. He used long stitches and didn't bother ironing the material. He was now ready to sew the prince's regal suit. This time he worked slowly, paying great attention to detail, and sewing with almost minute stitches. And after every few stitches, he would press the silk suit with a scorching hot iron.

At night, the wool suits made fun of the silk suit. "Do you think you are so special? In truth you really are not. See how he pierces you with his needle mercilessly, stitch after stitch! And if that were not enough to deflate some of your puffed up pride, think about that scalding hot iron he passes over you every few minutes! Of course, he pierced us too, but compassionately, and far less frequently. And surely out of love for us, he withheld that nasty old iron completely and totally! A sure sign indeed that he loves us more and chose us foremost over you!"

The silk suit didn't dare say a word. It wouldn't be right, he thought, to answer the fools according to their folly. He endured the humiliation in mute silence, accepting his travail with hope, faith, and love.

The servants' clothes were finished and hastily delivered to their owners, whereas the silk suit's quota of suffering had not yet been entirely filled. The tailor measured the suit on the lord now, and made all the last minute adjustments and repairs. After what seemed an eternity, the suit was finally completed to the tailor's satisfaction, at which time it was placed in the lord's clothes closet to await the great celebration. One last pass of the scorching iron was all that was required, and the prince outfitted himself in his splendid, regal garment.

The lord's birthday arrived, and his servants came dressed in their new wool garments in order to pay him homage. Together they blessed their master while their suits lifted up their eyes in astonishment. Beholding the lord's oriental silks now, there could be no more mistakes. They, who had suffered so much, were now stately garments, giving the lord the appearance of a king!

The garments could hold back no longer. They lifted up their eyes once more to the silk suit on the prince, and together addressed the ultimate question to it in unison: "The time has come for us to admit how very wrong we were. We no longer doubt that you are greater than we by far. But please allow us to understand: If you are so great and important, why did you have to suffer all that agony, oppression, and pain? Why were you pierced with needles and scorched with a searing iron?"

The silk garment answered them, "Simple garments of simple people you are, and with the minds of simple people you were graced. Don't you understand what you have said? It is because I am precious and important and worthy of adorning such a noble person that I had to be measured to his exact size and adjusted to fit him. That is why the tailor took such great pains over every stitch and pressed away each crease in me, to meticulously prepare me for my destiny — to make me a proper and fit garment for my master."

Ateres Tzvi, *Derush* 9

Blessed be He Who keeps His promise to Yisrael. Blessed be He. For the Holy One, Blessed be He, calculated the end [of their exile], to do as He had said to our father Avraham at the Covenant between the Portions, as it is written: "He said to Avram: 'Know for sure that your seed shall be a stranger in a land that is not theirs, and they will enslave them and afflict them four hundred years. But also that nation whom they shall serve, do I judge, and afterwards they shall go forth with great possessions.'" (*Bereishis* 15:13-14).

בָּרוּךְ שׁוֹמֵר הַבְטָחָתוֹ לְיִשְׂרָאֵל. בָּרוּךְ הוּא. שֶׁהַקָּדוֹשׁ בָּרוּךְ הוּא חִשַּׁב אֶת הַקֵּץ לַעֲשׂוֹת כְּמָה שֶּׁאָמַר לְאַבְרָהָם אָבִינוּ בִּבְרִית בֵּין הַבְּתָרִים. שֶׁנֶּאֱמַר וַיֹּאמֶר לְאַבְרָם יָדֹעַ תֵּדַע כִּי־גֵר יִהְיֶה זַרְעֲךָ בְּאֶרֶץ לֹא לָהֶם וַעֲבָדוּם וְעִנּוּ אֹתָם אַרְבַּע מֵאוֹת שָׁנָה: וְגַם אֶת־הַגּוֹי אֲשֶׁר יַעֲבֹדוּ דָּן אָנֹכִי וְאַחֲרֵי כֵן יֵצְאוּ בִּרְכֻשׁ גָּדוֹל:

They will enslave them...four hundred years.

It is well known that the amount of time that elapsed from our father Yaakov's descent into Egypt until the actual Exodus was 210 years. As Rashi points out, this is alluded to in Yaakov's statement to his children, "'Redu shama' (Go down there) [to Egypt]..." (*Bereishis* 42:2), the numerical value of "redu" being 210.

Theoretically, this need not have been the case. Had Hashem wished, He could have calculated differently. Yaakov's descent into Egypt could have marked the beginning of the 400 years of enslavement mentioned in the Covenant between the Portions. As it was, however, this 400-year period began exactly 190 years before with the birth of Yitzchak. This is the meaning of the phrase "chishev es ha-ketz" (calculated the end). The numerical value of "ketz" (end) is 190. In effect, we are thanking Hashem for calculating the "ketz" — that is, for including these 190 years in the calculation.

Rabbi Yosef Shaul Nathanzon of Lvov explains that Hashem never seriously considered the possibility of letting His children remain enslaved in Egypt for 400 years. As noted, He had already calculated the end and determined it would be in 210 years. If this is the case, though, the question naturally arises: Why did He imply that Yisrael's exile in a "land that is not theirs" would last for 400 years? Rabbi Nathanzon answers in the form of a parable.

There was once a merciful king who sat as chief justice of his tribunal. When trying a subject accused of breaking the law of the land, the king followed the normal procedure in all courts of law. First, he would summon the prosecutor to bring his charges against the accused. Then the advocate would defend him in an attempt to vindicate him. Witnesses would be called in, and evidence would be presented. Finally, the judges would meet with the king in his private chambers to arrive at a just verdict.

Once, one of the king's subjects was tried in this way, and the judges wanted to sentence him to ten years imprisonment. Identifying with the accused man's plight, the king wished to be lenient with him. He was prevented from doing this, however, for he did not wish to oppose his colleagues' decision. After all, a king must uphold justice in the administration of his kingdom. What could he do?

Addressing his fellow judges, he began, "When does a man sentenced to ten years in jail begin to feel the weight of imprisonment lighten? When does he begin to look up and start anticipating the day of his release? I would say by the time he reaches his seventh or eighth year."

The other judges nodded in agreement.

"This being the case," the king continued, "I suggest we sentence this man to twenty years. This way he will lose all hope, and we will be able to release him after eight years. The reason is simple: With all hope of premature release withheld from him, he will have suffered as much in his seventh and eighth years as a man sentenced to ten years suffers in the first years of his incarceration!"

Strictly speaking, we should have had to stay in Egypt approximately 300 years. Wishing to prevent our looking forward anxiously to the redemption as the end approached, Hashem informed Avraham Avinu that our sentence would last for a total of 400 years. In this way, the suffering we endured during our first 210 years was far greater, such that He was justified in reducing the original 300 year sentence to 210 years.

This is what the author of the Haggadah means when he continues, "And it is this [promise] which stood by our fathers and by us." That is, this profound insight into human nature, that we suffer infinitely more when we are kept in the dark regarding the duration of our suffering — to the point that all our hopes of a speedy redemption are dashed — this is the deep counsel Hashem used to rectify all our shortcomings and actually accelerate the Exodus.

How does this work? Exactly as it says in the Haggadah: "For not just one has risen up against us to destroy us, but in every single generation they rise up against us to destroy us." Living thus under the constant threat of annihilation, terrorized and panic-stricken — this was His way of cleansing us of our sins when all other ways failed. For in the end, all who have oppressed us have lost everything and sunk into oblivion. "And the Holy One, Blessed be He, delivers us from their hand."

Divrei Shaul 21a

To do as He had said to our father Avraham at the Covenant between the Portions.

In the Covenant between the Portions, Hashem said to Avraham, "I am the Eternal God who took you out of Ur Kasdim to give you this land as an inheritance" (*Bereishis* 15:7). "O' Hashem," Avraham asked, "how can I really be certain that it will be mine?"

Hashem replied to him, "Offer Me a prime heifer, a prime goat, a prime ram, a turtledove and a young pigeon."

Avraham offered all these to Him by splitting them in half and placing one half opposite the other. The birds, however, he did not split. Vultures descended on the carcasses, but Avraham drove them away.

When the sun was setting, Avraham fell into a trance and he was stricken by a deep, dark dread. Hashem said to Avraham, "Know for sure that your seed shall be a stranger in a land that is not theirs, and they will enslave them and afflict them four hundred years. But also that nation whom they shall serve, do I judge, and afterwards they shall go forth with great possessions" (*Bereishis* 15:13-14).

The sun set, and it grew very dark. A smoking furnace and a flaming torch passed between the halves of the animals. On that day, Hashem made a covenant with Avraham, saying, "To your descendants I have given this land, from the Egyptian River, as far as the great river, the Euphrates" (*Bereishis* 15:18).

The Gaon, Rav Aryeh Leib Tzintz of Platzk, asked the following three questions: Why did Hashem find it necessary to make a covenant with Avraham Avinu regarding the inheritance of the Land of Yisrael? Why did Avraham ask, "How can I really be certain that it will be mine?" Why was the answer given to him, "Know for sure that your seed shall be a stranger in a land that is not theirs?"

The Gaon answered with a parable.

There was once a king who was very fond of his minister. When the minister grew old and was about to die, the king wished to make his last hours more pleasant.

He paid him a visit and said, "As you know, I have an only daughter whom I love very dearly. She is the apple of my eye, embodying every fine virtue." The king hesitated, lest the shock of what he was about to say have the opposite effect of what he wanted to achieve. "I want you to know... I have now come to tell you that I have made up my mind. She will marry your grandson!"

The minister was shocked. Words failed him. For years his grandson had been suffering from a serious skin disease. As a result, his face was scarred. He was so deformed and ugly that nobody wished to associate with him. Trusting in the king's sincerity and knowing full well that he meant every word he said, the minister nevertheless feared that the other ministers would try to dissuade the king to change his mind. To allay the minister's apprehension, however, he immediately swore a solemn oath that he would never retract his promise.

Now the minister's fears were put to rest, but one thing still bothered him. It seemed strange to him that the king would give the hand of his only daughter, so enchantingly beautiful and perfect, to his grandson, cursed with such a wretched disease, an outcast among men.

The king knew what was on his mind. "Do you think that I will take him as he is? Not at all! First I will summon the finest doctors to cure him. Most certainly, the treatment will be long and painful. In the end, however, your grandson will be fully healed and a most fitting husband for my daughter!"

The Land of Yisrael is a holy land, set aside for sanctity, God's special "estate" in this world, which He constantly watches over. When Hashem promised this wondrous land to Avraham Avinu, the latter understood that his descendants would not be ready to inherit it for quite a long time. He also feared the accusations of the "ministers," the accusing angels in Hashem's heavenly tribunal. Perhaps his children's shortcomings would help them convince Hashem to go back on His promise!

What did Hashem do? He swore that He would never go back on His word. He made a covenant with Avraham that his children would eventually inherit the Land of Yisrael forever.

But Avraham still could not comprehend how his children would ever be fully worthy of such a precious gift. In answer to this, Hashem told him that he would refine them first by sending them into exile. Just as a furnace burns away the dross found in gold ore, exile would clean away every imperfection in his children. They would then be worthy of inheriting the promised land, Eretz Yisrael!

Birkas Ha-Shir

But also that nation whom they shall serve, do I judge.

Many have asked: If Hashem wished to subject Yisrael to Egyptian bondage, and the Egyptians were instrumental in fulfilling His wish, why were they punished for doing so?

The Maggid of Dubno provided his answer in the form of a parable.

A widower had an only son. The boy became his father's only consolation in life, and he pampered him to no end. For a number of years, father and son became more and more deeply attached.

Only when the time came to remarry did things begin to change. The father's new wife was jealous of his love for the boy. She perceived the boy as a spoiled brat to be dealt with harshly. Soon an outright battle broke out over the boy. His father would bring him gifts, while his stepmother deprived him of his basic needs. The stepmother did everything she could to cast the boy's behavior in a bad light. The father loyally defended him. This went on for many years.

Then the boy fell seriously ill. The father summoned the best doctors. They worked hard to save the boy and were successful in bringing his condition under control. Before leaving, they called the boy's father and stepmother aside and said, "Your son is still in critical condition. He is extremely weak, and may eat only tiny amounts of food. You must monitor every bite he takes and make sure he does not exceed the required amount."

The father took their warning seriously. When mealtime arrived, the stepmother would send in a large portion, and the father would cut it down to less than half!

The boy was confused and hurt. "Father, isn't it enough that my sickness makes me weak? Must you deprive me of the few morsels I need to survive? Until now, I would receive such portions from my stepmother. Now you are acting more cruelly towards me than she is!"

"No, my son," the loving father objected. "Do not be so quick to judge. Although our actions seem identical, and both of us have reduced your food intake, there is a world of difference in our intentions! She treats you with contempt and jealousy, whereas I am doing this out of love, and for your speedy recovery!"

Of course, Hashem decreed exile for us, and the Egyptians were instrumental in fulfilling that decree. But what a world of difference in their intentions! Hashem wished to refine us and draw our hearts close to Him for all eternity. He wanted us to cry out in our distress so that He could redeem us. The

Egyptians, on the other hand, subjugated us out of jealousy and hatred!

This is the meaning of Hashem's words to Nevuchadnetzar through His prophets: "I became angry with My people, [so] I desecrated My inheritance by delivering them into your hand. But you showed them no mercy. You laid your yoke heavily upon the aged" (*Yeshayahu* 47:6). And similarly: "I was angered a little, but they added evil to evil" (*Zecharyah* 1:14).

Kol Rinah Vi'Yeshuah 49a, 53b

Afterwards they shall go forth with great possessions.

Our Sages tell us that the "great possessions" promised to Avraham Avinu at the Covenant between the Portions was the Torah which his children received at the foot of Mount Sinai. But if this is indeed true, why were we commanded, before leaving Egypt, to ask the Egyptians for money and goods?

The Maggid of Dubno answered with one of his most famous parables.

A wealthy merchant needed a young boy to deliver packages to his customers' houses. It was vacation time, so he offered the job to his friend's son with the promise that he would be handsomely paid with a purse full of silver coins. The boy felt fortunate for being given the opportunity, and he worked earnestly for the entire vacation. When the time came for him to take his leave, it occurred to the merchant that a purse full of silver coins was too small a payment for the splendid services the boy had rendered him. He therefore put the silver aside, and instead wrote out a check for an amount many times the total value of the silver. But the boy, instead of thanking his employer for his generosity, sullenly stuffed the piece of paper into his pocket and went home weeping.

The next day, his father called at the merchant's house and said to the wealthy man, "You have been most generous to my son and I want to thank you. But the boy is still a child and does not understand the value of a check. All he knows was that he expected to receive a bag filled with shiny new coins, and that instead he got a plain sheet of paper. Therefore, I would be most grateful if you would let him have at least part of his wages in silver coins."

In the same manner did our father Avraham come to Hashem, saying, "You have been generous indeed in promising the Torah to my descendants. But the nation will be young and not mature enough to understand the value of the Torah. If they then have to depart from Egypt with empty hands, they will

Cover the matzos and raise the cup of wine:

AND it is this [promise] which stood by our fathers and by us, for not just one has risen up against us to destroy us, but in every single generation they rise up against us to destroy us, and the Holy One, Blessed be He, delivers us from their hand.

וְהִיא שֶׁעָמְדָה לַאֲבוֹתֵינוּ וְלָנוּ. שֶׁלֹּא אֶחָד בִּלְבָד עָמַד עָלֵינוּ לְכַלּוֹתֵנוּ. אֶלָּא שֶׁבְּכָל דּוֹר וָדוֹר עוֹמְדִים עָלֵינוּ לְכַלּוֹתֵנוּ. וְהַקָּדוֹשׁ בָּרוּךְ הוּא מַצִּילֵנוּ מִיָּדָם:

Put down the cup and uncover the matzos:

GO and learn what Lavan the Aramean planned to do to our father Yaakov. For while Pharaoh's decree applied only to the male children, Lavan sought to uproot all, as it says: **"...an Aramean near to ruin was my father, and he went down to Egypt and sojourned there as a stranger, few in number; and there he became a nation, great, strong and numerous"** (*Devarim* 26:5).

צֵא וּלְמַד. מַה בִּקֵּשׁ לָבָן הָאֲרַמִּי לַעֲשׂוֹת לְיַעֲקֹב אָבִינוּ. שֶׁפַּרְעֹה לֹא גָזַר אֶלָּא עַל הַזְּכָרִים וְלָבָן בִּקֵּשׁ לַעֲקוֹר אֶת הַכֹּל. שֶׁנֶּאֱמַר: **אֲרַמִּי אֹבֵד אָבִי וַיֵּרֶד מִצְרַיְמָה וַיָּגָר שָׁם בִּמְתֵי מְעָט וַיְהִי שָׁם לְגוֹי גָּדוֹל עָצוּם וָרָב:**

And he went down to Egypt — compelled by Divine decree.

And sojourned there as a stranger — this teaches that our father Yaakov did not go down to settle permanently in Egypt, but to stay there temporarily, as it says: "And they [the sons of Yaakov] said to Pharaoh: 'We have come to sojourn in the land, as there is no pasture for your servants' sheep, because the famine is severe in the land of Canaan; and now, please, let your servants dwell in the land of Goshen'" (*Bereishis* 47:4).

Few in number — as it says: "With seventy souls, your forefathers went down to Egypt, and now Hashem your God has made you as the stars of the heavens for multitude" (*Devarim* 10:22).

וַיֵּרֶד מִצְרַיְמָה. אָנוּס עַל פִּי הַדִּבּוּר:

וַיָּגָר שָׁם. מְלַמֵּד שֶׁלֹּא יָרַד יַעֲקֹב אָבִינוּ לְהִשְׁתַּקֵּעַ בְּמִצְרַיִם אֶלָּא לָגוּר שָׁם. שֶׁנֶּאֱמַר וַיֹּאמְרוּ אֶל פַּרְעֹה לָגוּר בָּאָרֶץ בָּאנוּ כִּי אֵין מִרְעֶה לַצֹּאן אֲשֶׁר לַעֲבָדֶיךָ כִּי־כָבֵד הָרָעָב בְּאֶרֶץ כְּנָעַן וְעַתָּה יֵשְׁבוּ נָא עֲבָדֶיךָ בְּאֶרֶץ גֹּשֶׁן:

בִּמְתֵי מְעָט. כְּמָה שֶׁנֶּאֱמַר בְּשִׁבְעִים נֶפֶשׁ יָרְדוּ אֲבֹתֶיךָ מִצְרָיְמָה וְעַתָּה שָׂמְךָ יהוה אֱלֹהֶיךָ כְּכוֹכְבֵי הַשָּׁמַיִם לָרֹב:

say, 'Indeed, Hashem has fulfilled part of His promise. We did become slaves. But what of the great wealth we were supposed to receive at the hour of our deliverance?'"

It is for this reason, the Talmud explains, that Yisrael was clearly commanded to take gold and silver vessels from the Egyptians. This would be tangible wealth that they could appreciate at that time. In this way, they would realize immediately that Hashem's promise to Avraham had been fulfilled.

It was only as Yisrael grew in wisdom that it came to understand that its true wealth lay not in the coins and trinkets gathered in Egypt, but in the Divine gift of the Torah which has stood by our side to this very day.

Emes L'Yaakov 14a

וַיְהִי שָׁם לְגוֹי. מְלַמֵּד שֶׁהָיוּ יִשְׂרָאֵל מְצֻיָּנִים שָׁם:

גָּדוֹל עָצוּם. כְּמָה שֶׁנֶּאֱמַר וּבְנֵי יִשְׂרָאֵל פָּרוּ וַיִּשְׁרְצוּ וַיִּרְבּוּ וַיַּעַצְמוּ בִּמְאֹד מְאֹד וַתִּמָּלֵא הָאָרֶץ אֹתָם:

וָרָב. כְּמָה שֶׁנֶּאֱמַר רְבָבָה כְּצֶמַח הַשָּׂדֶה נְתַתִּיךְ וַתִּרְבִּי וַתִּגְדְּלִי וַתָּבֹאִי בַּעֲדִי עֲדָיִים שָׁדַיִם נָכֹנוּ וּשְׂעָרֵךְ צִמֵּחַ וְאַתְּ עֵרֹם וְעֶרְיָה: וָאֶעֱבוֹר עָלַיִךְ וָאֶרְאֵךְ מִתְבּוֹסֶסֶת בְּדָמָיִךְ וָאֹמַר לָךְ בְּדָמַיִךְ חֲיִי וָאֹמַר לָךְ בְּדָמַיִךְ חֲיִי:

There he became a nation — this teaches that Yisrael were distinctive people there.

Great, strong — as it says: "And the Children of Yisrael were fruitful by multiple births, and they increased abundantly and became exceedingly strong and the land was filled with them" (*Shemos* 1:7).

And numerous — as it says: "I let you become as myriads, like the plants of the field, and you increased and grew big; and you came of age to wear jewelry of outstanding beauty, your breasts properly formed and your hair grown, but you were naked and bare" (*Yechezkel* 16:7). "And I passed over you and saw you wallowing in your blood; and I said to you: 'In your blood, live!' and I said to you: 'In your blood, live!'" (*ibid.*, 6).

"You were naked and bare."

Rabbi Yehudah Leib of Slonim told a story about a man whose rooster was stolen from him. He looked everywhere but did not find it. He decided to go to the slaughter house to look for it on the chance that the thief had taken it there.

And indeed, he did meet a fellow there holding a rooster ready to be slaughtered. Its tail was smashed and its feathers were plucked, but there was no mistaking it. That was his stolen rooster!

"Thief," the man called out, "that's my rooster. Give it back!"

"You're lying!" the thief countered, holding the rooster tightly with both hands. "The rooster is mine! Is this how your rooster's tail looked? Were its feathers plucked? I'm sorry, but you are falsely accusing me!"

"Obviously it was you who smashed its tail and plucked its feathers! As for the fact that you are presently holding it in your possession, that is no proof that it is yours. Set it free for a moment and let's see if it runs to me, its true owner, or to you!"

This is exactly how Micha'el, the heavenly advocate of Yisrael, stands in heaven and pleads for Hashem's people. The Accuser, on the other hand, opposes him and says, "You are full of lies and deceit. Look at them well! As long as they are in my custody, do they look like your Jews? They are indistinguishable from people of any other nationality. They have forgotten what it is to be Jewish. They can no longer be called the children of Avraham, Yitzchak, and Yaakov!"

"Correct," Micha'el answers, "they are naked of the mitzvos. But the reason for this is that you have deprived them of their true Jewish ornaments; you

have crushed their spirits and clipped their wings! Set them free for a moment, however, and let us see to whom they return — to their Father in heaven!"

The same situation existed in Egypt. We were naked of the mitzvos, sunken in forty-nine levels of immorality and spiritual impurity, until the Holy One, Blessed be He, revealed Himself to them in all His Glory! At that point, the truth was clear for all to see. To whom does this nation belong, and in whom does it place its hopes? The Holy One, Blessed be He! The prophet attested to this when he said: "God's word came to me saying: Go and proclaim in the ears of Yerushalayim, saying, Thus says God: I remember the devotedness of your youth, your love as a bride, how you followed after Me into the wilderness, into a land that was not sown!" (*Yirmeyahu* 2:1-2).

And so we are promised: "As in the days of your exodus from Egypt, I will show them wonders" (*Michah* 7:15). All Hashem has to do is reveal His light, the light of His unceasing providence, and we will immediately know to Whom we belong. We will again accept His sovereignty over us, this time forever!

Sippurei Maran Ha-Ramach 284

"You were naked and bare."

The Midrash (*Shemos Rabbah* 1:35) states: "God saw the Children of Yisrael, and God took note of it" (*Shemos* 2:25). [What did Hashem see; what did He take note of?] "I have indeed seen the suffering of My People in Egypt... I know their pains" (ibid. 3:7). "And God saw" — that they lacked any good deeds which would entitle them to be redeemed. Yechezkel refers to this: "I let you become as myriads, like the plants of the field, and you increased and grew big; and you came of age to wear jewelry of outstanding beauty, your breasts properly formed and your hair grown, but you were naked and bare" (*Yechezkel* 16:7). "Your breasts properly formed" refers to Moshe and Aharon, who were made ready to redeem them. "Your hair grown" — the time had come for redemption. "But you were naked and bare" — they did not possess any good deeds.

The Yeffes To'ar explains: "And God saw" — when He saw that they lacked any good deeds which entitled them to be redeemed, the Blessed Holy One knew that He must redeem them for the sake of His Name, and for the sake of the covenant He made with the Avos. The Maggid of Dubno explained this with a parable.

A young girl from a well-to-do family had been orphaned and left destitute.

Not being very capable, she could not successfully run a household. When she reached a marriageable age, no one could be found who would be suitable for her. The rabbi of the city, a wise and kind man, was advised of the situation. He immediately called together all the shadchanim (matchmakers) in the city and informed them that the young woman was indeed a relative of his, whom he had personally taken under his wing.

"I am her guardian," he said, "and she is under my direct care."

Once it was known that she was the relative of the beloved rabbi, and that he had taken her under his wing, she had no trouble finding a proper match. She even ended up marrying the son of a prominent family in the community!

In Egypt, we had sunk to the lowest level. In addition to being Pharaoh's slaves, we had lost all semblance of our Jewishness and forgotten who we were. We had absolutely no merit of our own with which to deserve redemption. What did the Holy One do? He spread His wing (His providential care) over us, and called us by His Name. With this, an entirely miraculous providence could be set into motion. We could be redeemed.

Acharis L'Shalom 12b

"In your blood, live!"

"In your blood, live!" (*Yechezkel* 16:6). The Maggid of Warsaw explained: Right there, in the very midst of your suffering, that is where the redemptive process begins! And the lesson is very clear: Do not fall into depression if pain, sickness, or any other kind of suffering overtakes you. On the contrary, know that it is a purification, sent to release you — a stimulus for you to grow beyond your present limitations!

This is like the city dweller who once traveled to a rural village to visit an old friend of his. The friend was not at home when he arrived, so the guest sat down to wait in his tree-filled yard. While enjoying the quiet and the fresh air of the countryside, he suddenly heard a strange buzzing sound. Before he saw what was making the noise, however, he felt a bee sting his hand. He jumped in pain!

Now he spied an entire swarm of them at the other end of the yard. Forgetting his pain for a moment, he thought: An army of pests! They must have stung my friend mercilessly! I must get rid of them!

He took a branch and lit it. Soon the entire yard was filled with smoke. Waving it frantically, he approached the beehive and succeeded in chasing away every last bee!

וַיָּרֵעוּ אֹתָנוּ הַמִּצְרִים וַיְעַנּוּנוּ וַיִּתְּנוּ עָלֵינוּ עֲבֹדָה קָשָׁה:

וַיָּרֵעוּ אֹתָנוּ הַמִּצְרִים. כְּמָה שֶׁנֶּאֱמַר הָבָה נִתְחַכְּמָה לוֹ פֶּן יִרְבֶּה וְהָיָה כִּי תִקְרֶאנָה מִלְחָמָה וְנוֹסַף גַּם הוּא עַל שֹׂנְאֵינוּ וְנִלְחַם בָּנוּ וְעָלָה מִן הָאָרֶץ:

וַיְעַנּוּנוּ. כְּמָה שֶׁנֶּאֱמַר וַיָּשִׂימוּ עָלָיו שָׂרֵי מִסִּים לְמַעַן עַנֹּתוֹ בְּסִבְלֹתָם וַיִּבֶן עָרֵי מִסְכְּנוֹת לְפַרְעֹה אֶת פִּתֹם וְאֶת רַעַמְסֵס:

"And the Egyptians ill-treated us, and they afflicted us and laid upon us hard bondage" (*Devarim* 26:6).

And the Egyptians ill-treated us — as it says: "Come, let us deal wisely with them, lest they multiply, and then, when circumstances bring about war, they too will join our enemies, or they will also fight against us, and move up out of their land" (*Shemos* 1:10).

And they afflicted us — as it says: "And they set over them fiscal officers in order to afflict them with their burdens, and they built storage cities for Pharaoh, Pisom and Raamses" (*Shemos* 1:11).

Before long, his friend returned and was happy to see him. He looked around, however, and immediately sensed that something was amiss.

"What's been going on here?" he asked when he noticed the bees were gone.

"O', I'm happy to inform you that I arrived just in time to do you a favor!" the guest proudly announced. "There were hundreds of insects flying around, an army of them, ready to wreak havoc. One of them even stung me on the hand! With the smoke of a burning branch, I managed to drive them away. You'll never have to suffer their stings again!"

His friend could not contain himself. "Woe is me! You have ruined me! You have decreed poverty for me and my family! Certainly, bees sting once in a while, but I was able to earn a living selling their sweet honey and making candles from their beeswax. Now it is all gone. You have ruined my entire livelihood!"

The hasty guest recognized the harmful aspect of the bees as revealed by their sting. He did not recognize the beneficial aspect of them that was hidden in their beehive (i.e., their honey).

In the same way, our life in exile and all the pain we suffer individually resembles the different aspects of the bee. We perceive the suffering as evil, but the truth is that it refines us. This is similar to a seed which must be placed in the earth in order to grow. First, the shell of the seed opens and a tiny shoot begins to grow upward. In essence, the seed has decomposed, but this very decomposition was necessary in order that it give birth to a strong, new plant. The same principle is embodied in the transformation of a lowly caterpillar into a magnificent butterfly. In the same way, our sinking to the lowest level in Egypt prepared us to become a Godly people capable of receiving the Torah on Sinai. This is the meaning of "In your blood, live!"

Chomas Ha-Da'as V'Ha-Emunah 66a

And laid upon us hard bondage — as it says: "And the Egyptians made slaves of the Children of Yisrael, with crushing harshness" (*Shemos* 1:13).

"And we cried out to Hashem, the God of our fathers, and Hashem heard our voice and saw our affliction and our misery and our oppression" (*Devarim* 26:7).

And we cried out to Hashem, the God of our fathers — as it says: "And it came to pass in the course of those many days that the king of Egypt died and the Children of Yisrael sighed from the slavery, and they cried, and their cry for help rose up to God from the slavery" (*Shemos* 2:23).

And Hashem heard our voice — as it says: "And God heard their groaning, and God remembered His covenant with Avraham, with Yitzchak and with Yaakov" (*ibid.*, 24).

And saw our affliction — this refers to the enforced disruption of normal family relations, as it says: "And God saw the Children of Yisrael, and God took note of it" (*ibid.*, 25).

And our misery — these are the children, as it says: "...every son that is born, you shall throw into the river, and every daughter you shall let live" (*Shemos* 1:22).

And our oppression — this is the pressure, as it says: "...and I have also seen the oppression with which the Egyptians oppress them" (*ibid.* 3:9).

"And Hashem brought us out from Egypt with a mighty hand and with an outstretched arm and with great awesomeness, and with instructive signs and with punishing miracles" (*Devarim* 26:8).

And Hashem brought us out from Egypt — not through an angel, not through a seraph, and not through a messenger. But it was the Holy One, Blessed be He, Himself in all His glory, as it says:

> **"And I will pass through the land of Egypt in this night, and I will smite every firstborn in the land of Egypt, from man to beast, and against all the gods of Egypt I will execute judgment, I, Hashem"** (*Shemos* 12:12).

וַיִּתְּנוּ עָלֵינוּ עֲבֹדָה קָשָׁה. כְּמָה שֶׁנֶּאֱמַר וַיַּעֲבִדוּ מִצְרַיִם אֶת בְּנֵי יִשְׂרָאֵל בְּפָרֶךְ:

וַנִּצְעַק אֶל יהוה אֱלֹהֵי אֲבֹתֵינוּ וַיִּשְׁמַע יהוה אֶת־קֹלֵנוּ וַיַּרְא אֶת־עָנְיֵנוּ וְאֶת עֲמָלֵנוּ וְאֶת־לַחֲצֵנוּ:

וַנִּצְעַק אֶל־יהוה אֱלֹהֵי אֲבֹתֵינוּ. כְּמָה שֶׁנֶּאֱמַר וַיְהִי בַיָּמִים הָרַבִּים הָהֵם וַיָּמָת מֶלֶךְ מִצְרַיִם וַיֵּאָנְחוּ בְנֵי־יִשְׂרָאֵל מִן־הָעֲבֹדָה וַיִּזְעָקוּ וַתַּעַל שַׁוְעָתָם אֶל־הָאֱלֹהִים מִן־הָעֲבֹדָה:

וַיִּשְׁמַע יהוה אֶת־קֹלֵנוּ. כְּמָה שֶׁנֶּאֱמַר וַיִּשְׁמַע אֱלֹהִים אֶת־נַאֲקָתָם וַיִּזְכֹּר אֱלֹהִים אֶת־בְּרִיתוֹ אֶת־אַבְרָהָם אֶת־יִצְחָק וְאֶת־יַעֲקֹב:

וַיַּרְא אֶת־עָנְיֵנוּ. זוֹ פְּרִישׁוּת דֶּרֶךְ אֶרֶץ. כְּמָה שֶׁנֶּאֱמַר וַיַּרְא אֱלֹהִים אֶת־בְּנֵי יִשְׂרָאֵל וַיֵּדַע אֱלֹהִים:

וְאֶת עֲמָלֵנוּ. אֵלּוּ הַבָּנִים. כְּמָה שֶׁנֶּאֱמַר כָּל־הַבֵּן הַיִּלּוֹד הַיְאֹרָה תַּשְׁלִיכֻהוּ וְכָל־הַבַּת תְּחַיּוּן:

וְאֶת לַחֲצֵנוּ. זֶה הַדְּחַק. כְּמָה שֶׁנֶּאֱמַר וְגַם־רָאִיתִי אֶת־הַלַּחַץ אֲשֶׁר מִצְרַיִם לֹחֲצִים אֹתָם:

וַיּוֹצִאֵנוּ יהוה מִמִּצְרַיִם בְּיָד חֲזָקָה וּבִזְרֹעַ נְטוּיָה וּבְמֹרָא גָּדֹל וּבְאֹתוֹת וּבְמֹפְתִים:

וַיּוֹצִיאֵנוּ יהוה מִמִּצְרַיִם. לֹא עַל־יְדֵי מַלְאָךְ וְלֹא עַל־יְדֵי שָׂרָף וְלֹא עַל־יְדֵי שָׁלִיחַ. אֶלָּא הַקָּדוֹשׁ בָּרוּךְ הוּא בִּכְבוֹדוֹ וּבְעַצְמוֹ. שֶׁנֶּאֱמַר:

> **וְעָבַרְתִּי בְאֶרֶץ־מִצְרַיִם בַּלַּיְלָה הַזֶּה וְהִכֵּיתִי כָל־בְּכוֹר בְּאֶרֶץ מִצְרַיִם מֵאָדָם וְעַד בְּהֵמָה וּבְכָל אֱלֹהֵי מִצְרַיִם אֶעֱשֶׂה שְׁפָטִים אֲנִי יהוה:**

And against all the gods of Egypt I will execute judgment, I, Hashem.

Rabbi David Abudraham asked: Is it not written, "When we cried out to Hashem, He heard our call and sent a malach to take us out of Egypt" (*Bemidbar* 20:16)? Doesn't this verse make it very clear that Moshe Rabbenu was the agent who brought us out of Egypt? How then can this be reconciled with the text of the Haggadah which states, "And against all the gods of Egypt I will execute judgment, I, Hashem"?

The Maggid of Dubno answered this difficulty with a parable.

A man's only son once fell deathly ill. He summoned the best doctors to treat him. He did not leave the boy alone for a moment. He also fed him the healthiest diet possible for his condition.

One day, the man received word that he had to travel to a neighboring city for business purposes. He informed the boy, saying, "My precious son, I have been called away on an emergency. I have asked my dear friend to take my place at your side. He will keep an eye on you and make sure you are given everything you need."

"No father," the boy cried, "do not go. Do not leave me all alone!"

He quieted the boy down and reassured him, "I have already spoken with my friend and informed him that I am depositing into his care a very precious treasure. He has promised me that he will feed you himself, with his own hands, and he will not leave your side!"

When the boy's fears were assuaged, the father took his leave. Days passed, and when he finally returned, he came to see his son. "Well, my boy, did my friend stand by his word? Did he fulfill his promise to me?"

"No father, not at all!" the boy complained. "He promised you that he would feed me with his own hands, but he used a fork and spoon!"

The father laughed, "A fork and spoon are merely extensions of the hand, my son! They do not constitute being fed by an agent!"

Moshe Rabbenu could never be considered as Hashem's messenger. The reason for this is simple: He nullified himself completely and absolutely before the Blessed One. He was no more than an extension of Hashem's hand.

This basic fact gives us insight into another statement by the Sages. In the Talmud (*Ta'anis* 2a-b), they assert, "The keys to rain (livelihood), childbirth, and the revival of the dead were never given over to a shaliach (agent)." Tosafos asks: Wasn't the key to rain given to Eliyahu Ha-Navi? Didn't Eliyahu revive Yonah? And didn't Elisha revive Chavakkuk from the dead?! Weren't they agents?

According to our explanation, however, the difficulty never even arises. Tzaddikim who nullify themselves entirely before their Creator are not called agents! This explains why, when Elisha wished to revive Chavakkuk, he gave his staff to his servant Gechazi and instructed him to refrain from speaking with anyone else on the way. This included not initiating a conversation with anyone nor answering anyone who addressed him. He was to proceed directly to the boy and place the staff on his mouth.

וְעָבַרְתִּי בְאֶרֶץ־מִצְרַיִם בַּלַּיְלָה הַזֶּה. אֲנִי וְלֹא מַלְאָךְ.
וְהִכֵּיתִי כָל־בְּכוֹר בְּאֶרֶץ מִצְרַיִם. אֲנִי וְלֹא שָׂרָף.
וּבְכָל־אֱלֹהֵי מִצְרַיִם אֶעֱשֶׂה שְׁפָטִים. אֲנִי וְלֹא הַשָּׁלִיחַ.
אֲנִי יהוה. אֲנִי הוּא וְלֹא אַחֵר:

And I will pass through the land of Egypt in this night — I, and no angel.
And I will smite every firstborn in the land of Egypt — I, and no seraph.
And against all the gods of Egypt I will execute judgments — I, and no messenger.
I, Hashem — it is I, and no other.

בְּיָד חֲזָקָה. זוֹ הַדֶּבֶר. כְּמָה שֶׁנֶּאֱמַר הִנֵּה יַד יהוה הוֹיָה בְּמִקְנְךָ אֲשֶׁר בַּשָּׂדֶה בַּסּוּסִים בַּחֲמוֹרִים בַּגְּמַלִּים בַּבָּקָר וּבַצֹּאן דֶּבֶר כָּבֵד מְאֹד:

With a mighty hand — this refers to the pestilence, as it says: "Behold, the hand of Hashem will be upon your property which you have in the fields, on the horses, on the asses, on the camels, on the cattle, and on the sheep, a very severe pestilence" (*Shemos* 9:3).

וּבִזְרֹעַ נְטוּיָה. זוֹ הַחֶרֶב. כְּמָה שֶׁנֶּאֱמַר וְחַרְבּוֹ שְׁלוּפָה בְּיָדוֹ נְטוּיָה עַל־יְרוּשָׁלָיִם:

And with an outstretched arm — this is the sword, as it says: "...and his drawn sword in his hand, outstretched over Yerushalayim" (*Divrei Hayamim* I, 21:16).

וּבְמֹרָא גָּדֹל. זֶה גִּלּוּי שְׁכִינָה. כְּמָה שֶׁנֶּאֱמַר אוֹ הֲנִסָּה אֱלֹהִים לָבוֹא לָקַחַת לוֹ גוֹי מִקֶּרֶב גּוֹי בְּמַסֹּת בְּאֹתֹת וּבְמוֹפְתִים וּבְמִלְחָמָה וּבְיָד חֲזָקָה וּבִזְרוֹעַ נְטוּיָה וּבְמוֹרָאִים גְּדֹלִים כְּכֹל אֲשֶׁר־עָשָׂה לָכֶם יהוה אֱלֹהֵיכֶם בְּמִצְרַיִם לְעֵינֶיךָ:

And with great awesomeness — this is the revelation of the Divine Presence, as it says: "Or has a god proved himself, to come to take a nation unto himself from out of the midst of another nation, with proofs of might, with signs and with instructive miracles, and with war and with a strong hand and with an outstretched arm and with great awesomeness, comparable to all that Hashem your God did for you in Egypt before your eyes?" (*Devarim* 4:34).

Gechazi transgressed Elisha's instructions. He spoke to people on the way. As a result, when he placed the staff on Chavakkuk's mouth, nothing happened. Only when Elisha came was he able to revive Chavakkuk.

The principle is clear: There is a difference between a "vessel" and a "messenger." A vessel exists solely for its contents; it exists solely to peform its functions. A messenger, on the other hand, while performing his intended function, also maintains his own independent existence.

Knowing that the key to reviving the dead could never be given over to a "messenger," Elisha wished to make Gechazi a "vessel." He therefore gave him his staff and commanded him not to say a word to another human being. This was a very important stipulation. Success depended on not speaking. Gechazi failed to understand this. Once he spoke to another person, he forfeited the privilege of being a vessel for Elisha. Speaking to others indicated that he could not be entrusted with such an important mission. Being filled with his own self-importance meant he could no longer be filled with the holy spirit of his master. Elisha had to come and revive Chavakkuk himself.

According to Kochav Mi'Yaakov, *Haftarah to Parashas Vayera*

"With a mighty hand and with an outstretched arm and with great awesomeness ."

There is a buildup here, from "mighty hand" to "outstretched arm" to "great awesomeness." Rabbi Yosef Shaul Nathanzon illuminated this buildup through the following parable.

A great king was informed that a spirit of unrest had begun to spread in one of his distant provinces. He immediately sent an entire regiment of the royal guard to fill the streets of the province. Their presence would bring fear into the hearts of the revolutionaries and discourage them from staging an open uprising.

The king was then informed that the situation had degenerated to the point where open revolution was imminent. The king sent orders for his regiment to conduct battle maneuvers where the entire civilian population could see them. A demonstration of the power of his army would surely impel the rebels to think twice before defying the crown.

Before long, another courier arrived, however, with news that the rebellion had broken out! There was fighting in the streets! The king immediately ordered five more regiments to converge on the province. In addition, the courier was instructed to return to inform the rebel chiefs that the king would be joining his troops. Nothing could stop him now from squashing the revolution and punishing its instigators!

Hashem used the same tactics to bring us out of Egypt. First, He gave Pharaoh a taste of His power by striking the Egyptian cattle with blight. This was a warning. When Pharaoh did not heed the warning, Hashem stretched forth His arm, with sword in hand, so to speak, and slew the Egyptian firstborn. This ocurred at midnight on Pesach, and it was a great blow to the Egyptians. Seeing such a demonstration of Divine power, they knew the end was imminent. Still, Hashem saw that they were not completely repentant. He therefore decided to appear, in all His awesome splendor and greatness. This is what the author of the Haggadah meant when he said, "With great awesomeness — this is the revelation of the Shechinah (Divine Presence)."

Divrei Shaul 29b

Blood, Frogs, Vermin.

Regarding the first plague, the Torah states: "[Aharon] held the staff up, and then struck the waters of the Nile in the presence of Pharaoh and his officials.

ובאתות. זה המטה. כמה שנאמר ואת־המטה הזה תקח בידך אשר תעשה בו את־האתת:

And with instructive signs — this is the staff, as it says: "and this staff shall you take in your hand, with which you should perform the signs" (*Shemos* 4:17).

ובמפתים זה הדם. כמה שנאמר ונתתי מופתים בשמים ובארץ.

And with punishing miracles — this is the blood, as it says: "I will do miracles in heaven and on earth:

One dips his finger into the cup and dabs a bit of wine onto his plate when saying each of the words "blood and fire and pillars of smoke," as well as when reciting each of the ten plagues and pronouncing "detzach, adash beachav," for a total of 16 times. Some have the custom of pouring from the cup rather than dabbing their finger. The cups are then refilled.

דם ואש ותמרות עשן:

blood and fire and pillars of smoke" (*Yoel* 3:3).

דבר אחר. **ביד חזקה** שתים. **ובזרע נטויה** שתים. **ובמרא גדל** שתים. **ובאתות** שתים. **ובמופתים** שתים: אלו עשר מכות שהביא הקדוש ברוך הוא על־המצרים במצרים ואלו הן:

דם. צפרדע. כנים. ערוב.
דבר. שחין. ברד. ארבה. חשך.
מכת בכורות:

An alternative explanation: **with a MIGHTY HAND** — two (Hebrew words imply two plagues); **and with an OUTSTRETCHED ARM** — two; **and with GREAT AWESOMENESS** — two; **and with instructive SIGNS** — two (plural); **and with punishing MIRACLES** — two (plural). These, then, are the ten plagues which the Holy One, Blessed be He, brought upon the Egyptians in Egypt, and they are as follows:

Blood, Frogs, Vermin, Wild Beasts,
Pestilence, Boils, Hail, Locusts, Darkness,
Slaying of the Firstborn.

The waters of the Nile were transformed into blood. The fish in the Nile died, and the river became so polluted that the Egyptians could no longer drink from the Nile's waters. There was blood everywhere in Egypt. But when the Egyptian scientists were able to reproduce the same effect with their hidden arts, Pharaoh became obstinate" (*Shemos* 7:20-22).

Regarding the second plague, as well, the Torah states: "Aharon held his hand out over the waters of the Nile, and the frogs emerged, covering Egypt. The scientists were able to reproduce the same effect with their hidden arts, making frogs emerge on Egyptian land..." (ibid. 8:2-3).

Regarding the third plague, the Torah states: "Aharon held out his hand with his staff, and struck the dust of the earth. The vermin [lice] appeared, attacking man and beast. Throughout all Egypt, the dust turned into lice. The scientists tried to reproduce lice with their hidden arts, but they could not.... It is a finger of God, they said to Pharaoh..." (ibid. 8:13-15).

The Gaon, Rabbi Simchah Flamm, asked: Why did Hashem choose blood and frogs as the first two plagues, knowing full well that the Egyptian scientists would be able to reproduce them? Why didn't He begin with lice so that they

would immediately recognize Hashem's power and exclaim, "It is a finger of God!"

He answered with a parable.

There was once an artist who lived in a small village. His portraits were masterpieces and his landscapes were breathtaking. Seeking wider recognition for his work, he decided to stage an exhibition and invite the press to cover the event. On second thought, he realized that the opinion of the local art critic wasn't worth much. What could he and his rather limited readership possibly understand about art? No, he would travel to the capital, the hub of national culture. There, more people would see the exhibit and his work would gain the recognition it deserved. But this idea, too, was limited to the boundaries of his own country. If he wanted international renown, he would have to go to Paris. If his work drew enough praise there, with the great international art critics applauding his genius, he might gain recognition as the greatest artist in the world. Then he would only have one problem: Upon returning to his hometown, he would first have to tell his fellow townsmen what Paris is, and how talented its artists are. Only then would they appreciate the true value of his work!

The point and purpose of all the miracles performed in Egypt, including the wondrous Eser Ha-Makkos (Ten Plagues) which Hashem visited upon the Egyptians, is stated in ascending order in the Torah. First Pharaoh is told: "So that you will know that there is none like Hashem our God" (*Shemos* 8:6). But perhaps His dominion is limited to Egypt? Pharaoh is further told: "So that you will realize that I am the Eternal God, right here on earth" (ibid. 8:16). But perhaps His dominion is limited to this earth? Pharaoh is finally told: "So that you will know that the whole world belongs to Hashem" (ibid. 9:29).

Where did Hashem choose to "publicize" the greatness of His Name, to make it known that the entire world is filled with evidence of this greatness, and that all of creation is mere clay in His hands? He chose Egypt. Egypt was the center of knowledge and science, the most advanced civilization in the ancient world. Its wise men were the greatest scientists of that age, as our Sages said: "Ten portions of magic [the ability to manipulate physical matter and its laws] came down to the world. Nine of these went to Egypt and one to the rest of the world" (*Kiddushin* 49b). When they would recognize that "Hashem is the Supreme Being, and there is none besides Him" (*Devarim* 4:35), everyone else would follow suit. When they would admit that their wisdom was like nothing in the face of the Creator of the world, all others would admit it as well.

But one problem remained. What was to prevent some historian some day from claiming that the Egyptians were a lowly people, without wisdom or knowledge? The entire proof of God's greatness, which depends on the recognition of the great Egyptian scientists, would collapse! It is for this reason that the Eser Ha-Makkos began with blood and frogs, plagues which the Egyptian scientists could duplicate, and thereby demonstrate their talents. Only then did Hashem choose vermin, a plague which even they could not reproduce!

Bris Avos 20b

Darkness.

"Hashem said to Moshe: Extend your hand out towards the heavens, so that darkness will be over the land of Egypt, darkness which will be palpable. Moshe extended his hand towards the heavens, and there was opaque darkness all throughout Egypt, lasting for three days. People could not see one another, and no one left his place for three days. Meanwhile, the Children of Yisrael had light in their dwellings" (*Shemos* 10:21-23).

The Midrash (*Shemos Rabbah* 14:2) asks: "Where did this darkness come from? Rebbi Yehudah answered: It was the primeval darkness of Heaven, as the Psalmist said, 'He made darkness His hiding place, His canopy enveloping Him' (*Tehillim* 18:12). Rebbi Nechemyah answered: It was the darkness of Gehinnom, which Iyov spoke about when he pleaded, 'Leave me alone, that I may take slight comfort before I go to the place from which no one returns, to the land of darkness and the shadow of death...' (*Iyov* 10:20-22)."

Quoting the Maharal, Rabbi Eliyahu Dessler explains: "Darkness" represents lack and nonexistence, of which there are two kinds that apply to mankind: First, man is a creature, that is, there was once a time when he was not yet created, when he did not yet exist. Second, man's actions lack in the sense that he can never attain ultimate perfection (there will always be a greater perfection that lies beyond whatever he attains). The first is called the "primeval darkness of Heaven," and the second is called "the darkness of Gehinnom."

According to this, the disagreement between Rabbi Yehudah and Rabbi Nechemyah is over which specific lack is better to focus on when one wishes to understand the human condition. This is why the Sages asked, "Where did this darkness come from?" They were not asking a technical question. Their intention was to examine the ultimate source of the darkness that permeates our lives.

רַבִּי יְהוּדָה הָיָה נוֹתֵן בָּהֶם סִמָּנִים:

דְּצַ"ךְ עֲדַ"שׁ בְּאַחַ"ב:

רַבִּי יוֹסֵי הַגְּלִילִי אוֹמֵר. מִנַּיִן אַתָּה אוֹמֵר שֶׁלָּקוּ הַמִּצְרִים בְּמִצְרַיִם עֶשֶׂר מַכּוֹת וְעַל הַיָּם לָקוּ חֲמִשִּׁים מַכּוֹת. בְּמִצְרַיִם מַה הוּא אוֹמֵר. וַיֹּאמְרוּ הַחַרְטֻמִּם אֶל־פַּרְעֹה אֶצְבַּע אֱלֹהִים הִוא. וְעַל־הַיָּם מַה הוּא אוֹמֵר. וַיַּרְא יִשְׂרָאֵל אֶת־הַיָּד הַגְּדוֹלָה אֲשֶׁר עָשָׂה יהוה בְּמִצְרַיִם וַיִּירְאוּ הָעָם אֶת־יהוה וַיַּאֲמִינוּ

Rabbi Yehudah made a mnemonic of their Hebrew initials, as follows:

DETZACH, ADASH, BEACHAV

Rabbi Yose the Galilean said: From what passage can you infer that the Egyptians were smitten with ten plagues in Egypt and with fifty plagues at the Sea? Of the plagues in Egypt, it says: "And those knowledgeable of the writings said to Pharaoh: 'It is a finger of God'..." (*Shemos* 8:15), while at the Sea, it is said: "And Yisrael saw the great Hand which Hashem had used upon Egypt; and the people feared Hashem and trusted in Hashem and in Moshe, His

This distinction between technical reasons for things and their true causes can be thus illustrated:

A young man once traveled far from his home town to learn in a famous yeshivah. When he arrived, the other students gathered around him and asked, "Why have you come?"

Instead of simply answering, "To learn Torah!" he replied that he had come because the train had brought him.

"But that is only how you got here!" they retorted. "We mean, why did you come?"

It seems like a simple distinction, but how often do we confuse the two in our daily lives? When someone falls ill, for instance, we do not attempt to discover the real reason — the why, but instead we investigate the technical reason — the how. We ask if he left the house without a coat on a cold day; we ask if he was sweating when he came into an air-conditioned room on a hot day. And when the answer is yes, we are satisfied. We now know why he got sick. But the truth is that we have not found out why, but how.

The Sages wished to teach us how to ask the real questions and how to find out the real answers. "Where did this darkness come from?" That is, what caused that darkness to come to the Egyptians? What was it meant to teach them?

based on Michtav Me-Eliyahu, Vol. II, p. 239

"And the people feared Hashem and trusted in Hashem and in Moshe, His servant."

Rabbi Shemuel Meltzen of Slutzk, student of the famed Gaon of Vilna, explained the profound nature of our faith in Hashem with the following parable.

servant" (*ibid.* 14:31). How many plagues were visited on them by a *finger*? Ten plagues. Thus, in Egypt the Egyptians were smitten with ten plagues, while at the Sea they were smitten [by the *hand*], with fifty plagues.

בַּיהוה וּבְמֹשֶׁה עַבְדּוֹ. כַּמָּה לָקוּ בְּאֶצְבַּע עֶשֶׂר מַכּוֹת. אֱמֹר מֵעַתָּה בְּמִצְרַיִם לָקוּ עֶשֶׂר מַכּוֹת וְעַל־הַיָּם לָקוּ חֲמִשִּׁים מַכּוֹת:

While any good king loves all his subjects, there is a special place in his heart for his soldiers, since they protect and fight on behalf of the crown. Still, only a great king who is graced with a powerful intellect and unusually vivid memory is capable of keeping every single one of his soldiers in his mind's eye when he sends them into battle.

A king of lesser stature, unable to manage such an overwhelming responsibility, might have a staff of advisors around him to apprise him of all that occurs on the battlefield. Each advisor would provide intelligence reports on all enemy maneuvers made in his section. Together, all the advisors would assist him in ascertaining the larger picture he needs in order to plan a comprehensive battle strategy. Then they would represent him on the battlefield, implementing his strategy to ensure ultimate victory.

A king of even lesser stature would not be able to piece together the various intelligence reports in order to coordinate a battle on several fronts. He would need an excellent commanding general, with whom he would stay in constant contact concerning every detail. If their connection were strong enough, such a king could retain control over his entire army through his commanding general.

This lessening in stature between the most intelligent king who can recall each individual soldier while still relating to his entire army and the king who relies totally on his commanding officer is similar to that implied in the following passage from the Talmud (*Makkos* 23b-24a):

> Rabbi Samlai expounded: 613 commandments were given to Moshe [on Sinai]. 365 [of these] are negative prohibitions corresponding to the 365 days of the solar year. 248 [of these] are positive injunctions corresponding to the 248 limbs of the human body. Rav Hamnuna said: The verse states, "Moshe prescribed the Torah to us, an eternal inheritance for the congregation of Yaakov" (*Devarim* 33:4). The first 2 commandments, "I am Hashem your God" and "Do not have any other gods before Me" were heard from the mouth of the Almighty. Afterwards, Moshe prescribed the remaining 611 commandments of the Torah [the numerical value of the word Torah is 611] to complete a total of 613.
>
> David came and condensed these [613] into 11. He wrote: "A Psalm of David. Hashem! Who can dwell in [close proximity to] Your Sanctuary? He who walks in

Rabbi Eliezer said: From what passage can it be inferred that each plague which the Holy One, Blessed be He, brought upon the Egyptians in Egypt was actually a fourfold one? For it says: "He lets break forth against them the glow of His anger: excess of wrath, and condemnation, and distress; a mission of messengers of evil" (*Tehillim* 78:49). [Excess of] wrath — one, condemnation — two, distress — three, a mission of messengers of evil — four. Thus, in Egypt the Egyptians were smitten with forty plagues, while at the Sea they were smitten with two hundred plagues (see above).

Rabbi Akiva said: From what passage can it be inferred that each plague which the Holy One, Blessed be He, brought upon the Egyptians in Egypt was actually a fivefold one? For it says: "He lets break forth against them the glow of His anger, excess of wrath, and condemnation, and distress; a mission of messengers of evil" (*ibid.*). [The glow of His] anger — one, [excess of] wrath — two, condemnation — three, distress — four, a mission of messengers of evil — five. Thus, in Egypt the Egyptians were smitten with fifty plagues, while at the Sea they were smitten with two-hundred-and-fifty plagues.

רַבִּי אֱלִיעֶזֶר אוֹמֵר. מִנַּיִן שֶׁכָּל מַכָּה וּמַכָּה שֶׁהֵבִיא הַקָּדוֹשׁ בָּרוּךְ הוּא עַל הַמִּצְרִים בְּמִצְרַיִם הָיְתָה שֶׁל אַרְבַּע מַכּוֹת. שֶׁנֶּאֱמַר יְשַׁלַּח־בָּם חֲרוֹן אַפּוֹ עֶבְרָה וָזַעַם וְצָרָה מִשְׁלַחַת מַלְאֲכֵי רָעִים. עֶבְרָה אַחַת. וָזַעַם שְׁתַּיִם. וְצָרָה שָׁלֹשׁ. מִשְׁלַחַת מַלְאֲכֵי רָעִים אַרְבַּע. אֱמֹר מֵעַתָּה בְּמִצְרַיִם לָקוּ אַרְבָּעִים מַכּוֹת וְעַל־הַיָּם לָקוּ מָאתַיִם מַכּוֹת:

רַבִּי עֲקִיבָא אוֹמֵר. מִנַּיִן שֶׁכָּל מַכָּה וּמַכָּה שֶׁהֵבִיא הַקָּדוֹשׁ בָּרוּךְ הוּא עַל הַמִּצְרִים בְּמִצְרַיִם הָיְתָה שֶׁל חָמֵשׁ מַכּוֹת. שֶׁנֶּאֱמַר יְשַׁלַּח־בָּם חֲרוֹן אַפּוֹ עֶבְרָה וָזַעַם וְצָרָה מִשְׁלַחַת מַלְאֲכֵי רָעִים. חֲרוֹן אַפּוֹ אַחַת. עֶבְרָה שְׁתַּיִם. וָזַעַם שָׁלֹשׁ. וְצָרָה אַרְבַּע. מִשְׁלַחַת מַלְאֲכֵי רָעִים חָמֵשׁ: אֱמֹר מֵעַתָּה בְּמִצְרַיִם לָקוּ חֲמִשִּׁים מַכּוֹת וְעַל הַיָּם לָקוּ חֲמִשִּׁים וּמָאתַיִם מַכּוֹת:

wholehearted integrity, deals righteously, and speaks truth in his heart. He who has no slander on his tongue, who has not acted wickedly towards his brother, nor cast disgrace upon his relative. He who despises a base man, but honors those who fear Hashem; who, though he swear to his own disadvantage, does not recant on his oath. He who has not lent his money with interest, nor taken a bribe against the innocent. Whoever does these things will never falter" (*Tehillim* 15).

Yeshayahu came and condensed these [11] into 6. He wrote: "He who walks righteously and speaks upright words, despises unfair gain, shaking his hands to avoid bribes, stops his ears from hearing libel, and shuts his eyes from seeing evil — he shall dwell on high... seeing the King in His glory" (*Yeshayahu* 33:15-17).

Michah came and condensed these [6] into 3. He wrote: "He has told you, O man, what is good, and what Hashem requires of you: Only to do justly, and to love mercy, and to walk humbly with your God..." (*Michah* 6:8).

Yeshayahu came back and condensed these [3] into 2. He wrote: "Thus says Hashem: Keep judgment and do justice, for My salvation is imminent, and My righteousness will soon be revealed..." (*Yeshayahu* 56:1).

Chavakkuk came and condensed these [2] into 1. He wrote: "The righteous shall live by his faith" (*Chavakkuk* 2:4).

The meaning of this passage in the Talmud is that the first generations were capable of contemplating all the details and interrelationships of the 613 commandments. The entire Torah was constantly in their thoughts. Then the

How Many Stages of Benevolence Did the Omnipresent Grant Us!

כַּמָּה מַעֲלוֹת טוֹבוֹת לַמָּקוֹם עָלֵינוּ:

Had He brought us out of Egypt and not executed judgment on the Egyptians	Dayenu.* דַּיֵּנוּ:	אִלּוּ הוֹצִיאָנוּ מִמִּצְרַיִם וְלֹא־עָשָׂה בָהֶם שְׁפָטִים
Had He executed judgment on them and not upon their idols	Dayenu. דַּיֵּנוּ:	אִלּוּ עָשָׂה בָהֶם שְׁפָטִים וְלֹא־עָשָׂה בֵאלֹהֵיהֶם
Had He destroyed their idols and not slain their firstborn	Dayenu. דַּיֵּנוּ:	אִלּוּ עָשָׂה בֵאלֹהֵיהֶם וְלֹא־הָרַג אֶת־בְּכוֹרֵיהֶם

* Dayenu — it would have sufficed for us

generations progressively diminished in stature until Chavakkuk came and said: If you will maintain good, strong ties with the commanding general, i.e., basic Jewish faith, you will succeed in keeping the entire Torah. This is the meaning of the verse, "The people feared Hashem and trusted in Hashem." How? By trusting "in Moshe, His servant!"

Emunah V'Hashgachah 2

Dayenu.

The holy master, Rabbi Abdallah Somech of Baghdad, told the following parable:

A sultan had a beloved friend. When the friend's son was kidnapped by a sheikh and held captive in his fortress, the sultan sent messengers to the sheikh warning him to release the boy immediately. In addition to refusing to comply with the sultan's wishes, the sheikh spoke arrogantly to the messengers, insulting the sultan and his friend to them, and then having them thrown out of his presence!

Upon hearing of such brazen insolence, the sultan was angered. He immediately dispatched his troops. They sieged the fortress, toppled its battlements, destroyed its foundations, located the dungeon in which the boy was held captive, and released him. The sheikh was also taken captive and sentenced to death.

Beholding the fate of the sheikh, the other sheikhs in the sultan's domain were seized with trembling and dread. Convening among themselves, the question was naturally raised: Why was the sultan exacting such harsh revenge? Was he primaily interested in releasing his friend's son or in punishing the sheikh for his insolence in order to show the rest of his subjects that no one rebels against the sultan's authority? How would they know which of these two possibilities was most impotant to the sultan?

Had He slain their firstborn and not given us their wealth	Dayenu.	דַּיֵּנוּ:	אִלּוּ הָרַג אֶת־בְּכוֹרֵיהֶם וְלֹא־נָתַן לָנוּ אֶת־מָמוֹנָם
Had He given us their wealth and not split the Sea for us	Dayenu.	דַּיֵּנוּ:	אִלּוּ נָתַן לָנוּ אֶת־מָמוֹנָם וְלֹא־קָרַע לָנוּ אֶת־הַיָּם
Had He split the Sea for us and not led us through it on dry land	Dayenu.	דַּיֵּנוּ:	אִלּוּ קָרַע לָנוּ אֶת־הַיָּם וְלֹא־הֶעֱבִירָנוּ בְתוֹכוֹ בֶּחָרָבָה
Had He led us through it on dry land and not drowned our tormentors in it	Dayenu.	דַּיֵּנוּ:	אִלּוּ הֶעֱבִירָנוּ בְתוֹכוֹ בֶּחָרָבָה וְלֹא־שִׁקַּע צָרֵינוּ בְּתוֹכוֹ
Had He drowned our tormentors in it and not provided our needs in the desert for forty years	Dayenu.	דַּיֵּנוּ:	אִלּוּ שִׁקַּע צָרֵינוּ בְּתוֹכוֹ וְלֹא־סִפֵּק צָרְכֵּנוּ בַּמִּדְבָּר אַרְבָּעִים שָׁנָה
Had He provided our needs in the desert for forty years and not fed us with mannah	Dayenu.	דַּיֵּנוּ:	אִלּוּ סִפֵּק צָרְכֵּנוּ בַּמִּדְבָּר אַרְבָּעִים שָׁנָה וְלֹא־הֶאֱכִילָנוּ אֶת־הַמָּן
Had He fed us with mannah and not given us Shabbos	Dayenu.	דַּיֵּנוּ:	אִלּוּ הֶאֱכִילָנוּ אֶת־הַמָּן וְלֹא־נָתַן לָנוּ אֶת־הַשַּׁבָּת
Had He given us Shabbos and not brought us near to Mount Sinai	Dayenu.	דַּיֵּנוּ:	אִלּוּ נָתַן לָנוּ אֶת־הַשַּׁבָּת וְלֹא־קֵרְבָנוּ לִפְנֵי הַר־סִינַי
Had He brought us near to Mount Sinai and not given us the Torah	Dayenu.	דַּיֵּנוּ:	אִלּוּ קֵרְבָנוּ לִפְנֵי הַר־סִינַי וְלֹא־נָתַן לָנוּ אֶת־הַתּוֹרָה

It was decided that the fate of the boy after being released was the key. If the sultan simply let the boy go after rescuing him, this was a sure sign that he had used him as an excuse to take revenge against the sheikh. But if the sultan took the boy under his wing, caring for his every need, and restoring him to his father with glory and honor, then he was clearly the main reason for all the sultan's actions!

Pharaoh enslaved Yisrael and treated them with unparalleled cruelty. The Holy One demanded their release. Pharaoh arrogantly declared, "Who is God that I should heed Him and let Yisrael go?" (*Shemos* 5:2). In response, the Holy One struck Pharaoh and his nation with ten plagues. He bared His holy arm and brought His children out of Egypt with wonders.

But there was still room for the question: Did the Holy One really do this for our sake? Or did He simply wish to crush Pharaoh's rebelliousness? The author of the Haggadah gives us the answer: If He had only drowned our oppressors in the Red Sea, we would have known that His main object was to punish the Egyptians. Since, however, He continued providing us with everything we needed for forty years in the wilderness; since, in addition, He gave us the Torah, brought us to the land of Yisrael, and built the Beis Ha-Mikdash for us — there is no doubt that that He did it all for us!

Kibbutz Chachamim 160

Had He given us the Torah and not brought us into Eretz Yisrael	Dayenu.	דַּיֵּנוּ:	אִלּוּ נָתַן לָנוּ אֶת הַתּוֹרָה וְלֹא הִכְנִיסָנוּ לְאֶרֶץ יִשְׂרָאֵל
Had He brought us into Eretz Yisrael and not built the Holy Temple for us	Dayenu.	דַּיֵּנוּ:	אִלּוּ הִכְנִיסָנוּ לְאֶרֶץ יִשְׂרָאֵל וְלֹא בָנָה לָנוּ אֶת בֵּית הַבְּחִירָה

Had He given us the Torah and not brought us into Eretz Yisrael, Dayenu.

We must try to understand. The land of Yisrael is our eternal inheritance. It was promised to our forefathers. At the Burning Bush, Hashem told Moshe: "Go, gather the elders of Yisrael, and say to them, 'The Eternal God, the God of your fathers appeared to me — the God of Avraham, Yitzchak and Yaakov.' Tell them: I have surely remembered you and all that is being done to you in Egypt. I declare that I will bring you out of the wretchedness of Egypt to the land of the Canaanites, the Hittites, the Amorites, the Perizzites, the Hivites, and the Yevusites — to a land flowing with milk and honey" (*Shemos* 3:16-17). The entire purpose of the Exodus was to bring us to the Holy Land!

In addition, a great number of the commandments depend upon our living in the land. The holiness of the land is essential in allowing us to reach the highest levels of prophecy! How, then, could we say, "Had He given us the Torah and not brought us into Eretz Yisrael, Dayenu!"?

Rabbi Binyamin, the Maggid of Zhlishtshik, answered with a parable:

A king wished to promote one of his ministers. He appointed him ruler over an entire province. It would have been enough had the king written an order announcing the minister's appointment and signed it. But when the king himself traveled to the province together with the new ruler, chose a special mansion for his residence, and saw to it that the new ruler was installed with pomp and ceremony — this was a clear indication of the special love the king had for this minister.

The same is true in our case. Had the Holy One not accompanied us into the land, but simply commanded us to conquer it and its thirty-one kings on our own, it would have been enough. It was a double favor He showed us when He told Yehoshua, "Be strong and courageous, since you will bring the Children of Yisrael to the land I promised them, and I will be with you" (*Devarim* 31:23). This revealed more love and care than we could ever have imagined!

Chelkas Binyamin 37b

Thus, we owe the Omnipresent a debt of gratitude, not for one, but for many and repeated benefits. For He brought us out of Egypt. And executed judgment on them. And destroyed their idols. And slew their firstborn. And gave us their wealth. And split the Sea for us. And led us through it on dry land. And drowned our tormentors in it. And provided our needs in the desert for forty years. And fed us with mannah. And gave us Shabbos. And brought us near to Mount Sinai. And gave us the Torah. And brought us into Eretz Yisrael. And built for us the Holy Temple to atone for all our sins.

עַל אַחַת כַּמָּה וְכַמָּה טוֹבָה כְפוּלָה וּמְכֻפֶּלֶת לַמָּקוֹם עָלֵינוּ. שֶׁהוֹצִיאָנוּ מִמִּצְרַיִם. וְעָשָׂה בָהֶם שְׁפָטִים. וְעָשָׂה בֵאלֹהֵיהֶם. וְהָרַג אֶת־בְּכוֹרֵיהֶם. וְנָתַן לָנוּ אֶת־מָמוֹנָם. וְקָרַע לָנוּ אֶת־הַיָּם. וְהֶעֱבִירָנוּ בְתוֹכוֹ בֶּחָרָבָה. וְשִׁקַּע צָרֵינוּ בְּתוֹכוֹ. וְסִפֵּק צָרְכֵּנוּ בַּמִּדְבָּר אַרְבָּעִים שָׁנָה. וְהֶאֱכִילָנוּ אֶת הַמָּן. וְנָתַן לָנוּ אֶת הַשַּׁבָּת. וְקֵרְבָנוּ לִפְנֵי הַר־סִינַי. וְנָתַן לָנוּ אֶת־הַתּוֹרָה. וְהִכְנִיסָנוּ לְאֶרֶץ יִשְׂרָאֵל. וּבָנָה לָנוּ אֶת בֵּית הַבְּחִירָה לְכַפֵּר עַל־כָּל־עֲוֹנוֹתֵינוּ:

"He brought us out of Egypt....And built for us the Holy Temple."

At the conclusion of Dayenu (It would have been enough for us!) we thank and praise Hashem for fifteen ways in which He showered us with His love.

The Maggid of Dubno asked: Since the whole purpose of the Exodus was to be fulfilled in the building of the Beis Ha-Mikdash, why did we agree to postpone its construction almost five hundred years after departing Egypt until the time of Shelomo Ha-Melech? He answered with the following comparison.

Imagine two young girls of marriageable age, one the daughter of a wealthy merchant and the other an orphan.

Imagine if the wealthy merchant asked, "My beloved daughter, would you agree to marry on the condition that your bridal gown, your Shabbos clothes, and your Yom Tov wardrobe, as well as your living arrangements, would not be given to you for at least two years?"

She would certainly reply, "No, Father! Please prepare my dowry before the wedding, as is customary. Find an apartment, as well, and only afterwards shall we celebrate my marriage!"

An orphan girl, on the other hand, especially one who had been thrown into a dungeon and whose life had been embittered with backbreaking work, would respond differently to the same offer. If a gentleman would come to redeem her from her torments, release her from her enslavement, and ask whether she would agree to marry his son on the same conditions offered the daughter of the wealthy merchant, she would not hesitate for a moment. She would marry with great joy, and her gratitude would be everlasting!

In *Shir Ha-Shirim* 4:8, Hashem speaks to His beloved people, "Come with Me from Levanon, o' My bride, come from Levanon!" In the Midrash (*Shemos Rabbah* 23:5), Rabbi Levi says: It is customary to bedeck a bride before ushering her under the wedding canopy. The Holy One did not do so. Rather, He spoke to the Congregation of Yisrael, saying, "Come from "Levanon" — I have come to take you away from the mud and "levenim" (bricks) of Egypt to make you My bride!

The words "Levanon" and "levenim" are surely related. The only problem is that the word "Levanon" is generally associated with the Beis Ha-Mikdash. "Levanon" is thus interpreted as "White House" or "House that whitens the sins of Yisrael" (*Gittin* 57a). Here, on the other hand, it seems to be associated with the Egyptian exile. How can these two usages be reconciled?

According to our parable, however, the intention here is both meanings. Indeed, the Holy One Himself promised to bring us to the Land of Yisrael and build the Temple for us. Our midrash thus continues: But why does the verse repeat itself, "Come with Me from Levanon, o' My bride, come from Levanon"? The first alludes to the Beis Ha-Mikdash which is called Levanon. "Come with Me from Levanon, o' My bride" thus refers to the Shechinah (Divine Presence) accompanying us in our exile from our Temple and our Land. The second "come from Levanon" alludes to the Holy One taking us out of exile, which is also called Levanon.

How then did we agree to wait so long before the very purpose for which we had left Egypt was fulfilled? Like the orphan girl in the parable, we rejoiced in the actual redemption from Egyptian bondage, in the freedom from the backbreaking work of having to bake bricks. At that point, we could hardly ask for more. Dayenu!

Kol Yeshorer 23a

And He gave us their wealth.

This refers to the wealth which the Egyptians gave us when we left their land, as it is written, "The Egyptians were also urging the people to hurry and leave the land...The Children of Yisrael then did as Moshe had said. They requested silver and gold articles and clothing from the Egyptians. Hashem granted them favor in the eyes of the Egyptians, and they agreed to their request. [The Israelites] thus drained Egypt of its wealth" (*Shemos* 12:33-36).

The Maggid of Dubno drew attention to the fact that Hashem did not bless us with wealth that we had earned, but rather, we were granted it as a gift by our

oppressors. [Although we had worked as slaves and deserved compensation, this was not the intention of the Egyptians when they gave us their silver and gold.]

This same thought is repeated in another context. When we were about to enter the Promised Land, Moshe informed us, "When Hashem your God brings you to the land He swore to give to your forefathers, Avraham, Yitzchak, and Yaakov, [you will find] great, thriving cities which you did not build. [You will find] houses stocked with all good things which you yourself did not stock, bored cisterns which you did not quarry, vines and olive trees which you did not plant..." (*Devarim* 6:10-11).

This principle is not limited to us only in the collective. It is written: "The wealth of the sinner is laid up for the righteous" (*Mishlei* 13:22). Similarly, "[The wicked] may prepare [a garment], but the righteous will wear it and the innocent will divide his silver" (*Iyov* 27:17). This is the principle behind Achashverosh giving Queen Esther Haman's mansion, as Achashverosh said: "See, I have given Haman's house to Esther" (*Esther* 8:7).

The question, the Maggid asked, is why? Why is this principle followed? He answered with a parable.

A rich man had two sons. One son was upright and God-fearing, the second was drawn after immoral ways.

The father summoned his wicked son to him. "Look," he said to him, "I own a large lot. It is located in an excellent neighborhood. I want you to build me a magnificent house on that lot. All the money I have is at your disposal!"

The wicked son thanked his father and immediately set to work. He hired the best architects and contractors. He used the best and most expensive materials obtainable. The entire city was abuzz with talk about the mansion that was going up at an incredible speed.

News of this reached the good son. He turned to his father and asked in astonishment, "Father! How could you choose my corrupt brother over me?"

"Trust me," his father replied. "I have only your best interests in mind." Satisfied with his father's answer, the upright son returned to his studies.

The building was almost finished, but the wild life that the wicked son led was taking its toll. His health deteriorated and his general condition worsened. Within a short time he died. The magnificent house thus went straight to the good son.

"Now I know," the good son exclaimed, "why my father did what he did. How wise my father is! First of all, in addition to the fact that I now own a most wondrous home, I also benefited from the fact that the entire time my

brother was overseeing the construction I was able to continue my studies uninterrupted! Secondly, had I been given the task of constructing a building, I would never have built such a palace. Since I have no concept of luxury, I would have built a simple home fit for my own needs and standards. Now that my brother built it, there is not a single item lacking in it. I truly have the best of both worlds!"

David Ha-Melech wrote, "Set a table before me — comparable to [that of] my enemies" (*Tehillim* 23:5), then "my cup will surely overflow" (ibid.).

This is how Yisrael inherited the wealth of the Egyptians and of the Canaanites. This is how Mordechai and Esther inherited Haman's mansion. This is the meaning of the verse, "[Hashem] gave them the lands of the nations and they inherited the toil of [many] peoples, that they might observe His decrees and keep His Torah" (*Tehillim* 105:44-45).

Kol Rinah Vi'Yeshuah 54a

And gave us their wealth.

The Maggid of Dubno told another parable along the same lines.

On a visit to the royal capital, a young scholar returned from the study hall to his lodgings one evening. On his way, he passed the king's palace. As he passed, he spied a gang of thieves who had dug a tunnel under the king's treasury and were in the act of emptying the entire vault!

He sneaked away before they noticed him. Breathing a sigh of relief, he offered a little prayer, "How grateful I am that You have not placed my portion among the likes of these men. I hasten to the reward of the next world, while they hasten to a pit of destruction!"

He arrived at his inn, tired and hungry. To his surprise, the thieves arrived shortly after him. They too were truly famished after a hard night's work. They ordered a large meal — at the king's expense!

The waiter approached the scholar and requested his order. "Nothing," he replied.

The waiter shrugged his shoulders and walked away. The scholar smiled, remained at his table, and waited patiently. Why should he pay for his meal when he knew exactly what was going to happen? In a few moments, a meal fit for royalty would be spread out in front of the thieves. Shortly after that, the king's guards would come after them and the entire meal would be left for him! Again, this is the meaning of the verse, "The wealth of the sinner is laid up for the righteous" (*Mishlei* 13:22).

Kol Negidim 99a

And gave us their wealth. And split the sea for us.

The Torah states: "The Children of Yisrael did as Moshe said. They requested/borrowed ('vayishalu') silver and gold articles and clothing from the Egyptians. Hashem granted them favor in the eyes of the Egyptians. They granted their request/they lent them ('vayashilum")....They thus drained Egypt of its wealth" (*Shemos* 12:33-36).

The Maggid of Dubno asked: How can we say that Hashem "gave" us the wealth of the Egyptians? True, paralleling the word "vayishalu" (they requested), "vayashilum" can be translated as "they granted their request." However, "vayishalu" can also be translated as "they borrowed," and "vayashilum" can be translated as "they lent them." Whichever way we look at it, lending or even granting a request is not the same as giving a gift. How can we say that He "gave" us their wealth?

Of course, there is one other possibility. Perhaps "their wealth" does not refer to the silver and gold we took out of Egypt. Perhaps it refers to the treasures that washed up on the shores of the Red Sea after the Egyptians' demise. If this were so, however, why would the author of the Haggadah write, "And gave us their wealth. And split the Red Sea for us"? We must conclude that he is referring only to the silver and gold we took out of Egypt.

The answer to our first question must therefore be sought by asking yet another, more fundamental, question: Why did Moshe tell us to "borrow" silver and gold? Why not ask the Egyptians to give them to us outright?!

He provided the answer to both questions in the form of a parable.

A merchant's business affairs obliged him to make plans to stay in a distant city for an entire year. In order to make ends meet, he rented his own house to a tenant for the period in question. Unexpectedly finishing his business in ten months, he returned home. The tenant refused to vacate before the appointed time, however, so he was left with nowhere to go.

The merchant turned to the tenant and tried to arouse his sympathies. The latter maintained he had a right to stay until the end of the rental period. Under no circumstances would he vacate the house. Finally, he changed his tune when the owner offered him more than double the rent he was paying to get him to vacate the premises.

Anyone witnessing this transaction would have been dumbfounded. Why should the owner humble himself so much? Should he be forced to haggle and to beg? After all, he is the owner! Let him call the authorities and have the "squatter" thrown out on his heels!

But no, this is not the right way. True, he is the owner, but he did rent his

house out for an entire year. From that moment on, the renter became the "owner" of the house. There is no choice. Either the agreement must be upheld or he must strive to convince his tenant to willingly concede by offering him a hefty sum in return.

Our Sages say that the Holy One does not exact payment from a nation until its quota of transgressions has been reached (*Sotah* 9a). He does not collect from them little by little, as He does with Yisrael. Rather, He waits until the end and finishes them off all at once. This is actually the secret of Yisrael's continued existence in contrast with the rise and fall of other nations to the point of disappearing from the stage of history. Only Yisrael continues, even after the most tragic and trying times. Other nations rise to meteoric success and then plunge overnight into oblivion.

Egypt is a case in point. According to our tradition, the old Egyptian Empire collapsed seven days after the Exodus, during the crossing of the Red Sea. At that moment, their quota of transgressions was filled.

If so, why did Yisrael leave when there was just one more week to go? Why didn't they wait a little longer? The Egyptians would then have been destroyed by their wickedness. At that point, as the Psalmist says: "The snare would have been broken, and we would have escaped" (*Tehillim* 124:7).

The answer is that our own quota also was just about filled. We, too, were in danger of sinking beyond the forty-ninth level of Egyptian impurity. If we would have remained one more moment, we might not have made it out.

We can now understand the answer to our questions. By all rights, the great wealth of the Egyptians was ours. However, ownership would take on legal or official status only after their quota of transgressions had been filled. This would not take place for another seven days, when we actually crossed the sea and the Egyptians were drowned. It is for this reason that Hashem instructed us through Moshe to borrow their belongings for a short time, i.e., until the seventh day of Pesach. At that time, it would revert to its rightful owners!

Ohel Yaakov, *Bo*

And gave us Shabbos. And brought us near to Mount Sinai.

After crossing the Red Sea, Yisrael traveled for three days until they arrived at Marah, a desert oasis whose waters were bitter or tainted. First, Hashem

instructed Moshe to cast a tree into the waters to make them sweet and drinkable. Then, as the Torah states: "There He commanded... [the Jewish People] a decree and a law" (*Shemos* 15:25). Our Sages (*Sanhedrin* 56b) have informed us that one of the things Hashem commanded us at Marah was the Shabbos. This was before we arrived at Sinai. The question is: Why wasn't the commandment to observe the Shabbos given with the other commandments at Sinai?

The holy Rabbi Chayim of Tchernovitz answered this question with a parable.

There was once a pharmacist who was successful in concocting all types of remedies. No one needed these remedies where he lived, however, and none of his fellow townsmen ever bought his products. One day, he heard about a distant city on the coast. There, no medications were available, and therefore, many of its inhabitants were maimed and diseased. He decided to go there to sell his remedies for a high price.

Upon arriving, he set up his stand in the main marketplace. One day passed. Then two.

He called out, "Whoever wants an elixir of life, let him come to me!"

But nobody came to him to buy his remedies.

The reason for this was that the people in this city knew absolutely nothing about the existence of such things. They lived so far away from where the ingredients of these remedies grew that they were under the impression that no such cures for their maladies existed. They thought that someone injured or ill had no hope of ever being healed. They had never seen it, so they thought it didn't exist.

What did the pharmacist do? Looking around the marketplace, his eyes came to rest upon a man whose entire body was covered with wounds. Without asking for a cent, but simply to demonstrate the efficacy of his remedies, he gently administered one of them to this man until one of his wounds healed. Seeing is believing. The man immediately asked to purchase enough medicine to heal all of his wounds.

Seeing this, others also made their way to him, asking to be healed. Before long, he became extremely rich by selling all his remedies. But of all the people in that city, the first man was most grateful, for the pharmacist had healed him without demanding payment.

The same applies to an even greater extent regarding our holy Torah. The Torah contains many cures, deliverances, and redemptions. Speaking for the

Torah, Shelomo Ha-Melech wrote, "My son, heed my words, incline your ear to my sayings. Remove them not from before your eyes, safeguard them in your heart. For they are life to those who discover them and healing to all their flesh" (*Mishlei* 4:20-22). All kinds of spiritual and material blessings are hidden in the Torah.

Knowing this, the angels had originally lobbied for the Torah to remain in heaven. When Hashem was about to give the Torah to Moshe on Mount Sinai, they protested, saying, "O' God, our Master, Your Name is too powerful to rule on the earth. Establish it in the heavens above... What is mortal man that You think of him, and the finest human that You even consider him?" (*Tehillim* 8:2, 5).

In order to bring the Torah down, Moshe had to overcome their arguments. He said, "Is there envy among you? Do you have an evil inclination?" (*Shabbos* 88b). "Do you have diseases among you? Do you require remedies? These things are only needed among us mortals."

There was only one problem. When Hashem took us out of Egypt with the intention of giving us the Torah on Sinai, we still had no way of appreciating its value and its sweetness.

What did He do? He commanded us to observe the Sabbath even before we arrived at Sinai. After experiencing our first Shabbos and tasting its awesome sweetness, we began to appreciate the Torah. We were drawn to its sweetness with love.

Sidduro shel Shabbos 1:2:9

And gave us the Torah.

The Talmud (*Shabbos* 88b) records the following:

> Rabbi Yehoshua ben Levi said: When Moshe ascended to heaven, the ministering angels said to the Holy One, "Master of the world, can one born of a human mother stand among us?"
>
> "He has come to receive the Torah," He answered them.
>
> "The Torah!" the angels protested. "Your hidden treasure! The treasure which You stored away nine hundred and seventy four generations before the creation of the world — and You wish to give it to one of flesh and blood! 'O' God, our Master, Your Name is [too] powerful [to rule] on the earth. Establish Your Splendor in the heavens above...What is mortal man that You think of him, and the finest human that You even consider him?' (*Tehillim* 8:2, 5)."

The Maggid of Dubno asked: Why didn't Hashem acquiesce to their protestations? The answer is hinted in the very way they presented their case.

It is similar to what happened in the story about a man who owned a beautiful silver Chanukah menorah. An inheritance from his parents, he cherished the menorah greatly. Difficult times came, however, and he found himself sorely in need of money. He then was forced to put the menorah up for sale.

Two buyers showed up, both of whom agreed to pay the same price. One was a poor man and the other rich. The poor man had heard about the menorah's former illustrious owners. It had been lit by true spiritual giants. He wished to light the same menorah they had used.

The rich man had different reasons. He was fascinated by the menorah's craftsmanship. He appreciated it as a piece of art.

"In my care, the menorah will last a long time. I will place it in a special glass case. It will thus never lose its shine. Using it will ruin its luster. It may became soiled."

The owner of the menorah replied, "Is it a work of art? It was meant to serve as a menorah for Chanukah lights. Its beauty and its craftsmanship are secondary to the function it was made to serve."

Like this rich man, the angels wished to guard the Torah, "Hashem's hidden treasure." They saw its light and its splendor, and they wished to keep it for themselves.

The Holy One therefore ordered Moshe to prove to them that they were wrong. The Talmud continues:

> Moshe said, "Master of the world, what is written in the Torah which You are giving me? 'I am Hashem your God who has taken you out of the land of Egypt.'"
>
> Moshe now turned to the angels and said, "Did you go down to Egypt? Were you subjugated by Pharaoh? Why should the Torah remain with you?
>
> "What else is written in the Torah? 'Do not have any other gods before Me.' Do you live among idolatrous nations?
>
> "What else is written in it? 'Do not take Hashem's Name in vain.' Do you do business [that you might come to swear falsely by His Name]?
>
> "What else is written in it? 'Remember the Sabbath day to keep it holy.' Do you work, that you should need [one day a week] to rest?
>
> "What else is written in it? 'Honor your father and mother.' Do you have parents?
>
> "What else is written in it? 'Do not murder. Do not commit adultery. Do not steal...' Do you have jealousy among you? Do you possess an evil inclination?"

At that, the Talmud concludes, the angels conceded to the Holy One. They repeated, "O' God, our Master, Your Name is powerful throughout the earth"

(*Tehillim* 8:10), but they did not add, "Establish Your Splendor [solely] in the heavens above" (ibid. 8:5).

The Torah was meant to guide our lives in the path of righteousness and integrity. It was meant to help us distinguish between wrong and right, clean and unclean, permitted and forbidden. It therefore had to be given to mankind, to those who could lead their lives in accordance with its principles.

Kochav Mi'Yaakov, *Haftarah of Vayikra*

And gave us the Torah.

The Talmud (*Shabbos* 88a) records the following:

> It is written: "They stood underneath the mountain" (*Shemos* 19:17; Rashi ad loc.). Rabbi Avidimi ben Chama ben Chasa said, "This teaches us that the Holy One [lifted Mount Sinai and] held it over them like a pail. He then coerced them [to accept the Torah, saying:] If you accept My Torah, fine. If not, this will be your burial ground."
>
> Rabbi Acha said, "This provides a great excuse for [Yisrael not to keep] the Torah." [Rashi: They will now be able to answer that they were coerced into accepting the Torah!]"

In another place (*Avodah Zarah* 2b), the nations of the world use this claim against us: "The nations say: Master of the world, why didn't You lift a mountain up and hold it over us? [Why didn't You coerce us into accepting the Torah?]"

According to the Talmud, Hashem answered them thus: "Did you keep the [seven Noachide] commandments that I did give you?" And He proceeded to reprove them. In the following parable, the Maggid of Dubno gave yet another explanation.

Two mothers once came to a doctor. One mother explained how her infant had become ill and had refused to eat for the past few days. The doctor prescribed certain medications, and warned the mother not to force-feed her baby.

"When he wants to eat, he will show you he is hungry. Then you can feed him," he explained.

The second mother said that ever since she had weaned her baby, he had refused to eat a thing. He just cried constantly.

"Open his mouth by force," the doctor ordered her, "and make him eat!"

The two mothers were astonished by the different answers. "We both asked the same question," they exclaimed. "Why did you give us such different answers?"

"Yes, the questions were identical," the doctor explained, "but the causes were different. The first child is sick, suffering from an intestinal disorder. The treatment for his illness is to give his digestive system a good rest. He should not be forced to eat. The second child, on the other hand, is healthy and he is hungry, as well. The reason he refuses to eat is because he is used to his mother's milk. Compared to it, all other foods seem inedible to him. He must, therefore, be made to taste the food he is presently refusing, until he realizes that it tastes good and is good for him. He will then ask to eat more without the slightest coercion."

Never having tasted the sweetness of the Torah, Yisrael was reluctant to accept it. They therefore had to be coerced into accepting it. But this was only at first. Afterwards, as the Talmud (*Shabbos* 88a) continues, they accepted it willingly and joyously in the days of Esther and Mordechai. The other nations, however, will only be able to accept the truth of the Torah when the Mashiach comes. Until that time comes, they are incapable of appreciating it, and are not forced to accept it.

Kol Rinah Vi'Yeshuah 60a

And built for us the Holy Temple to atone for all our sins.

Let us understand something about this part of the Haggadah. We have just thanked and praised Hashem for the fifteen ways in which He showered us with His love. In all but the last one, the reason we are thankful is not specified. It is not stated that Hashem gave us the Shabbos to be "an eternal sign between Himself and us." It is not stated that He gave us the Torah in order to "instill eternal life into our hearts." Only with regard to the Beis Ha-Mikdash, Hashem's Chosen House, is the reason given — "to atone for all our sins."

This is referring to the First Temple. It could perhaps even be referring to the Second Temple. The problem arises, however, with regard to the Third Temple. The problem is that when the Third Temple will be built, Mashiach already will have come, and we will no longer have an evil inclination (*Sukkah* 52a). Without an evil inclination, "[the possibility of] sin will cease to exist on the earth, and wicked men will be no more" (*Tehillim* 104:35).[1] What will the

[1] The Talmud (*Berachos* 10a) tells the famous story of Rebbi Meir and his wife Bruria. Some rough youths in the neighborhood bothered Rebbi Meir. He then prayed for them to die.

Third Temple accomplish if its only function will be "to atone for all our sins"?

Before we answer this question, we must delve into David Ha-Melech's relationship with the Beis Ha-Mikdash. In his psalms, David wrote, "A Song of Ascents by David: I rejoiced when they said to me, 'Let us go to the House of Hashem!'" (*Tehillim* 122:1). The Talmud (*Makkos* 10a) explains: "David said before the Holy One: Master of the world, I have heard [wicked] men talking, saying, 'When will this old man die so that his son Shelomo can finally come and build the Holy Temple, and we will be able to go up there thrice annually?' I heard them speaking thus, and I rejoiced!"

The Holy One answered David, "One day in your courtyards surpasses a thousand [anywhere else]" (*Tehillim* 84:11). David, one day of your Torah study is better than a thousand sacrifices which your son Shelomo will offer before Me on the altar [when he builds the First Beis Ha-Mikdash].

Two questions arise: Why did David rejoice? And furthermore, why didn't Hashem allow David to build the Beis Ha-Mikdash in the first place? The Maggid of Dubno answered these questions with the following parable:

A king once hired a renowned chef to run his kitchen. The chef fulfilled his duties faithfully. He baked delicious cakes, cooked tasty dishes, and concocted irresistable spiced drinks. Not only was the king's table filled with all kinds of festive dishes every day of the week, each dish was as healthy as it was delicious.

Years passed and the chef grew old and weak. He still spent time in the kitchen, he still oversaw everything that was done and made sure that it was all according to the king's satisfaction. In the meantime, however, the king understood that the chef's health was waning. He therefore took steps to hire the best doctor in the kingdom. The doctor was found, and he signed a contract. In the contract, it was agreed that he would set up his practice in the king's palace. This would not go into effect, however, until the old chef passed away!

Word got around about the contract. Anxious for the new doctor to move to the palace, some of the king's servants were overheard saying, "It would be good if that old chef would die, so that the doctor would come!"

News of this reached the king's ears. He called the servants in and rebuked them: "Fools! Did you think it was by sheer whim that I decided to bring the new doctor in only after the chef's death? Perhaps you thought there

---

Bruria challenged him on this. She said, "Is it written: 'Sinners ("chotim") will cease to exist'? No, it is written: 'Sins ("chata'im") will cease to exist'! Once 'sins cease to exist,' then 'wicked men ("resha'im") will be no more.' Pray, rather, that they return in teshuvah!" He did, and they did!

wasn't enough room in my palace to house both of them at the same time and pay them their full salaries? No! That is not the reason I have made such an arrangement. On the contrary, as long as the chef is alive and continues to oversee all food preparation, I am certain that not even a single one of you will become sick and require the services of a doctor! After he passes away, however, the food we eat will not be as healthy. I am merely preparing for the eventuality of us becoming ill by hiring the best doctor in the kingdom! My true wish is that the chef live for a long time. May he continue keeping us healthy with his food for many a day to come!"

In David's times, when Torah was learned the way it was supposed to be learned and people acted righteously, there was no need for a Beis Ha-Mikdash. This is what Hashem meant when He said to David, "One day of your Torah study is better than a thousand sacrifices which your son Shelomo will offer before Me on the altar [when he builds the First Beis Ha-Mikdash]." Shelomo Ha-Melech expressed the same idea when he said, "To do charity and justice is more acceptable to Hashem than sacrifice" (*Mishlei* 21:3). It was for this reason that David Ha-Melech rejoiced. Certainly, he was bothered by what people were saying. But Hashem saw this and assured him that, on the contrary, his service was more important than building the Beis Ha-Mikdash!

This sheds light on what the author of the Haggadah is telling us. How thankful we must be to Hashem for all the good He has done for us! He led us through the desert wilderness like a father leads his beloved son. He bequeathed the Torah to us, He brought us to His promised land. If we would have taken full advantage of all He gave us, we ourselves would have become a Sanctuary for His presence.

Indeed, this will be the situation in the future. The Third Beis Ha-Mikdash will not be the same as the first two. The only reason we needed them was to atone for all our sins. In the future, there will be no sins. We will be Hashem's Temple, as the verse states, "Let them make [themselves] a Temple for Me, and I shall dwell in their midst" (*Shemos* 25:8).

Kochav Mi'Yaakov, *Haftarah of Shemini*

...the Holy Temple to atone for all our sins.

The Maggid of Zalozitsch asked a number of bothersome questions: Could it be that the sole purpose of the Beis Ha-Mikdash was to atone for our sins? We know that there will be a Third Beis Ha-Mikdash despite the fact that there will no longer be an evil inclination. Furthermore, it was not the Beis Ha-Mikdash itself that atoned for our sins, but the altar. Indeed, it is known that under certain circumstances "we may sacrifice on the altar even in the absence of a Temple" (*Zevachim* 62b). Lastly, why does the author of the Haggadah call it Beis Ha-Bechirah (the Chosen House) rather than Beis Ha-Mikdash (the Holy Temple)?

He answered all these questions based on a famous parable told by the holy Ba'al Shem Tov.

A peasant once rebelled against the king, desecrating a monument dedicated to the king's glory. Hearing of this, the king did not punish him. Instead, he elevated the peasant step by step, until he became the king's chief assistant.

The more good the king showered on this peasant and the more he elevated him to new heights, the more the peasant saw the glory of the king and his servants, as well as their ways. This caused the peasant to suffer tremendous shame. He realized that he had rebelled against a great, merciful king, who, instead of punishing him, had bestowed so much good upon him.

The king, however, had done this deliberately. If he had killed this rebel, his suffering would only have lasted a very short time. This way, he was made to suffer all his days. The higher he was raised, the more he suffered, since he had the audacity to rebel against such a benevolent king!

This is why we recount fifteen kindnesses for which we are indebted to the Eternal One. With each additional kindness, we suffer greater shame for every time we have rebelled against our King who is so good and merciful! When we finally remember the supreme kindness He showed us — choosing to dwell in our midst despite our unworthiness (this is why the Beis Ha-Mikdash is called the Chosen House) — we realize the magnitude of His kindness. Our shame is then so great that it "atones for all our sins"!

Be'er Mayim 79b

RABBAN Gamliel used to say: Whoever does not explain the following three things at the Pesach festival has not fulfilled his obligation, namely:

PESACH, MATZAH, and MAROR.

רַבָּן גַּמְלִיאֵל הָיָה אוֹמֵר. כָּל שֶׁלֹּא־אָמַר שְׁלֹשָׁה דְבָרִים אֵלּוּ בַּפֶּסַח לֹא־יָצָא יְדֵי חוֹבָתוֹ. וְאֵלּוּ הֵן.

פֶּסַח. מַצָּה. וּמָרוֹר:

PESACH the Paschal lamb that our fathers used to eat at the time when the Holy Temple was still standing — for what reason? Because the Holy One, Blessed be He, passed over the houses of our fathers in Egypt, as it says: "And you shall say: 'It is a meal of a salvation performed through a hesitating pass-over, dedicated to Hashem Who hesitated as He passed over the houses of the Children of Yisrael in Egypt when He mortally smote the Egyptians and our houses He saved.' And the people bowed and prostrated themselves" (*Shemos* 12:27).

פֶּסַח שֶׁהָיוּ אֲבוֹתֵינוּ אוֹכְלִים בִּזְמַן שֶׁבֵּית הַמִּקְדָּשׁ הָיָה קַיָּם עַל־שׁוּם מָה. עַל־שׁוּם שֶׁפָּסַח הַקָּדוֹשׁ בָּרוּךְ הוּא עַל בָּתֵּי אֲבוֹתֵינוּ בְּמִצְרַיִם. שֶׁנֶּאֱמַר וַאֲמַרְתֶּם זֶבַח־פֶּסַח הוּא לַיהוה אֲשֶׁר פָּסַח עַל־בָּתֵּי בְנֵי־יִשְׂרָאֵל בְּמִצְרַיִם בְּנָגְפּוֹ אֶת־מִצְרַיִם וְאֶת־בָּתֵּינוּ הִצִּיל וַיִּקֹּד הָעָם וַיִּשְׁתַּחֲווּ:

The leader of the Seder lifts the broken middle matzah for all the participants to see.

MATZAH unleavened bread — this matzah which we eat — for what reason? Because the dough of our fathers did not have time to become leavened before the King of kings, the Holy One, Blessed be He, revealed Himself to them and redeemed them. As it says: "And they baked the dough which they had brought forth from Egypt into unleavened cakes, for it was not leavened, because they had been driven out of Egypt and could not tarry, and even provisions they had not prepared for themselves" (*ibid.* 12:39).

מַצָּה זוֹ שֶׁאָנוּ אוֹכְלִים עַל שׁוּם מָה. עַל שׁוּם שֶׁלֹּא הִסְפִּיק בְּצֵקָם שֶׁל אֲבוֹתֵינוּ לְהַחֲמִיץ עַד שֶׁנִּגְלָה עֲלֵיהֶם מֶלֶךְ מַלְכֵי הַמְּלָכִים הַקָּדוֹשׁ בָּרוּךְ הוּא וּגְאָלָם. שֶׁנֶּאֱמַר וַיֹּאפוּ אֶת־הַבָּצֵק אֲשֶׁר הוֹצִיאוּ מִמִּצְרַיִם עֻגֹת מַצּוֹת כִּי לֹא חָמֵץ כִּי גֹרְשׁוּ מִמִּצְרַיִם וְלֹא יָכְלוּ לְהִתְמַהְמֵהַּ וְגַם־צֵדָה לֹא־עָשׂוּ לָהֶם:

This matzah which we eat — for what reason?

As always, the author of the Haggadah is precise in stating his case. First he says, "This matzah which we eat." Only then does he ask, "For what reason?" This comes to teach us that it is well and fine to try to understand the reasons behind the commandments. We are allowed and even encouraged to do so. But it is secondary, however, to their fulfillment. First we must eat the matzah. Afterwards, there is time to ask why.

This lesson is forcefully illustrated in the following parable by Rabbi Simcha Bunim of Peshischa.

A landlord (paritz) purchased a prize stallion at great expense. He brought the steed into his barn and hired a special guard to watch over it by night.

The first night, the paritz could not sleep. After all, he worried, maybe the guard fell asleep or maybe thieves came and stole his horse!

He went down to the courtyard and approached the barn. His fears were allayed and he was immediately reassured when he saw the guard on duty. In the moonlight, however, he noticed that the guard was troubled. His brow was wrinkled, as if he was bothered by something.

"What is bothering you?" the paritz inquired.

"I was thinking," the guard answered, "about when a nail is pounded into a wooden wall. Where does the wood that was there go when the nail takes its place?"

"An interesting problem," the paritz agreed. "It is well and fine that you are thinking such deep thoughts in the middle of the night. Surely they will prevent you from falling asleep on the job!"

He took leave of the guard and returned to his room. Time passed, but he was still worried. He could not sleep, so he went down again to the courtyard. He found the guard at the entrance to the barn. Everything was in order. His brow, however, was wrinkled in thought.

"What is the problem this time?" the paritz asked.

"I cannot figure it out. When a person eats a round cookie with a hole in the middle, where does the hole disappear to?"

The paritz was taken aback. He had never been bothered by such a question. This guard of mine, he thought to himself, must be a great philosopher. The best thing about it is that he stays awake while he thinks these thoughts!

He returned to his room. The guard did not sleep, but neither did the paritz. In fact, it seemed to him that he was hearing suspicious noises down below. He hurried to the courtyard. He found the guard, his brow wrinkled, totally astonished.

"What are you thinking of now?" he asked.

"I am standing here in total astonishment," the guard answered. "The barn is locked, the guard is standing at his post, and the horse is gone. How did it happen?"

This is truly a philosophical question, much deeper than the earlier ones. If he would only take a little stroll around the back of the barn, however, he would learn the answer. While he was contemplating all these deep thoughts, robbers broke through the back wall and removed the stallion without the least bit of interference.

We learn from this that we must first perform mitzvos and learn to stay on our guard. After we have mastered this, there will be plenty of time to ask philosophical questions.

Siach Tzaddikim 127

For what reason?

In our tradition, whenever a reason is given for a commandment, we are not to assume it is the only reason. Just as Hashem is infinite, so are His reasons. We know that there are mysteries in the Torah to which only the greatest tzaddikim were privy.

A proof of this, found in our Haggadah, is the fact that we were commanded to eat matzos on Pesach night long before we actually left Egypt on the fifteenth of Nissan. Already on the first of Nissan we were commanded, "Eat matzos for seven days" (*Shemos* 12:15). Similarly, "From the fourteenth day of the first month in the evening until the night of the twenty-first day of the month, you must eat matzos. During [these] seven days, no leaven may be found in your homes..." (ibid. 12:18-19). All this despite the fact that the "revealed reason" for eating matzos on Pesach was: "Because the dough of our fathers did not have time to become leavened before the King of kings, the Holy One, Blessed be He, revealed Himself to them and redeemed them" (Haggadah).

The Maggid of Dubno explained this with a parable.

A king wished to encourage people to move to agricultural settlements near the border of his country. He issued an official proclamation that all who settled there would be exempt from military service.

In those days, military service was decided according to a lottery. All males up to the age of thirty were eligible. It was not uncommon for the heads of families to be taken for ten years of military service, leaving their wives and children behind. Understandably, many feared this terrible possibility. When they heard of the king's offer, masses of people streamed to the border settlements.

Among them was one particular family: a father, a mother, and one child, a five-year-old boy. The moment they were assigned a place to live, they unpacked their belongings and lay down to rest.

In the morning, the boy arose first. As was his custom, he asked his father for five cents to buy some sweets at the candy shop.

His father answered him, "My son, in this settlement there are no sweets and there is no candy store."

The boy cried and complained, "If so, let us return to our home in the city! Why have you brought me to a place where there are no sweets?"

The leader of the Seder lifts the maror for all the participants to see.

MAROR the bitter herbs — this maror which we eat — for what reason? Because the Egyptians embittered the lives of our fathers in Egypt, as it says: "And they [the Egyptians] embittered their lives with hard labor, with mortar and bricks and with all manner of work in the field; they embittered all their work which they made them do, with harshness" (*ibid.* 1:14).

מָרוֹר זֶה שֶׁאָנוּ אוֹכְלִים עַל־שׁוּם מָה. עַל־שׁוּם שֶׁמֵּרְרוּ הַמִּצְרִים אֶת־חַיֵּי אֲבוֹתֵינוּ בְּמִצְרַיִם. שֶׁנֶּאֱמַר וַיְמָרְרוּ אֶת חַיֵּיהֶם בַּעֲבֹדָה קָשָׁה בְּחֹמֶר וּבִלְבֵנִים וּבְכָל עֲבֹדָה בַּשָּׂדֶה אֵת כָּל־עֲבֹדָתָם אֲשֶׁר עָבְדוּ בָהֶם בְּפָרֶךְ:

The boy's father tried to calm him down. "Don't cry, my son," he said. "There are no sweets here, but there are open fields unlike anything you could find in the city. There are beautiful hills and knolls, with flowers everywhere. Why don't you go outside and pick some colorful, sweet-smelling flowers?"

But the boy cried even more. "What will I do with pretty-colored flowers? Can I eat them? Is a flower a substitute for a sweet candy?"

The boy was right. Flowers are no substitute for candy. But can the father explain to a five year old what it is to serve in the military? Would the child understand?

And if a five year old cannot understand his twenty-five-year-old father, is it any wonder that we cannot understand the mind of the Infinite One? Could He possibly explain to us all the reasons He had for giving us the mitzvos, when those very reasons transcend all thought?

Chomas Ha-Da'as V'Ha-Emunah 16a

This maror which we eat — for what reason?

The Haggadah continues: This maror herb which we eat, what is the reason for it? It is because the Egyptians embittered the lives of our ancestors in Egypt. It is thus written: "And they [the Egyptians] embittered their lives with hard labor, with mortar and bricks and with all manner of work in the field; they embittered all their work which they made them do, with harshness" (*Shemos* 1:14).

Rabbi Naftali, author of *Maskil La'Eitan*, was bothered by a seeming contradiction between this passage and the following passage from the Midrash (*Shemos Rabbah* 19:7):

"You must keep this law [of the Pesach festival] on its appointed day from year to year" (*Shemos* 13:10). MASHAL: A king wished to marry a noblewoman from a distant land. She was to reach him by sea. During the voyage, many waves passed over her. In the end, she arrived in peace and prepared to meet the king. Upon hearing of the difficulties she had endured, the first thing the king said was, "Try not to remember the waves that passed over you. Remember rather the day you arrived safely, and observe it as a day of rejoicing each year." This is what the Holy One said to Yisrael when He appeared to them to redeem them. How many waves had passed over them before He delivered them! He therefore cautioned them to rejoice each year [on Pesach night].

It seems, Rabbi Naftali said, that we are not to commemorate our suffering. Rather, we are to commemorate the day we were redeemed from it. Why, then, do we eat bitter herbs to commemorate how "the Egyptians embittered the lives of our Fathers in Egypt"? He answered this with a parable which explained what the above midrash really meant.

A king wished to marry a noblewoman from a distant land. She set off to reach him by sea. Suddenly, a storm came up. The ship rose to the heavens and descended to the depths. It was about to split in half from such a beating when, through God's grace, the storm subsided, saving the lives of all aboard.

Two days later, the ship ran aground, tearing a big hole in its hold. Water began pouring in. The crew worked for hours bailing water, and they waited for high tide to carry the ship out to sea. Once they were freed from the reef, they worked to patch up the hole. After hours of backbreaking work, they succeeded in doing so, at least partially.

Everybody realized that their salvation was only temporary. Eventually, they knew, the patch would wear out and the water would come flooding in. When they spied another ship on the horizon, they signaled, and it began sailing towards them. To their dismay, it was a pirate ship. Everyone aboard was taken hostage. Their own ship sunk right after the last of them made it onto the second vessel.

The pirates sailed to the closest country where they could sell their hostages on the slave market. In the meantime, the king's betrothed miraculously managed to escape their clutches. After many trials and tribulations, she finally succeeded in crossing the border to her fiance's country and made her way straight to his palace.

Out of thanks to God, she decided to commemorate her many deliverances. The first day of thanksgiving was to be on the anniversary of the day the storm subsided. The second day of thanksgiving was to be on the day the hole in the ship's hold was patched up. The third day was to be on the day they

בְּכָל דּוֹר וָדוֹר חַיָּב אָדָם לִרְאוֹת אֶת־עַצְמוֹ כְּאִלּוּ הוּא יָצָא מִמִּצְרַיִם. שֶׁנֶּאֱמַר וְהִגַּדְתָּ לְבִנְךָ בַּיּוֹם הַהוּא לֵאמֹר בַּעֲבוּר זֶה עָשָׂה יהוה לִי בְּצֵאתִי מִמִּצְרָיִם. לֹא אֶת־אֲבוֹתֵינוּ בִּלְבָד גָּאַל הַקָּדוֹשׁ בָּרוּךְ הוּא אֶלָּא אַף אוֹתָנוּ גָּאַל עִמָּהֶם. שֶׁנֶּאֱמַר וְאוֹתָנוּ הוֹצִיא מִשָּׁם לְמַעַן הָבִיא אוֹתָנוּ לָתֶת לָנוּ אֶת הָאָרֶץ אֲשֶׁר נִשְׁבַּע לַאֲבוֹתֵינוּ:

In every single generation one is obligated to look upon himself as if he personally had gone forth out of Egypt, as it says: "And you shall relate to your child on that day, saying: 'It is because of this that Hashem acted for me when I came forth out of Egypt'" (*ibid.* 13:8). Not only our fathers did the Holy One, Blessed be He, redeem, but us, too, He redeemed together with them, as it says: "And He brought *us* out from there that He might bring us home to give to us the land which He had sworn to our fathers" (*Devarim* 6:23).

were taken captive by the pirates [and thus saved from their sinking ship]. The fourth day was set for the day she escaped from the pirates.

Hearing this, the king said, "No, my beloved, why should you commemorate every single wave [sorrow] that passed over you? Commemorate just one single day, the day you entered my palace and left all those sorrows behind. On this day, remember them all. Recount all the miracles God performed for you and thank Him for each time He delivered you from danger."

This is the intention of the midrash, and this is why the Sages connected it to the verse: "You must keep this law [of the Pesach festival] on its appointed day from year to year" (*Shemos* 13:10). In Hebrew, the words "from year to year" are "miyamim yamimah." Although the proper translation is as we have rendered it, "miyamim yamimah" can also be rendered as "from day to day." That is, we are to commemorate one day alone for Pesach. On that day, however, we are to be thankful for every single "day," for each and every time we were saved from mortal danger, from every bitter trial. On this day, we commemorate everything, from the hardship symbolized by the bitter herbs to the deliverance symbolized by the matzos.

Midrash Haggadah 41

In every single generation one is obligated to look upon himself as if he personally had gone forth out of Egypt.

We learn from this that the mitzvah of recounting the Exodus is not merely to read the Haggadah! It has to penetrate our hearts. We must feel and relive

it with joy and with thanksgiving! If we will recount it this way, our faith will grow stronger in leaps and bounds. We will feel uplifted in our serving Hashem.

This is exactly how the Alter of Kelm used to interpret the phrase in the Haggadah, "He who elaborates upon the story of the departure from Egypt is worthy of praise." In Hebrew, the expression "worthy of praise" is "harei zeh meshubach." In the Talmud, the word "meshubach" is always used in connection with the appreciation of value, as when something improves, its value appreciates. In this sense, the Alter of Kelm said, "He who elaborates upon the story of the departure from Egypt — because his heart overflows with excitement — becomes a better person. His service to God appreciates in value — he becomes invaluable."

On the other hand, a person who does not see himself as going out of Egypt, whose heart remains unaffected by the story of the Exodus, who reads the Haggadah without digesting its meaning and its message — such a person is the subject of the following parable told by Rabbi Yaakov Levitt of Bialishtok.

A villager became ill and bedridden. The doctor came to examine the man, and he determined that his condition was serious. He wrote out a prescription in which he listed the various medications that would be needed to restore him to health. Before departing, he instructed the family, "Give this prescription to the patient three times a day, in the morning, at noon, and in the evening. Dissolve it in a cup of water. The patient will be fine."

The man's wife took the prescription, paid the doctor, and followed his instructions to the letter. She tore the prescription into small pieces, dissolved one piece at a time in water and gave it to the sick man to drink.

His family hoped for a speedy recovery. Their spirits fell, however, when they saw that not only was his condition not improving, but it was actually worsening by the hour!

They rushed to the doctor and accused him of lying to them. What had happened to his promise? What kind of a doctor was he? He took their money, and didn't help the patient!

The doctor hurried to the man's side. He asked to see the prescription. He was sure that the medicine he had prescribed was exactly what the patient needed, but perhaps he had made some mistake.

"The prescription is all gone," the family told him.

He didn't quite understand.

They explained to him that they had followed his instructions to a tee. They had given the patient a portion of the prescription three times a day, one piece every few hours.

The doctor was stunned. "You foolish people," he exclaimed, "you come to me with complaints, blaming me because the medicine didn't work? Can a man be cured by placing a piece of paper in his mouth? I never meant for him to ingest the prescription, but rather the medicines prescribed on it. If he would have taken that medicine, he would have been better by now."

Recalling the Exodus is important enough that we were commanded to do it twice daily, once in the morning and once at night. In addition to this, every Shabbos and every Festival commemorates the Exodus. Moreover, the Seder night is totally dedicated not only to recalling the Exodus but to reliving it. If the Torah considers it so important, it must mean that a person can change, can impove, by doing it. The problem is that we read through the Haggadah... and nothing happens! We seem to have forgotten that we must ingest, not the prescription, but its contents and its message.

Pe'er Yisrael 57

In every single generation one is obligated to look upon himself as if he personally had gone forth out of Egypt.

The key word here is "chayav" (obligated). It appears twice: "In every generation one is chayav to look upon himself as if he personally had gone forth out of Egypt," and "Therefore we are chayav to avow thanks, to praise... and celebrate Him Who wrought all these miracles for our fathers and for us."

Rabbi Chayim Elazar from Munkatch asked a very penetrating question on this passage.

We are told that recounting the story of the Exodus is a mitzvah; elaborating on it is praiseworthy. But who among us has raised himself to the level of actually envisioning the Esser Ha-Makkos (Ten Plagues) and of seeing Hashem's powerful hand and outstretched arm? Who among us has genuinely felt as though he had been delivered from slavery with miracles and supernatural wonders? And if we have felt even a small part of all this, have we been thankful enough?

In answer, he told the story of Rabbi Yeshaya, the great genius of Prague, whose son passed away while in his prime. When Rabbi Yeshaya received the news, he immediately quoted the rabbinical injunction: "One is chayav to bless [Hashem] for bad tidings just as he is for the good" (*Berachos* 9:5).

The matzos are covered and the cup is lifted and held until the closing sentence "Who has redeemed Yisrael" (according to some customs it is put down after "Halleluyah" and the matzos are uncovered, then lifted again for the berachah "Who redeemed us..." and the matzos covered once again).

THEREFORE we are obliged to avow thanks, to praise His mighty acts, to laud, glorify, exalt, proclaim His might, bless, extol and celebrate Him Who wrought all these miracles for our fathers and for us. He brought us forth from slavery into freedom, from sorrow into joy, from mourning into festivity, and from darkness into great light, and from subjugation into redemption. Let us therefore recite before Him a new song: Halleluyah!

לְפִיכָךְ אֲנַחְנוּ חַיָּבִים לְהוֹדוֹת לְהַלֵּל לְשַׁבֵּחַ לְפָאֵר לְרוֹמֵם לְהַדֵּר לְבָרֵךְ לְעַלֵּה וּלְקַלֵּס לְמִי שֶׁעָשָׂה לַאֲבוֹתֵינוּ וְלָנוּ אֶת־כָּל הַנִּסִּים הָאֵלֶּה הוֹצִיאָנוּ מֵעַבְדוּת לְחֵרוּת מִיָּגוֹן לְשִׂמְחָה מֵאֵבֶל לְיוֹם טוֹב וּמֵאֲפֵלָה לְאוֹר גָּדוֹל וּמִשִּׁעְבּוּד לִגְאֻלָּה וְנֹאמַר לְפָנָיו שִׁירָה חֲדָשָׁה הַלְלוּיָהּ:

That is, we must recognize that our suffering, too, is from Hashem. We must accept everything He does with love, and at the same time know that He loves us and has not abandoned us.

It is not by chance that our teachers used the word chayav when speaking of receiving bad tidings. Since it involves such a high level of service, one that is difficult to attain at the very moment we are in our greatest distress, most people remain chayav because they have not fulfilled their obligation perfectly.

The same is true in our case, the Munkatcher continued. "In every single generation one is chayav to look upon himself as if he personally had gone forth out of Egypt." And we are all "chayav to avow thanks, to praise His mighty acts, to laud, glorify, exalt, proclaim his might, bless, extol and celebrate Him Who wrought all these miracles for our fathers and for us." The reason is clear. As much as we try to relive the experience, we remain sorely lacking in our service, and hence we remain obligated.

The same is true of another injunction: "For it is the chovah (obligation) of all creatures [who stand] before You, Hashem our God, and God of our ancestors, to offer thanks, to praise..." (*U'bemak'halos*). As much as we will praise Him, we will always remain lacking, unable to fully express the proper gratitude, as we say: "If our mouths were filled with singing like [water fills] the sea, and our tongues with ecstatic song like the multitude of its waves, and our lips with praise like the expanse of the heaven, and our eyes shone like the sun

הַלְלוּיָהּ הַלְלוּ עַבְדֵי יהוה הַלְלוּ אֶת־שֵׁם יהוה: יְהִי שֵׁם יהוה מְבוֹרָךְ מֵעַתָּה וְעַד־עוֹלָם: מִמִּזְרַח שֶׁמֶשׁ עַד־מְבוֹאוֹ מְהֻלָּל שֵׁם יהוה: רָם עַל־כָּל־גּוֹיִם יהוה. עַל הַשָּׁמַיִם כְּבוֹדוֹ: מִי כַּיהוה אֱלֹהֵינוּ. הַמַּגְבִּיהִי לָשָׁבֶת. הַמַּשְׁפִּילִי לִרְאוֹת בַּשָּׁמַיִם וּבָאָרֶץ: מְקִימִי מֵעָפָר דָּל. מֵאַשְׁפֹּת יָרִים אֶבְיוֹן: לְהוֹשִׁיבִי עִם־נְדִיבִים. עִם נְדִיבֵי עַמּוֹ: מוֹשִׁיבִי עֲקֶרֶת הַבַּיִת אֵם־הַבָּנִים שְׂמֵחָה הַלְלוּיָהּ:

Halleluyah! Praise by proclaiming His mighty acts, o' servants of Hashem, praise by proclaiming His mighty acts, the Name of Hashem. Blessed be the Name of Hashem from this time forth and unto eternity. True from the rising of the sun until its setting, the Name of Hashem is lauded in praises of His mighty acts. For Hashem is high above all nations, His glory is beyond the heavens. But Who is like Hashem our God, Who though enthroned on high, looks down so low, into the heavens and upon the earth? He raises out of the dust him who has sunk low and lifts the defenseless up from the dunghill. To set him next to princes, next to the princes of his people. He causes the barren woman of the house to sit as a joyous mother of children; Halleluyah! (*Tehillim* 113).

and the moon, and our hands spread out like the [wings of] soaring eagles, and our feet swift like deer, we would still be unable to thank You sufficiently, Hashem, our God and God of our ancestors, or to bless Your Name, our King, for even one of the thousand, million, billion times You did favors, miracles, and wonders for our ancestors and for us!"

Sha'ar Yissachar, *Aggadeta D'Pischa* 78

True from the rising of the sun until its setting, the Name of Hashem is lauded.

The Maggid of Dubno asked: Why is Hashem's Name praised, why not Hashem Himself? And furthermore, how is it possible to say that Hashem's Name is praised from the rising of the sun in the east until its setting in the west? Aren't many of the nations still sunk in some level of idol worship? How can they be said to "praise Hashem's Name"?

But, the Maggid said, let us answer the first question by telling a parable about the second.

A great king was known as a kind and just ruler. He cared about his subjects, considered their problems, and worked for their benefit. He eased their burdens, judged them charitably, and did everything he could for their good. Everyone praised him; all his subjects loved him.

One day, news arrived that an upstart from a distant city had begun impersonating the king. Masses of people had surrounded him, showered expensive gifts upon him, honored him, and carried him on their shoulders.

בְּצֵאת יִשְׂרָאֵל מִמִּצְרָיִם בֵּית יַעֲקֹב מֵעַם לֹעֵז: הָיְתָה יְהוּדָה לְקָדְשׁוֹ יִשְׂרָאֵל מַמְשְׁלוֹתָיו: הַיָּם רָאָה וַיָּנֹס. הַיַּרְדֵּן יִסֹּב לְאָחוֹר: הֶהָרִים רָקְדוּ כְאֵילִים. גְּבָעוֹת כִּבְנֵי צֹאן: מַה לְּךָ הַיָּם כִּי תָנוּס. הַיַּרְדֵּן תִּסֹּב לְאָחוֹר: הֶהָרִים תִּרְקְדוּ כְאֵילִים. גְּבָעוֹת כִּבְנֵי־צֹאן: מִלִּפְנֵי אָדוֹן חוּלִי אָרֶץ. מִלִּפְנֵי אֱלוֹהַּ יַעֲקֹב: הַהֹפְכִי הַצּוּר אֲגַם־מָיִם. חַלָּמִישׁ לְמַעְיְנוֹ־מָיִם:

When Yisrael went forth from Egypt, the House of Yaakov from a people of alien tongue. Yehudah became His sanctuary, Yisrael His sphere of dominion. The Sea saw it and fled, the Jordan sought to turn backward. The mountains skipped like rams, the hills like young sheep. What ails you, o' Sea, that you flee, o' Jordan, that you turn backward; o' mountains, that you skip like rams, o' hills, like young sheep? Tremble, o' earth, before the Master, before the God of Yaakov. Who turns the rock into a pool of water, pebbles into a fountain of water (*ibid.* 114).

All of the king's subjects were certain that the real king would be furious. They were sure that he would order the man's punishment. Instead, he was very calm. A wide smile of satisfaction even crossed his lips!

"What is the meaning of this? Why is his majesty smiling?" they asked in bewilderment.

He answered, "Certainly, the people of that city are foolish for falling into the impostor's trap. He, as well, is guilty and should be punished. Still, I am happy, for now I know how much they revere me and are willing to honor me!"

The prophet said in Hashem's Name: "From the rising of the sun until its setting, My Name is great among the nations, and in every place incense is offered in My Name, even pure meal offerings" (*Malachi* 1:11). How could this be? Is their incense really offered up in Hashem's Name?

But the truth is that even those nations who serve foreign deities really do serve Hashem indirectly. Certainly in one sense, they mistake their particular god for the ultimate Ruler, the true God. But in actuality, even those who honor a false god do so only because they think it is the true God. If this is so, then it is true that "from the rising of the sun until its setting, the Name of Hashem is lauded." For what is a false god if not one that takes the real God's Name for itself?

Ohel Yaakov, *Beshallach*

When Yisrael went forth from Egypt, the House of Yaakov from a people of alien tongue.

The Maggid of Dubno pointed out that in Hebrew "from a people of alien

tongue" is "me'am lo'ez." According to the Aramaic, this is "me'amei barbera'ei," (from a barbaric people). A barbaric people is cruel and brutal. Why, he asked, did the Psalmist wish to emphasize this particular trait of the Egyptians?

He answered with a parable.

The king's son fell ill, and his condition worsened until he was on the brink of death. The king summoned the greatest doctor in the land.

He examined the boy and said, "I must operate on your son right now, without delay."

"Do this, and I will make you the richest man in the kingdom," the king assured him.

"I have not yet finished saying what I have to say," the doctor continued. "In most cases, I operate on a patient after I have administered the anesthesia. Then the patient does not feel a thing. Your son's condition is so serious, however, that I fear putting him to sleep lest he never regain consciousness!"

The king had no words; his face turned pale.

"I have no choice," the doctor continued, "but to operate on your son without using anesthesia."

The king shuddered, but he said, "Do what is right in your eyes, just make sure he gets better!"

"If so," the doctor rejoined, "I have two requests. First, you must leave the room and go as far away as possible, so that you will not hear his cries and not even think of interfering when he calls for your help. His life depends upon it."

"I will do so," the king replied. "And the second request?"

"Find me a giant of a man, a heartless fellow, an insensitive, cruel, sadistic type, who will hold your son down during the operation and not allow him to make the slightest move!" the doctor explained.

The king immediately issued the order that an animal of a man fitting the above description be found and brought to him without delay. Before long, an evil pirate, a depraved man with a vile heart, was brought before the king.

"See," he boasted to everyone within hearing distance, "out of everyone in the kingdom, only I was called in to save the king's son! No one else can compare with me!"

Those present nodded and said, "Not only are you wicked, but you're stupid on top of it! Don't you know that the only reason you've been called in to save the king's son is because you are the meanest and vilest man in the kingdom?"

בָּרוּךְ אַתָּה יהוה אֱלֹהֵינוּ מֶלֶךְ הָעוֹלָם אֲשֶׁר גְּאָלָנוּ וְגָאַל אֶת אֲבוֹתֵינוּ מִמִּצְרַיִם וְהִגִּיעָנוּ הַלַּיְלָה הַזֶּה לֶאֱכָל בּוֹ מַצָּה וּמָרוֹר. כֵּן יהוה אֱלֹהֵינוּ וֵאלֹהֵי אֲבוֹתֵינוּ יַגִּיעֵנוּ לְמוֹעֲדִים וְלִרְגָלִים אֲחֵרִים הַבָּאִים לִקְרָאתֵנוּ לְשָׁלוֹם שְׂמֵחִים בְּבִנְיַן עִירֶךָ וְשָׂשִׂים בַּעֲבוֹדָתֶךָ וְנֹאכַל שָׁם מִן הַזְּבָחִים וּמִן הַפְּסָחִים (יֵשׁ אוֹמְרִים בְּמוֹצָאֵי שַׁבָּת: מִן הַפְּסָחִים וּמִן הַזְּבָחִים) אֲשֶׁר יַגִּיעַ דָּמָם עַל קִיר מִזְבַּחֲךָ

BLESSED be You, Hashem our God, King of the universe, Who redeemed us and redeemed our fathers from Egypt and enabled us to attain this night, on which to eat matzah and maror. So Hashem, our God and God of our fathers, enable us to attain other festivals of assembly and of pilgrimage which approach us in peace, rejoicing in the building of Your city and joyful in Your sacrificial service; and we shall eat there from the sacrifices and from the Pesach offerings (on *Motzai Shabbos* some say: from the Pesach offerings and from the sacrifices) whose blood will be sprinkled on the sides of Your altar for gracious acceptance, and we shall thank You with a new

When Hashem searched among the nations of the ancient world for one that would subjugate His beloved children and prepare them to become His treasure for all eternity and receive His Torah, He found no more fitting a candidate than the Egyptians. We might have thought that they were chosen because they possessed some special good quality. Exactly the opposite was true!

Kochav Mi'Yaakov, *Haftarah of Vayishlach*

Joyful in Your sacrificial service.

The difference between the joy of the righteous and that of the wicked is that the joy of the righteous is true and honest. Concerning the righteous, it is written, "We will rejoice and delight in You" (*Shir Ha-Shirim* 1:4). Their soul rejoices in Hashem alone — in serving Him, in fulfilling His will, in following His commandments, which bring joy to the heart.

The wicked, on the other hand, are really very sad at heart. They experience very little pleasure in life, and this is why they are constantly seeking new pleasures, external stimuli — food, wine, music, adventure — anything to satisfy that deep craving in their souls.

The prophet spoke of such people when he lamented: "Woe to them who rise up early in the morning, that they may chase after strong drink; who continue into the night, until wine enflames them. They bring lyre, lute, tambourine, flute, and wine to their feasts, but they disregard Hashem's craftsmanship, pay no attention to his handiwork" (*Yeshayahu* 5:11-12). This need to seek outside entertainment is a sign of inner emptiness. It is also the subject of a parable given by the Maggid of Dubno.

A father and son were traveling together, and stopped at an inn on the way.

The innkeeper served them a heavily spiced meat dish. The father refused to eat it, but the smell of the spices wafted into his son's nostrils and made his mouth water.

"Why don't you eat, Abba?" the boy asked. "The smell of this food is irresistable!"

"That's the problem, my son," the father replied. "The meat is spoiled. It has already become putrid and begun to stink. The spices testify to this. If the meat was good, not nearly as much spice would be needed!"

For one who wishes to nurture a rich inner life, so many of the distractions of modern life are unnecessary. They are insidious because they not only cover up an inner emptiness, but they are partially responsible for creating the vacuum of meaning so prevalent today.

The Kohanim in the Beis Ha-Mikdash illustrated the opposite of this. If they drank even the smallest amount of an intoxicating beverage, they were forbidden from entering the Temple and performing their service (*Vayikra* 10:9; Sifra, Rashi ad. loc.; Rambam, *Biyas Ha-Mikdash* 1:1-5). As the Psalmist said, the Beis Ha-Mikdash was "the joy of the whole earth" (*Tehillim* 48:3). The delight of doing Hashem's will and serving Him in joy was there. For one to have entered the Temple under the influence of strong drink would have meant that the joy of serving Hashem was not sufficient for him, and that he required some chemical stimulant in order to feel that joy.

This is illustrated in the story of Nadav and Avihu. The Torah relates that they each took an incense burner and "placed fire upon it" (ibid. 10:1). They then entered the Holy of Holies and offered this unauthorized fire. Fire then shot out from between the Cherubim on the Golden Ark and consumed their insides.

In the Midrash, at least twelve opinions are given with regard to what exactly Nadav and Avihu did wrong. Rabbi Eliezer says: (1) They gave a halachic ruling in the presence of their teachers.

Bar Kappara added four more reasons: (2) They entered unauthorized into the Holy of Holies; (3) they brought an unauthorized offering; (4) the fire they used was unauthorized, having been taken from outside the Mishkan; (5) they had not conferred with each other, but acted independently.

Rabbi Mani, Rabbi Yehoshua, Rabbi Yochanan, and Rabbi Levi added four more reasons: (6) They had drunk intoxicating wine before entering the Holy of Holies; (7) they were not wearing the proper vestments; (8) they entered without first washing their hands and feet; (9) they were without children. Abba Chanin added: (10) They were unmarried.

song for our redemption and for the deliverance of our souls. Blessed be You, Hashem, Who has redeemed Yisrael.	לְרָצוֹן וְנוֹדֶה לְךָ שִׁיר חָדָשׁ עַל גְּאֻלָּתֵנוּ וְעַל פְּדוּת נַפְשֵׁנוּ. בָּרוּךְ אַתָּה יהוה גָּאַל יִשְׂרָאֵל:

One should intend to fulfill the requirement of drinking the second of the four cups of wine.

Blessed be You, Hashem our God, King of the universe, Who creates the fruit of the vine.	בָּרוּךְ אַתָּה יהוה אֱלֹהֵינוּ מֶלֶךְ הָעוֹלָם בּוֹרֵא פְּרִי הַגָּפֶן:

The required amount of the second cup is drunk, within the required period of time, while reclining to the left.

Rabbi Yehoshua ben Nechemyah added: (11) They thought or spoke disrespectfully about Moshe and Aharon, saying, "When will these two old men finally die so that we can take control of this congregation?"

Rabbi Berachyah added: (12) On Mount Sinai, they had acted disrepectfully in the presence of the Divine One (*Vayikra Rabbah* 20:6-10; listed in *Michtav Me-Eliyahu* 2:245).

The sixth reason interests us here: They had drunk intoxicating wine before entering the Holy of Holies. The Torah states that "they offered unauthorized fire," or literally, "strange fire" (*Vayikra* 10:2). What connection is there between this fire and entering the Holy of Holies under the influence of intoxicating wine?

We must conclude that they are one and the same. The Torah is not only referring to physical fire, but to the fire of joy and passion that a Jew, especially a Kohen, should feel while serving Hashem! By drinking intoxicating wine, Nadav and Avihu demonstrated that, even with all their greatness, they were insensitive to the sheer joy and delight of serving Hashem. True joy can never be externally stimulated; it must come from the inside, it must pour forth from a person's heart and soul.

And how can we tell the difference between a person who feels true joy and one who feels counterfeit joy? The difference might not be noticeable in the way each one acts. Both might seem uncontrollably happy. Both might lose a little of their normal composure. After all, joy is an overwhelming experience!

How, then, can we know? We can tell if we look at them the next day. A hangover is the first sign that his "joy" was not true joy. True joy lasts. Even when the initial exhilaration ends, the deep abiding sense of thankfulness and peace linger on.

Kol Rinah Vi'Yeshuah 49b

Rochtzah

רָחְצָה

From the time the hands are washed until after eating the korech, no unnecessary speaking is allowed. Therefore, the leader of the Seder should now explain to all the participants (especially children) all the instructions they will need to know concerning the eating of the matzah and the maror.

It is unlikely that there will be enough matzah on the Seder plate for all of the assembled. Furthermore, since the leader of the Seder is required to distribute from his matzah to those assembled, to have to measure and distribute the required amount after the blessing would constitute an unnecessary lapse of time between the berachah and the fulfilling of the mitzvah. Therefore, it is advisable that everyone have the measured, required amount of matzah from other, shemurah matzos before him (see Required Measurements and Amounts, page 37, before he goes to wash his hands. After the leader of the Seder will have recited the berachah and have measured the required amount for himself, he will easily and quickly be able to distribute bits of the leftover matzah to all assembled to eat together with their portions.

All present wash their hands (a washbasin is brought to the leader of the Seder) and recite the following berachah (one who washed his hands before the karpas and is sure that they have been kept clean, should first contaminate them by touching his shoe or the like):

BLESSED be You, Hashem our God, King of the universe, Who has sanctified us by His commandments and commanded us concerning the washing of the hands.

בָּרוּךְ אַתָּה יהוה אֱלֹהֵינוּ מֶלֶךְ הָעוֹלָם אֲשֶׁר קִדְּשָׁנוּ בְּמִצְוֹתָיו וְצִוָּנוּ עַל נְטִילַת יָדָיִם:

Motzi

מוֹצִיא

If the leader of the Seder is to make the berachos over the matzah and maror for all assembled (as is the custom in many homes), then he and they must have that in mind while the berachos are being made, and everyone should have in mind that it is his intention to fulfill his duty to eat matzah on Pesach night.

The leader of the Seder, or each participant, if he is to make his own berachos, takes all three matzos in his hand (the two whole ones for lechem mishneh and the broken one between them for lechem oni) and says the following berachah:

BLESSED be You, Hashem our God, King of the universe, Who causes bread to grow forth from the earth.

בָּרוּךְ אַתָּה יהוה אֱלֹהֵינוּ מֶלֶךְ הָעוֹלָם הַמּוֹצִיא לֶחֶם מִן הָאָרֶץ:

Matzah

מַצָּה

He now releases the bottom matzah from his grip and says the following berachah, with the intention that it refer also to the matzah of the korech and afikoman which will be eaten later on:

BLESSED be You, Hashem our God, King of the universe, Who has sanctified us by His commandments and commanded us concerning the eating of matzah.

בָּרוּךְ אַתָּה יהוה אֱלֹהֵינוּ מֶלֶךְ הָעוֹלָם אֲשֶׁר קִדְּשָׁנוּ בְּמִצְוֹתָיו וְצִוָּנוּ עַל אֲכִילַת מַצָּה:

In some communities the matzah is dipped in salt, but in most it is not.

The required amounts of matzah are then eaten by all of the participants, while reclining on the left side, within the required period of time.

Maror

מָרוֹר

The leader of the Seder takes a kezayis of maror dips it briefly in charoses, and shakes off the excess charoses. After putting aside one such kezayis for himself, he proceeds to distribute similar portions to all present. Everyone should have in mind that it is his intention to fulfill the requirement of eating maror on Pesach night. He, or each participant, if he is making his own berachos, then says the following berachah with the intention that it refer also to the maror of the korech which will be eaten later on:

BLESSED be You, Hashem our God, King of the universe, Who has sanctified us by His commandments and commanded us concerning the eating of maror.

בָּרוּךְ אַתָּה יהוה אֱלֹהֵינוּ מֶלֶךְ הָעוֹלָם אֲשֶׁר קִדְּשָׁנוּ בְּמִצְוֹתָיו וְצִוָּנוּ עַל אֲכִילַת מָרוֹר:

All the assembled eat their portions of maror, not reclining, within the required period of time.

Korech

כּוֹרֵךְ

The leader of the Seder takes a kezayis of the third, unbroken matzah, places upon it a kezayis of maror, dips it in the charoses (some shake off the charoses and some do not), and distributes similar portions to the other participants. Before eating the korech the following is said:

This is in remembrance of the Temple, according to the custom of Hillel. Thus did Hillel at the time when the Temple was standing: He would combine (the Paschal lamb,) the matzah and the maror and eat them together in order to fulfill what is written: "...with unleavened bread and bitter herbs shall they eat it" (*Bemidbar* 9:11).

זֵכֶר לְמִקְדָּשׁ כְּהִלֵּל. כֵּן עָשָׂה הִלֵּל בִּזְמַן שֶׁבֵּית הַמִּקְדָּשׁ הָיָה קַיָּם. הָיָה כּוֹרֵךְ (פֶּסַח) מַצָּה וּמָרוֹר וְאוֹכֵל בְּיַחַד. לְקַיֵּם מַה שֶּׁנֶּאֱמַר עַל־מַצּוֹת וּמְרֹרִים יֹאכְלֻהוּ:

Everyone eats his portion, while reclining to the left, within the required period of time.

He would combine (the Paschal lamb,) the matzah and the maror and eat them together.

Rabbi Shelomo Kluger of Brodi asked: Why did Hillel choose to combine the matzah and bitter herbs together?

He answered: The Mishnah (*Berachos* 9:3, 54a) states: One who approaches his home town, hears the sound of wailing, and prays, "May it be Your will that these [cries] are not from the members of my household," has prayed in vain. As the commentators explain, uttering a prayer about something that is already a reality is a contradiction in terms.

How then should one react in such a situation? The Talmud (*Berachos* 60a) cites the case of Hillel: Hillel the Elder was approaching his home town when he heard the sounds of wailing coming from the city [from the direction of his home]. He said, "I am certain that this is not coming from my house." Regarding a person [with such implicit trust in Hashem], the verse states, "One whose heart trusts firmly in Hashem need never fear evil tidings!" (*Tehillim* 112:7).

Through Hillel's exemplary behavior, the Talmud teaches us how we should act in similar circumstances. And yet it says in Chumash that even Yaakov Avinu feared his brother Esav, and said, "How can I be sure that Hashem's promise to protect me is still in force? Haven't I sinned in the meantime, and perhaps become unworthy of His aid?" How could Hillel have been so sure? How can any of us be sure?

The answer is that Hillel knew something about the members of his family. He knew that if some calamity befell them, God forbid, they would not scream and wail. He had already taught them that — no matter what — everything is for the good. One must accept all that comes with love and faith in the Master of the world.

The Talmud (*Berachos* 60b) thus states: Rabbi Acha asked in the name of Rabbi Levi: What is the meaning of the verse, "I will sing about [Your] love, I will sing about [Your] judgment; to You, Hashem, I will sing" (*Tehillim* 101:1)? The meaning is: I will sing to Hashem whether He shows me love or judgment.

Similarly, David Ha-Melech uses the same expression three times in one psalm: "I will call *in the Name of Hashem*." Each of these occurs in a different context:

(1) "I found myself in the midst of sorrow and agony, and I called *in the Name of Hashem*" (*Tehillim* 116:3-4).

(2) "I shall raise the cup of salvation's many forms and call *in the Name of Hashem!*" (ibid. 116:13).

(3) "I will bring You offerings to acknowledge my debt of gratitude, and call *in the Name of Hashem!*" (ibid. 116:17).

There is a progession here: First, David calls out for Hashem's help in the midst of pain. Second, he calls out in gratitude for all the times Hashem has delivered him in the past, and prays that He will continue to deliver him in the future. Finally, he calls out in joyous recognition of Hashem's being with him at all times.

Now, it is known that maror (bitter herbs) alludes to bondage and suffering, while matzah alludes to freedom and redemption. Since Hillel embodied the ability to see Hashem's lovingkindness in everything, and he knew that ultimately all is for the good, it is therefore clear why Hillel was especially suited to combine the bitter herbs and the matzah into one sandwich!

Ma'asei Yedei Yotzer 69b

"With unleavened bread and bitter herbs shall they eat it."

Rabbi Yisrael Yaakov Yaffe HaKohen of Manchester also told a true story that illustrates the connection between matzah (redemption), maror (suffering), and the Jewish People!

An article appeared in the Hebrew weekly *Ha-Zeman* in the year 1896 (folio 72). It was about the famous Jewish doctor, Dr. Aharon Gordon, who was in Spain in 1652. At that time, it was still forbidden for a Jew to tread on Spanish soil. One who did received the death penalty.

Only the descendants of the Marranos still lived in Spain at that time. Forever in fear of being caught, they observed what commandments they could in secret.

Dr. Gordon tried his best to conceal his identity while trying to figure out how he could safely leave the country. As the holiday of Pesach neared, however, he realized that he would have to spend it in Spain. The problem was, how could he keep the laws of Pesach in this inhospitable land?

He went to the marketplace, intending to buy green vegetables in order to fulfill the mitzvah of eating bitter herbs. Suddenly he saw a distinguished officer ride into the marketplace on horseback. The man dismounted and went to the section where green vegetables were sold. He bought a large quantity of bitter herbs, got on his horse, and rode off.

It did not take long for Dr. Gordon to figure out what he had just seen. He managed to follow the officer to his house and knocked on his door. When the

Shulchan Orech — שֻׁלְחָן עוֹרֵךְ

It is customary to eat eggs at the beginning of the meal and not to eat roasted meat of any kind. Some do not dip any food. Although one may not drink wine between the first and second cups or between the third and fourth, at the meal, between the second and the third cups, one is permitted to do so provided that he is cautious not to become drowsy as a result. One should recline throughout the meal unless it is uncomfortable. One may not eat so much that he has no appetite for the afikoman.

One should be careful to finish the meal early enough for the afikoman to be eaten before midnight. The meal is not to be considered as a "break" in the Seder, and, consequently, as a time for levity, lightheadedness and idle talk. On the contrary, it is a part of the service and should be treated with the proper dignity and in the festive yom tov spirit. It is appropriate to discuss the Exodus and to sing zemiros of thankfulness to Hashem during this time.

Tzafun — צָפוּן

At the end of the meal, everyone must eat a kezayis of the afikoman in remembrance of the Korban Pesach. It is preferable to eat a second kezayis in remembrance of the matzah which was eaten with it.

The pieces of afikoman are broken from the larger part of the broken middle matzah which was hidden away at the beginning of the Seder for this purpose. If it is lost or there is not enough for all of the participants, any shemurah matzah may be used.

It is customary to allow the children to "steal" the afikoman at the beginning of the Seder and to "buy" it back from them now to show how precious this mitzvah is to us. However, the bargaining should not take too long, so as not to delay the eating of the afikoman before midnight.

All the participants should eat the required amount of the afikoman while reclining to the left and within the required period of time, having in mind that it is their intention to fulfill their duty to eat the afikoman.

After the afikoman, it is forbidden to eat or drink anything except for the last two cups of wine, and water, tea, or the like.

Barech

בָּרֵךְ

A Song of Ascents. When Hashem will turn once more to the return of Tzion, we will have been like those who dream. Then our mouth will fill with laughter and our tongue with exultation; then they will say among the nations: "Hashem has done great things with these." Hashem has done great things with us at all times; we have remained glad. Turn, Hashem, to our captivity once more, as the springs in the South. Those who sow in tears will reap in exultation. Though he who bears the measure of seed goes on his way weeping, he shall surely come home with exultation, bearing his sheaves (*Tehillim* 126).

שִׁיר הַמַּעֲלוֹת בְּשׁוּב יהוה אֶת שִׁיבַת צִיּוֹן הָיִינוּ כְּחֹלְמִים: אָז יִמָּלֵא שְׂחוֹק פִּינוּ וּלְשׁוֹנֵנוּ רִנָּה אָז יֹאמְרוּ בַגּוֹיִם הִגְדִּיל יהוה לַעֲשׂוֹת עִם אֵלֶּה: הִגְדִּיל יהוה לַעֲשׂוֹת עִמָּנוּ הָיִינוּ שְׂמֵחִים: שׁוּבָה יהוה אֶת שְׁבִיתֵנוּ כַּאֲפִיקִים בַּנֶּגֶב: הַזֹּרְעִים בְּדִמְעָה בְּרִנָּה יִקְצֹרוּ: הָלוֹךְ יֵלֵךְ וּבָכֹה נֹשֵׂא מֶשֶׁךְ הַזָּרַע בֹּא־יָבֹא בְרִנָּה נֹשֵׂא אֲלֻמֹּתָיו:

The third cup is filled for birkas hamazon. If the cup is not clean, it must first be washed and rinsed. It is customary to wash the hands with mayim acharonim. Although a guest is usually honored with leading birkas hazimun, on Pesach night it is customary for the leader of the Seder to do so, although he may appoint another participant. One should have in mind that he is fulfilling the requirement of reciting birkas hamazon. The cup is held throughout birkas hamazon and one should not recline.

man answered, the doctor said, "Look, I am a Jew, like yourself! Allow me to celebrate the Pesach holiday with you!"

The officer was astonished. "How did you discover my secret?" he asked Dr. Gordon.

The doctor smiled, "I saw you buy maror. Wherever there are bitter herbs, there you can find Jews."

Knesses Yisrael 71

When Hashem will turn once more to the return of Tzion, we will have been like those who dream.

The Maggid of Dubno explained: It is one of the fundamental teachings in Judaism that history has a direction and a Director. Hashem steers the drama of world history towards its finale — the Final Redemption. Each and every generation is given its unique role to play in this great unfolding drama.

For the most part, Hashem's plan is hidden from our view. Even our prophets were not told exactly how history would unfold. For this reason, there are many historical events which we cannot understand or put into context, and

therefore they pain us. Only when Hashem gathers together His dispersed nation and restores His Shechinah (Divine Presence) to Tzion will we see how all the pieces fit together. We will then understand how fitting was the dark night of history that preceded the dawn. "We will have been like those who dream. Our mouths will be filled with laughter and our tongues with joyous song" (*Tehillim* 126:1-2).

The Maggid illustrated this with a parable which was later made famous by Rabbi Elchanan Wasserman ז"ל. Rabbi Wasserman told it to his students prior to his demise at the hands of the Nazis.

A city dweller went to see the countryside for the first time in his life. While taking a stroll, he saw a farmer at his daily chores. He approached the farmer and asked to be taught about farming.

The farmer took him to his field and asked him what he saw. "A beautiful piece of land," he replied, "lush with grass and pleasing to the eye."

The visitor was aghast to see the farmer begin plowing the grass under, turning the beautiful field into row after row of shallow brown furrows.

"You've ruined the field!" the city dweller exclaimed.

"Be patient, you'll see," was the farmer's only reply.

The farmer then showed his guest a sack of wheat grain and said, "Tell me what you see." The city dweller described their shape and color, and then watched in shock as the farmer walked back and forth across the field, dropping the grains into the furrows and covering them with dirt.

"Hey, what are you doing?" the city dweller yelled. "You're wasting good food!"

"Be patient," the farmer replied. "You'll see."

Time passed, and the farmer took the city dweller out to the field. Now he saw the ground full of wheat rippling in the gentle wind.

Realizing his mistake, he apologized to the farmer and said, "Now I see that you have made the field more beautiful than ever. Truly, farming is an amazing art!"

"No," said the farmer. "We are not done yet. You must still be patient."

More time passed and the stalks were fully grown. The farmer then took his sickle and began cutting down all the wheat. The city dweller was agitated.

As before, however, the farmer told him to be patient and hold his peace. The farmer then gathered and bound the stalks into sheaves. He began to beat and crush them mercilessly until they became a mass of straw and loose kernels. The city dweller protested.

"Be patient," he was told.

The farmer separated the wheat kernels from the straw and placed them all

together in a large pile. Then he shoveled them into his wagon and transported the entire load to his mill. There, he ground the beautiful kernels into "dust" (flour).

The city dweller was beside himself. The farmer's only reply, "be patient," was wearing thin.

The farmer placed the "dust" into sacks and brought it home. He then took some of it and mixed it with water into a lump of "clay" (dough). He pounded the "clay" for a while and then placed it on a table to rise. While the "clay" was rising, the farmer kindled a fire in his oven. When he was satisfied that the oven was hot enough, he placed the "clay" into the oven.

The city dweller screamed, "Are you mad? After all that work, you burn what you have made?"

"Haven't I told you to be patient?" was all the farmer replied.

Only when he saw the luscious hot bread emerge from the oven, and smelled its irresistible fragrance, did the poor city dweller finally understand in retrospect all that the farmer had done.

When the prophet Amos tried to describe what would happen in the end of days, he said, "Behold, days are coming, says Hashem, when the plowman will meet the reaper, and the treader of grapes will meet the sower of seeds..." (*Amos* 9:13). That is, the start and end will fit together; the long intricate plan of history will be grasped in a flash of illumination.

All the various stages of Yisrael's painful exile — the plowing, the sowing, the reaping, the grinding, and the burning — each of which was viewed as tragic and destructive — will be recognized as necessary stages in a greater process. The larger picture of Yisrael's history will be understood.

At that time, "I [Hashem] will bring back the captivity [exiles] of My people Yisrael....I will plant them in their land, and they shall never again be plucked up from their land which I have given them" (ibid. 9:14-15). In the meantime, we must be patient, have faith, and know that everything Hashem does is for the good.

Kochav Mi'Yaakov, *Haftarah of Acharei Mos*

Then our mouth will fill with laughter and our tongue with exultation.

The Maggid of Dubno explained with a parable.

A certain drunk arrived at the inn for his nightly spree. Meeting his friends there, he ordered a round for all of them.

"Innkeeper, give them all a drink on my account," he shouted boisterously.

The innkeeper saw that he was already a little loaded. Now he's being generous, he thought to himself. He wants to squander all his hard-earned money on this bunch of low-lifes. Tomorrow, when he wakes up and realizes what he's done, he'll regret having wasting so much on them. The innkeeper decided to disregard the order.

The drunk ordered again. When he saw the innkeeper ignore him, his temper flared. He called out, "By my life, you won't see me come into this barn anymore!"

The innkeeper acted like he didn't hear. He was sure that when the poor fellow woke up in the morning he would regret his words and actually be grateful to the innkeeper for saving him so much money.

The Jewish People, in exile from our land and ourselves scattered, are like this wretched drunk. In our spiritual torpor, we crave all kinds of physical pleasures, but the Holy One does us a favor by withholding them from us. Of course we are very upset by such treatment, and we register our complaints daily. In the future, however, we will acknowledge His wisdom and fairness, and thank Him a million times over for not giving us everything we thought we wanted.

This is the meaning of the psalm: "When Hashem will turn once more to the return of Tzion, we will have been like those who dream" — the slumber and dream of exile. At that time, "our mouth will filled with laughter and our tongue with exultation!" — thanksgiving to Hashem for the hidden providence that accompanied and sustained us everywhere in our exile.

Our joy will be contagious. Mankind as a whole will also recognize how the entire panorama of history revolved around the tiny nation of Yisrael in exile. We will be eternally grateful. Even the tears we cried will turn into tears of joy.

The prophet also said: "Hashem's redeemed will return, and they will come singing to Tzion...they shall experience [the highest] joy and happiness, and grief and sadness will flee" (*Yeshayahu* 35:10, 51:11). That is, when Hashem redeems Yisrael (and this includes many souls who are presently totally unaware of His existence), we will all appreciate the great love He showed us even during our most bitter trials. At that time, our joy will be so great that the grief and sadness we experienced in the midst of exile will flee and evaporate, as if they never existed.

Kol Bochim 89b

Those who sow in tears will reap in exultation.

The troubles experienced in exile are precursors of the benefits of the Final Redemption. For this very reason, "When Hashem will turn once more to the return of Tzion, we will have been like those who dream. Then our mouth will fill with laughter and our tongue with exultation" (*Tehillim* 126:1-2). When the historical drama draws to a close, we will understand how all of the difficulties and afflictions we suffered were for our benefit. The Psalmist likens this to a farmer "who bears the measure of seed [and] goes on his way weeping" (ibid. 126:6). At first, he sows with tears in his eyes, concerned lest the seeds he plants will go to waste. Only when he sees every one of them blossom will he "come home with exultation, bearing his sheaves" (ibid.).

The prophet Yeshayahu alluded to this as well. Speaking of the Final Redemption, he said, "I will rejoice exceedingly in Hashem (Yud-Keh-Vav-Keh), my soul will delight in my God (Elokai)" (*Yeshayahu* 61:10). The Divine Name Yud-Keh-Vav-Keh represents middas ha-rachamim, Hashem's attribute of mercy, and Elokai represents middas ha-din, the Divine attribute of justice (Rashi on *Bereishis* 1:1). Only when the complete extent of Hashem's mercy is revealed with the onset of redemption will we fully appreciate and even rejoice in His justice. For we will understand that one was a preparation for and precursor of the other.

Yeshayahu continued, using the same metaphor that David Ha-Melech had used before him: "For as the earth brings forth her growth, and as the garden causes its seeds to grow, so the Eternal God will cause righteousness and glory to spring forth before all the nations" (ibid. 61:11). Here again we learn that redemption resembles a farmer's large harvest after a long winter of uncertainty, when all he planted appeared to rot away in the earth, and the seasons that followed, when he could see the produce growing to his delight. Even so is our exile a preparation for the redemption.

We therefore follow a general principle whenever a portion of the Torah is read which contains rebuke. "The reader must not stop in the middle, but rather... finish the entire portion in one reading. Why? Rav Chama bar Guriya explained: It is written, 'My son, do not reject the correction of your Father, nor have contempt ("tikotz") for His rebuke' (*Mishlei* 3:1). This teaches us that we are not to divide or break His rebuke up into small segments ('kotzin kotzin')" (*Devarim Rabbah* 4:1; *Sofrim* 12:1).

Why did Rav Chama bar Guriya feel it necessary to add to the simple meaning of the word "tikotz" in his explanation above? What did he wish to teach us?

He was teaching us that we must bless Hashem for all that seems evil just as we bless Him and acknowledge His kindness for all that seems good (*Berachos* 9:5, 54a). How? With unwavering trust and conviction that all evil is necessary for reaching ultimate good. This certainly does not mean that evil is not evil — only that it should not to be taken at face value. It is for this reason that we are enjoined "not to stop in the middle, but rather contemplate the portion in its entirety, and finish it in one reading." We will then surely reach the good part, begin to hear and feel the consolation, and see the Redemption brought closer.

The two meanings of "tikotz" ("to have contempt" and "to break into little segments") are thus seen to be connected: If we see the curses and afflictions that strike us as unrelated and disconnected ("kotzin kotzin"), we will have contempt for them ("tikotz"). If, on the other hand, we contemplate them in their larger context, as a form of preparation for the ultimate redemption, we will take strength and rejoice.

The Maggid of Dubno illustrated this with a parable:

Wishing to order a special suit for his son's wedding, a villager came to the city in search of a tailor. People directed him to the right part of town where he found a whole row of tailor shops. Entering one of them, he saw the proprietor take a beautiful piece of cloth and begin cutting it up into pieces.

Unable to believe his eyes, the man shouted, "Stop, what are you doing? You are ruining a perfectly good piece of material!"

The tailor smiled and answered, "How fitting the proverb that states: 'Don't show a fool a job half-done!' Wait here and I will show you how all these little pieces fit together into one suit which will be an honor to the one who wears it!"

Kochav Mi'Yaakov, *Haftarah of Lech Lecha, Vayishlach, Shemos*

Those who sow in tears will reap in exultation.

The Maggid of Dubno told another parable illustrating the same idea.

While walking through the marketplace, a man lost his wallet containing one hundred rubles. The moment he became aware of it, he started retracing his steps. Instead of finding his own wallet, however, he found someone else's. This wallet contained two hundred rubles! He took solace in this, but still regretted having lost the first hundred.

Another man purchased seeds at the local granary. He carefully placed the seeds in his knapsack and headed home. He was unaware that the knapsack

had a hole in it. As he walked, half the seeds fell to the ground. By the time he arrived home and realized what had happened, there was nothing he could do.

When passing along the same road two months later, however, he saw that the seeds had sprouted into full-grown sheaves. He cut them and sold the wheat at a nice profit. His consolation was complete. He did not complain, for he understood that without the initial loss he would have had no profit.

The same applies to Yisrael's exile among the nations. The pain and loss incurred during exile were the forerunners of redemption. Behind the scenes, all of history has been one long, "underground" redemptive process. When we finally wake up from our "dream," we will actually rejoice over everything that happened to us. The prophet alluded to this when he said, "I thank You, Hashem, though You showed me anger, for Your anger will be turned away and You will comfort me" (*Yeshayahu* 12:1). That is, when Hashem will relent from His anger, we will thank Him and rejoice retroactively, for we will realize that the losses and afflictions of exile were intrinsic to the redemptive process.

Ohel Yaakov, *Re'eh*

Blessed be You... Who nourishes the whole world with His goodness, with favor, lovingkindess and compassion.

We now recite the first blessing in Birkas Ha-Mazon. The Maggid of Dubno illustrated the point of this blessing with the following parable:

On their way from one city to the next, a group of merchants came to an inn. They were accompanied by a poor beggar. When the merchants entered the inn, the beggar remained outside in the courtyard. He had no money to pay for a meal, so he took a dry piece of bread out of his knapsack and began eating it. After "lunch" he felt tired, so he stretched out under a shady tree and fell asleep.

The next day, the innkeeper invited all his guests to a seudas mitzvah in honor of his son's bris. The beggar washed his hands and took a seat along with the other guests.

One of the merchants asked him, "What makes today different from all other days? Yesterday you remained outside in the courtyard, while today you join us."

"Yesterday," the beggar replied, "you paid for your meals. Being poor I was unable to do the same. Today, however, everyone is invited to participate in the celebration without paying. That's a free meal that even I deserve!"

If there are at least three adult males eating together at the Seder, the assembled say the following (if there are at least ten adult males, the words in parentheses are added):

Leader: Gentlemen, we wish to say Grace.
The others respond: Blessed be the Name of Hashem from this time forth and unto eternity.
The leader repeats the above verse and says: With your permission, let us bless Him (our God) from Whose bounty we have eaten.
The others respond: Blessed be Him (our God) from Whose bounty we have eaten, and through Whose goodness we live.
The leader repeats the above verse and says:

Blessed be He, and Blessed be His Name.

רַבּוֹתַי נְבָרֵךְ:
יְהִי שֵׁם יהוה מְבֹרָךְ מֵעַתָּה וְעַד עוֹלָם:
בִּרְשׁוּת מָרָנָן וְרַבָּנָן וְרַבּוֹתַי נְבָרֵךְ
(אֱלֹהֵינוּ) שֶׁאָכַלְנוּ מִשֶּׁלּוֹ:
בָּרוּךְ (אֱלֹהֵינוּ) שֶׁאָכַלְנוּ מִשֶּׁלּוֹ וּבְטוּבוֹ חָיִינוּ:

בָּרוּךְ הוּא וּבָרוּךְ שְׁמוֹ:

BLESSED be You, Hashem our God, King of the universe, Who nourishes the whole world with His goodness, with favor, lovingkindness and compassion. He gives food to all flesh because His lovingkindness endures forever. And through His great goodness we have never lacked nor shall we ever lack food, for His great Name's sake. For He is God Who feeds and sustains all beings, does good to all and prepares food for all His creatures which He has created. Blessed be You, Hashem, Who gives food to all.

בָּרוּךְ אַתָּה יהוה אֱלֹהֵינוּ מֶלֶךְ הָעוֹלָם הַזָּן אֶת הָעוֹלָם כֻּלּוֹ בְּטוּבוֹ בְּחֵן בְּחֶסֶד וּבְרַחֲמִים הוּא נוֹתֵן לֶחֶם לְכָל־בָּשָׂר כִּי לְעוֹלָם חַסְדּוֹ. וּבְטוּבוֹ הַגָּדוֹל תָּמִיד לֹא חָסַר לָנוּ וְאַל־יֶחְסַר לָנוּ מָזוֹן לְעוֹלָם וָעֶד. בַּעֲבוּר שְׁמוֹ הַגָּדוֹל כִּי הוּא אֵל זָן וּמְפַרְנֵס לַכֹּל וּמֵטִיב לַכֹּל וּמֵכִין מָזוֹן לְכָל־בְּרִיּוֹתָיו אֲשֶׁר בָּרָא. בָּרוּךְ אַתָּה יהוה הַזָּן אֶת־הַכֹּל:

We thank You, Hashem our God, because You have given as a heritage to our fathers a desirable, good and spacious land; and because You brought us forth, Hashem our God, from the land of Egypt and delivered us from the house of bondage; as well as for Your covenant which You have sealed in our flesh; and for Your Torah which You have taught us; for Your statutes which You have made known to us; and for the life, favor, and lovingkindness which You have bestowed upon us; and for the food, for You feed and sustain us constantly every day, in every season, and at every hour.

נוֹדֶה לְּךָ יהוה אֱלֹהֵינוּ עַל שֶׁהִנְחַלְתָּ לַאֲבוֹתֵינוּ אֶרֶץ חֶמְדָּה טוֹבָה וּרְחָבָה. וְעַל שֶׁהוֹצֵאתָנוּ יהוה אֱלֹהֵינוּ מֵאֶרֶץ מִצְרַיִם וּפְדִיתָנוּ מִבֵּית עֲבָדִים וְעַל בְּרִיתְךָ שֶׁחָתַמְתָּ בִּבְשָׂרֵנוּ וְעַל תּוֹרָתְךָ שֶׁלִּמַּדְתָּנוּ וְעַל חֻקֶּיךָ שֶׁהוֹדַעְתָּנוּ וְעַל חַיִּים חֵן וָחֶסֶד שֶׁחוֹנַנְתָּנוּ וְעַל אֲכִילַת מָזוֹן שָׁאַתָּה זָן וּמְפַרְנֵס אוֹתָנוּ תָּמִיד בְּכָל־יוֹם וּבְכָל עֵת וּבְכָל שָׁעָה:

This is the meaning of, "Blessed be You, Hashem our God, King of the universe, Who nourishes the entire world with His goodness, with favor, lovingkindness and compassion." We are all guests at the table of the Holy One.

Kol Ha-Tor 37a

A desirable, good and spacious land.

A rich merchant once traveled to Eretz Yisrael and before departing stopped in to visit the Rizhiner Rebbe, of blessed memory. In reply to the rebbe's question of whether he liked it there, he answered quietly that he didn't find very much to like.

The rebbe then told him the following story: There was once a rich landowner who married off all his daughters to young, promising scholars. Not one to scrimp on anything, he provided all the clothing and jewelry his daughters would need to appeal to their husbands.

When his youngest daughter came of age, no fitting scholar could be found for her. He was forced to marry her off to an ignorant tailor. Of course, he wished to bedeck her with the finest clothing and jewelry, but his daughter said, "Father, my sisters needed to adorn themselves with such things in order to find favor in their husbands' eyes [due to their higher caliber]. I am marrying this tailor, however, and for him, I am pretty enough as I am."

The rebbe concluded, "This is the story of our beloved land. For those who recognize her special loftiness, she adorns herself and reveals herself in all her splendor. With simple folk, on the other hand, she does not reveal her radiance, and they don't see anything special in her."

Sippurei Maran Ha-Ramach 241

And for the food, for You feed and sustain us constantly.

The Maggid of Dubno said: A person generally buys simple glasses and keeps them in the kitchen cupboard when he's not drinking from them — until they break, that is, as all glasses seem prone to do. But a person who is personally invited by the king to take part in a royal feast, and who is presented with a beautiful glass chalice as a token of the king's friendship — such a person will cherish his glass and place it in a special case for all to see. He will not regard it as a drinking glass, but as a special showpiece.

The same applies to us. When we eat, we should not only rejoice in the particular food. We should rather be cognizant of the fact that this food comes from Hashem. Seeing it as a token of Hashem's love will increase our pleasure immeasurably.

This is the meaning of the verse, "You shall rejoice in all the good which Hashem your God has granted you..." (*Devarim* 26:11). The joy comes from knowing the One who is giving us our food. The food is not an end in itself,

but a token of His unceasing care. We therefore thank Him "for the food, for you feed and sustain us constantly every day, in every season, and at every hour!"

Kochav Mi'Yaakov, *Haftarah of Nitzavim*

And for the food, for You feed and sustain us constantly.

The Maggid of Dubno illustrated this point with yet another jewel of a parable:

A widower had an only son from his deceased wife. He loved the boy more than anything else. Time passed and he married a second wife, a widow with an only daughter. It wasn't long before the husband saw indications that his new wife favored her daughter over his son. She, on the other hand, suspected him of the reverse! They truth is, they were both right. Even without intending it, a person tends to feel closer and pay more attention to his own flesh and blood. No matter, a certain amount of tension could be felt in the house at all times as a result of this partiality.

Time passed, and the two children grew up. It was agreed that they would marry each other. After the wedding, the new couple set up house and loved and cared for each other. The proud parents lavished their love upon both of the newlyweds. Ever since then, peace reigned and happiness prevailed. Their children, who until then had been the cause of tension between them, were now the cause of their mutual delight.

Hashem created man with both a soul and a body — with both spiritual and material aspirations. Between these two "marriage partners," however, there is a great deal of tension. The soul has no desire other than to attach herself to her Creator, to refine and elevate herself, to experience the light and joy of the Divine Presence, to learn His Torah, and fulfill His will. The body, on the other hand, enjoys its own pleasures, has its own desires and wants, and is occupied at all times in trying to fulfill them. How can there ever be peace between them?

There is one way. A person must recognize the One who supplies all of his wants. He must direct his thanks to Him alone for everything he has. In this way, his most mundane, physical needs will lead him straight to the service of the Blessed Holy One, the Source of all. Then the soul and the body can rejoice together! This is what we should have in mind when we thank Hashem in Birkas Ha-Mazon "for the food, for You feed and sustain us constantly."

Ohel Yaakov, *Ekev*

For all this, Hashem our God, we thank You and bless You, Blessed be Your Name by the mouth of all living things constantly and forever, even as it is written: "When you have eaten and are satisfied, you shall bless Hashem your God for the good land which He has given you." Blessed be You, Hashem, for the land and for the food.

וְעַל הַכֹּל יהוה אֱלֹהֵינוּ אֲנַחְנוּ מוֹדִים לָךְ וּמְבָרְכִים אוֹתָךְ יִתְבָּרַךְ שִׁמְךָ בְּפִי כָּל־חַי תָּמִיד לְעוֹלָם וָעֶד. כַּכָּתוּב וְאָכַלְתָּ וְשָׂבָעְתָּ וּבֵרַכְתָּ אֶת־יהוה אֱלֹהֶיךָ עַל־הָאָרֶץ הַטֹּבָה אֲשֶׁר נָתַן־לָךְ. בָּרוּךְ אַתָּה יהוה עַל הָאָרֶץ וְעַל הַמָּזוֹן:

"When you have eaten and are satisfied, you shall bless Hashem your God."

The Maggid of Dubno said: Eretz Yisrael and Am Yisrael are meant for each other, as the Sages commented on the verse, "Stand and measure the land" (*Chavakkuk* 3:6) — the Holy One measured all the lands and found none as fitting for His People as the Land of Yisrael (*Yalkut Shimoni* 2:563).

This can be likened to any suit that a tailor sews to fit a man. The Holy One "sewed" Eretz Yisrael to fit the exact measurements of Am Yisrael. It is a land that is suited to holiness, to Torah, and to the creation of a model society which will serve as an inspiration for all mankind.

Proof for this can be deduced from the Torah's laws concerning metzora (leprous marks in the walls of houses) — laws which are unique to Eretz Yisrael. It is written: "Hashem spoke to Moshe and Aharon, saying: When you come to the land of Canaan, which I am giving you as an inheritance, I may place the mark of the leprous curse in a house....The owner of the house shall come and tell the Kohen....The Kohen shall give orders that the house be emptied out....He shall then examine the mark....[If the mark is leprous] the Kohen shall quarantine the house for seven days....[If the mark has spread,] the Kohen shall give orders to remove the stones which are marked..." (*Vayikra* 14:33-40).

The Talmud (*Arachin* 15b) points out that the word "metzora" is an acrostic for "motzi ra" or "motzi shem ra" — speaking slander. The plague of metzora on a person's house, on his clothes, or finally (if he still refused to take the hint) on his body, was a sign of Hashem's displeasure for his having spoken slander about another Jew.

The Midrash (*Vayikra Rabbah* 17:6; Rashi, *Vayikra* 14:34) informs us of another, more hidden, aspect of metzora. Hearing of Yisrael's successful exodus from Egypt and imminent entry into their land, the Canaanites hid treasures of gold in the walls of their houses during the entire forty years that Yisrael was in the wilderness. Seeing this, Hashem said, "How will I fulfill My promise to Yisrael? '[You will find] houses filled with all good things that you did not put

there...' (*Devarim* 6:11). I shall cause those very places where they have hid their treasures to be marked with leprosy. Yisrael will then remove the stones and find the treasures...."

These two seemingly conflicting aspects of metzora, the Maggid said, are one. They are similar to a man whose hand had lost all sensation. The doctors treated it and gave him the following prognosis: "The nerves in your hand are dead. There is a chance, however, that you will recover. If you should begin feeling pain, know that you are on your way to regaining the use of your hand!"

One day, the man began to feel excruciating pain in his hand. Instead of lamenting, he jumped for joy! The pain was a sure sign that his hand was still a part of his body and joined to all his other senses.

Leprous marks on the houses of Eretz Yisrael were a sign of Hashem's displeasure with us — a sign that we had better correct our ways. On the other hand, if the very houses reacted to our sins, it also indicated that our bond with the land was still intact.

If, on top of this, we found treasures in the walls of the houses, this was an extra kindness. It showed that behind every barrier that stood between us and Hashem, something precious was concealed — that even behind the signs of Hashem's displeasure we would always find a sign of His love.

Kol Bochim 86b

You shall bless Hashem your God.

The Maggid of Dubno said: An experienced merchant once had a brilliant idea for attracting the many merchants who had come from afar to the big city in order to make their annual purchases. He would fill his store with the most sought-after merchandise and build an inn above the store where he would offer free food and drink. This alone would attract the merchants. After partaking of a free meal, they would then naturally want to purchase his goods. In this way, he would surely get all their business.

A group of beggars arrived in town together with the merchants. Hearing about where they could obtain a free meal, they proceeded to pack into the inn. They ordered the choicest dishes and drank the best wine. Realizing what was happening, the owner went upstairs and asked them to vacate the premises.

"Preferential treatment!" the beggars cried out. "Why should we be asked to leave while the merchants eat here for nothing?"

"Do you really think that the merchants don't pay for their food?" the

Have compassion, Hashem our God, on Yisrael Your People, and on Yerushalayim Your city, and on Tzion, the Abode of Your glory, and on the kingdom of the house of David, Your Anointed, and on the great and the holy House over which Your Name was proclaimed. Our God, our Father, tend us, feed us,

רַחֵם יהוה אֱלֹהֵינוּ עַל יִשְׂרָאֵל עַמֶּךָ וְעַל יְרוּשָׁלַיִם עִירֶךָ וְעַל צִיּוֹן מִשְׁכַּן כְּבוֹדֶךָ וְעַל מַלְכוּת בֵּית דָּוִד מְשִׁיחֶךָ וְעַל הַבַּיִת הַגָּדוֹל וְהַקָּדוֹשׁ שֶׁנִּקְרָא שִׁמְךָ עָלָיו. אֱלֹהֵינוּ אָבִינוּ רְעֵנוּ זוּנֵנוּ פַּרְנְסֵנוּ

owner asked. "Well, you are mistaken! They pay very good money when they purchase merchandise in my store. You, on the other hand, who have no intention of buying anything downstairs, have no permission to satisfy your stomachs at my expense."

The Sages said it: Eating and drinking without blessing is tantamount to stealing from the Holy One, Blessed be He (*Berachos* 35a). Hashem provides food and sustenance for all, and for our own benefit He asks only one thing — that we recognize Him as our Provider! This recognition is what distinguishes us from thieves in the palace of the King.

Kochav Mi'Yaakov, *Haftarah of Vayikra*

Have compassion... on the great and the holy House... tend us, feed us, sustain us....

The Ahavas Yisrael, the holy Vizhnitzer Rebbe, asked: Isn't it customary to begin by asking for something small and only then to enlarge upon the initial request? Doesn't a poor man first ask for a piece of bread, and only then for something to accompany it? And yet, we begin this blessing with our highest and most sublime requests for the coming of the Mashiach and the rebuilding of the Beis Ha-Mikdash! Immediately following this, we list our more mundane requests for nourishment, basic livelihood, alleviation of misery, quick relief from all our present troubles, and finally to be saved from the basic disgrace of having to borrow money in order to stay alive. How can we make sense of this?

He answered with the following parable:

A patient suffering from a serious illness was brought to the doctor. After a thorough examination, the doctor confirmed that the patient's weak condition required extended rest in a convalescent home in the mountains. "He needs the pure mountain air, the healthy food, and complete rest. His health will then be restored and he will return to his former strength," the doctor concluded.

Suddenly, the doctor noticed a wound on the patient's leg. He spent the next thirty minutes lancing it to drain out the pus, cleaning it, treating it with a powerful disinfectant, and bandaging it. When he finished, he breathed a sigh of relief.

The family, in the meantime, had been watching the entire procedure with bated breath.

"Is it serious, doctor? Is there anything to worry about?" they asked.

"No, not at all. The wound itself was harmless. However, it was worrying our patient here. If I had not taken proper care of it, it might have disturbed his relaxation and prevented him from regaining his health!"

The same is true for us. Whether or not most of us are able to articulate it, our true aspiration, for ourselves and our families, is to grow spiritually. On the national scale, this involves the blossoming of our highest potential as a people — the worldwide solidarity of the Jewish People, our prophesied return to our ancient homeland, the rebuilding of the Third Beis Ha-Mikdash, the raising up of a generation of great Jewish leaders, among whom will be many sages, prophets, and a Redeemer; the complete redemption of our people and of the entire world, the revelation of Malchus Shamayim (the Heavenly Kingdom), the advent of the World-to-Come, etc. — in short, all the things we pray for in Birkas Ha-Mazon!

As long as we are worried about our daily livelihood, however, and distressed about our basic security, both in our land and throughout the Diaspora, it is understandably very difficult for us to give our attention to these other requests. As our Sages said: "Three things can make a person lose his sanity and drive him away from his Creator — idolatry, an evil spirit, and the torments of poverty" (*Eruvin* 41b).

It is for this reason that we first state our most spiritual requests. However, we immediately add a prayer that the burden of making a living be eased so that we will have the peace of mind to put our energies where we are supposed to put them.

Netzach She'b'malchus 125

Along similar lines, it is told that the holy Rabbi David of Lelov was once traveling in the freezing winter, accompanied by some of his Chassidim. They all shivered from the cold and tried to gather close to one another to protect the rebbe from the biting wind.

sustain us, and nourish us, and relieve us, and speedily grant us relief, Hashem our God, from all our troubles. And, Hashem our God, let us not be in need of the gifts of human hands, or of their loans, but only of Your hand, which is full, open, holy and generous, so that we may not be ashamed nor blush with shame forever and ever.	וְכַלְכְּלֵנוּ וְהַרְוִיחֵנוּ וְהַרְוַח־לָנוּ יהוה אֱלֹהֵינוּ מְהֵרָה מִכָּל צָרוֹתֵינוּ. וְנָא אַל־תַּצְרִיכֵנוּ יהוה אֱלֹהֵינוּ לֹא לִידֵי מַתְּנַת בָּשָׂר וָדָם וְלֹא לִידֵי הַלְוָאָתָם כִּי אִם לְיָדְךָ הַמְּלֵאָה הַפְּתוּחָה הַקְּדוֹשָׁה וְהָרְחָבָה שֶׁלֹּא נֵבוֹשׁ וְלֹא נִכָּלֵם לְעוֹלָם וָעֶד:

Seeing an inn in the distance, the Chassidim said, "Rebbe, there's an inn! We can warm ourselves there by the fire and drink something hot!"

"Yes, you are right," the rebbe said. "The only problem is, what shall we drink until we get there?"

The Chassidim understood that the rebbe was speaking on more than one level. Getting safely to the inn was a metaphor for the Redemption, may we be worthy of its light soon, in our days! The question the rebbe asked, however, was: How shall the Jewish People survive until that glorious day? We therefore request that until the building of "the great and the holy House over which Your Name was proclaimed. Our God, our Father, tend us, feed us, sustain us, and nourish us, and relieve us, and speedily grant us relief, Hashem our God, from all our troubles."

Divrei David

So that we may not be ashamed nor blush with shame forever and ever.

The words "l'olam va'ed," the Chafetz Chayim explained, refer to the afterlife, the World-to-Come. We ask not to feel shame through all eternity.

It can be likened to a three-year-old girl who enjoys hour upon hour of playing with her favorite doll. But if we would present a similar doll to her on her twentieth birthday, she would surely think it was some kind of a joke.

Similarly, when we pass from this world and arrive in heaven, we will surely look upon so much of what we did as child's play. And here, we are not speaking of the things we did wrong, but of our mitzvos, the good deeds we performed. We will look back and see how few they were and how small they were. We will then feel considerable shame. Even the times we said Birkas Ha-Mazon, when we asked "so that we may not be ashamed nor blush with shame forever and ever," won't we be ashamed of how little we thought about what we were saying?

Sichos Ha-Chafetz Chayim 42

On Shabbos add:

רְצֵה וְהַחֲלִיצֵנוּ יהוה אֱלֹהֵינוּ בְּמִצְוֹתֶיךָ וּבְמִצְוַת יוֹם הַשְּׁבִיעִי הַשַּׁבָּת הַגָּדוֹל וְהַקָּדוֹשׁ הַזֶּה כִּי יוֹם זֶה גָּדוֹל וְקָדוֹשׁ הוּא לְפָנֶיךָ לִשְׁבָּת־בּוֹ וְלָנוּחַ בּוֹ בְּאַהֲבָה כְּמִצְוַת רְצוֹנֶךָ וּבִרְצוֹנְךָ הָנִיחַ לָנוּ יהוה אֱלֹהֵינוּ שֶׁלֹּא תְהֵא צָרָה וְיָגוֹן וַאֲנָחָה בְּיוֹם מְנוּחָתֵנוּ וְהַרְאֵנוּ יהוה אֱלֹהֵינוּ בְּנֶחָמַת צִיּוֹן עִירֶךָ וּבְבִנְיַן יְרוּשָׁלַיִם עִיר קָדְשֶׁךָ כִּי אַתָּה הוּא בַּעַל הַיְשׁוּעוֹת וּבַעַל הַנֶּחָמוֹת:

Be pleased, Hashem our God, and fortify us by Your commandments and by the commandment pertaining to the seventh day, this great and holy Shabbos, for this day is great and holy before You, that we may refrain thereon from every manner of work and rest upon it in love in accordance with the commandment of Your will. In Your favor, Hashem our God, grant us rest so that there be no distress, no grief or sighing on the day of our rest, and let us, Hashem our God, behold the consolation of Tzion, Your city, and the rebuilding of Yerushalayim, the city of Your Sanctuary, for You are the Master of all salvation and the Master of all consolation.

May the Compassionate One let us inherit that day which shall be all Shabbos and rest for life everlasting.

While Shabbos in this world is called a "taste of the World-to-Come," the World-to-Come is called "a day which shall be all Shabbos" (*Berachos* 61a).

The Maggid of Kaminetz elaborated on a parable from *Midrash Koheles* in order to stress the importance of utilizing our time on Shabbos to elevate ourselves spiritually.

In a king's palace, by an open window, hung a golden cage. Inside this golden cage was a rare and beautiful songbird. All of the other birds in the kingdom heard about this bird. They came from far and wide to pay their respects to him.

Admiring his cage of pure gold, and the choice food he was served in golden cups, they exclaimed, "How fortunate you are, and how good is your portion! How fortunate you are to be provided with all you need from the king's own table. You will never suffer any want! It is fitting for you to sing and to rejoice! It is not so with us," they continued. "During the hot summer months, we manage to gather enough to keep our souls alive. Soon, however, the winter will be upon us. Snow will cover the ground and freeze all life. How difficult it will be for us to find food then!"

But the songbird answered in a bitter voice, "Do not envy me, my brothers. What good is it to be trapped in this cage of gold with all the food in the world? If I cannot unfold my wings and fly, if my freedom is denied me, I would rather die! I would exchange this for a life of deprivation; I would suffer the ravages of winter's cold, and summer's burning heat, if only I could enjoy freedom again!"

The other birds heard and nodded in agreement.

The songbird continued, "Perhaps one of you could do me a favor. I have a sister who nests in a great oak in yonder White Forest. She is very wise. Who will go and inform her of the tragedy that has befallen me? Perhaps she will be able to advise and enlighten me."

One of the birds felt compassion for the songbird and flew straightaway to the White Forest, to inform his sister of his plight. Upon hearing the evil tidings, she ceased her sweet song and fell from her branch to the ground. There she remained motionless...

Seeing this, the messenger bird was deeply affected. She returned to the songbird in the palace, in shock and in mourning.

He saw her and asked, "Did you speak with my sister? Did you relate to her all that has befallen me?"

The bird sighed and could not answer.

"Tell me, please," the songbird entreated. "Do not withhold a thing from me!"

The messenger bird sadly related what had happened. Finally, unable to hold back her tears, she concluded, "And then she fell to the ground, dead."

The songbird was deeply moved. He mourned bitterly and refused to eat or drink. The king's servants who cared for the bird discerned the change which had taken place in his disposition.

"The songbird is sick," they concluded.

Indeed, the songbird no longer sang. He just sat all day in silent mourning.

"The songbird is dying," the servants whispered among themselves.

And so it was, one morning the songbird was discovered lying still on the floor of its golden cage, its life spirit departed. The king's servants opened the cage and cast the songbird's body out of the window onto the ground.

Then, suddenly, the songbird began to move. He was coming back to life! He spread his wings and flew high up into the sky, singing an awesome song whose sweetness had never been heard before!

The songbird flew straight to the White Forest, to the great oak, and reunited with his sister. He thanked her for her sage advice — to act dead in order to regain his freedom!

Alexander the Great asked the Sages, "What shall a man do to live?"

They answered, "Let him die" (*Tamid* 32a).

This world is like a dream that passes quickly. If a person spends all his time in bringing home money to furnish his house and to put bread on the table, he is likened to the songbird locked up in its cage. When will he be able to grow and improve himself spiritually? When will he accumulate his spiritual fortune? And when the day comes, and his soul rises up to stand before the Heavenly throne, what shall he take with him?

It is for this reason that Hashem gave us one day in the week on which we can "die" a little bit with respect to the follies of this world and stop the mad race to accumulate wealth and honor. On this day, we wake up to take stock

of ourselves and devote ourselves to attaining the true riches which we were born to attain. In this way we shall pave the way for a life of happiness that will last far beyond the gilded confines of this world. We shall prepare for the "day shall be all Shabbos" and tranquillity for life in this world and in the eternal World-to-Come!

Ateres Tzvi, *Derush Yud*

...which shall be all Shabbos and rest for life everlasting.

What is this rest all about? Surely it involves the cessation of all worldly activities. As Rabbi Avraham ibn Ezra wrote in his classic *Ki Eshmerah Shabbos,* "On Shabbos, it is forbidden to seek distracting entertainment, to carry on my usual activities, or even to speak about what I need to buy, about business matters or earthly kings...." The problem with this definition, however, is that it tells us what we cannot do, not what we should and can do! Without a positive definition, the concept of Shabbos rest might just become an excuse to sleep all day! Ibn Ezra therefore continued, "I will therefore [make it my business to] meditate on God's Torah, for only thus will I truly become wise!"

The following parable of the Maggid of Dubno brings this point home.

A young man once set out in search of his fortune. He traveled from country to country until he established himself in business in one of the biggest centers of commerce in Europe.

Years went by, but he still felt a tremendous yearning for his own country and his own hometown. He constantly thought about his relatives and former acquaintances back home. He promised himself: Someday, when I get the chance, I'm going to return home for a visit. In addition to this, he was always on the lookout for someone from back home, someone who could give him some news about all the people whose memories remained etched in his mind from childhood, someone who could tell him who got married, who died, who became rich, and who became poor.

One gloomy, winter day, a poor beggar going from house to house asking for charity knocked on his door. Shivering as a result of being exposed to the rain and biting cold, he held out his hand expecting a coin. The businessman looked closely at his face and recognized him.

"Aren't you Chayim, from my old hometown?"

"Yes," the beggar answered, "that's me."

"Come in, come in," the businessman urged, "you must be freezing from the cold. Be my guest, sit down and tell me everything about our home."

"If you recognize me," the beggar replied, "then give me a fitting sum and I shall be on my way. I have no time to speak, you see. I must continue collecting coins so that I can eat. I must move on, you see, for time is money."

"How much do you make in one day?" the businessman asked.

"Sometimes two gold pieces and sometimes three," the beggar answered.

"Here, take three coins, an entire day's work, and come in. Spend the day with me now. You can relax here. My house is warm; I will serve you hot food. I want you to tell me all about back home."

The beggar accepted the offer — it was impossible to refuse. He finally entered, dripping water all over the floor, until he was able to take off some of the top layers of his rags. He then sat down by the hot stove and allowed his weary bones to relax.

He began telling about whoever he could think of. After a while, however, he became drowsy. His words began to slur as his eyelids closed, his head slouched over onto his chest, and he dozed off.

"Wake up, wake up!" the businessman nudged him.

The beggar opened an eye and smiled.

"Listen, dear friend," the businessman said in a serious tone, "it is cold and rainy out there. I brought you in, I saved you an entire day of traipsing around collecting pennies in order to hear details from you about my family and acquaintances back home. I didn't pay you to sit here and fall asleep! Wake up now and continue speaking. Afterwards there will be plenty of time to eat, drink, and sleep!"

Every morning we pray, "My God, the Divine soul You placed within me is pure! You created it, You formed it, You breathed it into me, and You sustain it within me. You will also one day take it from me, and only restore it to me in the Ultimate Future ("asid lavo"). As long as the soul is within me, I thank You, Hashem, my God and God of my ancestors, Director of all events, Master of all souls. Blessed are You, Hashem, who restores the souls to [our] lifeless bodies!"

Hashem implanted a holy soul within each of us, an extension of His own Divinity. Like the businessman in this parable, Hashem is interested, so to speak, in hearing everything about the soul's accomplishments during its sojourn in this world. However, during our stay here, we become too preoccupied with worldly matters and with trying to eke out a living. As a result, the soul within us is literally in exile and unable to feel its connection to the Divine. What did Hashem do about this?

He promised a double portion of bread on Shabbos, as the song states, "On

Our God and God of our fathers, may our remembrance and the consideration of us and the remembrance of our fathers, and the remembrance of Mashiach the son of David Your servant, and the remembrance of Yerushalayim, Your holy city, and the remembrance of all Your people, the House of Yisrael, rise and come, reach You and be seen, be accepted and heard, considered and remembered for deliverance and for well-being, for favor and lovingkindness, for compassion, for life and for peace on this day of the Festival of Unleavened Bread. Remember us this day, Hashem our God, for good, be mindful of us for blessing, and save us for life; and in the promise of salvation and compassion, spare us and favor us, and be compassionate with us and save us, for our eyes look up to You; for You, o' God, are a gracious and compassionate King.

And rebuild Yerushalayim, the city of holiness, speedily in our days. Blessed be You, Hashem, Who in His compassion rebuilds Yerushalayim, Amen.

Blessed be You, Hashem our God, King of the universe, o' God, our Father, our King, our Mighty One, our Creator, our Redeemer, our Maker, our Holy One, the Holy One of Yaakov, our Shepherd, the Shepherd of Yisrael, o' King, Who is kind and Who does good to all! He alone has done good to us day after day; it is He alone Who does good; and it is He alone Who will do good to us in the future. He alone has caused our destiny to bear ripe fruit; it is He alone Who causes it thus to ripen; and He alone, will continue to cause it thus to ripen, for favor, and for lovingkindness and compassion, and for relief, rescue and success, for blessing and salvation, for consolation, sustenance and nourishment, and for compassion, and for life, and for peace and all good. And with all the good may He never cause us to become wanting.

אֱלֹהֵינוּ וֵאלֹהֵי אֲבוֹתֵינוּ יַעֲלֶה וְיָבֹא וְיַגִּיעַ וְיֵרָאֶה וְיֵרָצֶה וְיִשָּׁמַע וְיִפָּקֵד וְיִזָּכֵר זִכְרוֹנֵנוּ וּפִקְדוֹנֵנוּ וְזִכְרוֹן אֲבוֹתֵינוּ וְזִכְרוֹן מָשִׁיחַ בֶּן דָּוִד עַבְדֶּךָ וְזִכְרוֹן יְרוּשָׁלַיִם עִיר קָדְשֶׁךָ וְזִכְרוֹן כָּל עַמְּךָ בֵּית יִשְׂרָאֵל לְפָנֶיךָ לִפְלֵיטָה לְטוֹבָה לְחֵן וּלְחֶסֶד וּלְרַחֲמִים לְחַיִּים וּלְשָׁלוֹם בְּיוֹם חַג הַמַּצּוֹת הַזֶּה. זָכְרֵנוּ יהוה אֱלֹהֵינוּ בּוֹ לְטוֹבָה וּפָקְדֵנוּ בוֹ לִבְרָכָה וְהוֹשִׁיעֵנוּ בוֹ לְחַיִּים וּבִדְבַר יְשׁוּעָה וְרַחֲמִים חוּס וְחָנֵּנוּ וְרַחֵם עָלֵינוּ וְהוֹשִׁיעֵנוּ כִּי אֵלֶיךָ עֵינֵינוּ כִּי אֵל מֶלֶךְ חַנּוּן וְרַחוּם אָתָּה:

וּבְנֵה יְרוּשָׁלַיִם עִיר הַקֹּדֶשׁ בִּמְהֵרָה בְיָמֵינוּ. בָּרוּךְ אַתָּה יהוה בּוֹנֵה בְרַחֲמָיו יְרוּשָׁלָיִם אָמֵן:

בָּרוּךְ אַתָּה יהוה אֱלֹהֵינוּ מֶלֶךְ הָעוֹלָם הָאֵל אָבִינוּ מַלְכֵּנוּ אַדִּירֵנוּ בּוֹרְאֵנוּ גּוֹאֲלֵנוּ יוֹצְרֵנוּ קְדוֹשֵׁנוּ קְדוֹשׁ יַעֲקֹב רוֹעֵנוּ רוֹעֵה יִשְׂרָאֵל הַמֶּלֶךְ הַטּוֹב וְהַמֵּטִיב לַכֹּל שֶׁבְּכָל יוֹם וָיוֹם הוּא הֵטִיב הוּא מֵטִיב הוּא יֵיטִיב לָנוּ. הוּא גְמָלָנוּ הוּא גוֹמְלֵנוּ הוּא יִגְמְלֵנוּ לָעַד לְחֵן וּלְחֶסֶד וּלְרַחֲמִים וּלְרֶוַח הַצָּלָה וְהַצְלָחָה בְּרָכָה וִישׁוּעָה נֶחָמָה פַּרְנָסָה וְכַלְכָּלָה וְרַחֲמִים וְחַיִּים וְשָׁלוֹם וְכָל טוֹב וּמִכָּל טוּב לְעוֹלָם אַל יְחַסְּרֵנוּ:

Shabbos, I shall always find rest and tranquillity for my soul. Behold, my holy God bequeathed it to the first generation [that left Egypt]. He signified [its importance] by doubling the manna-bread that fell on the sixth day of the week. In the same way, He doubles my portion every Friday [in preparation for Shabbos]" (*Ki Eshmerah*).

This double portion was to teach us that Shabbos is the source of sustenance for the entire week, and therefore a special time set aside to nurture our connection with the Divine through davening, learning Torah, and family singing and celebration. This is the meaning of the verse, "You may do work during the six weekdays, but the seventh day is the Sabbath of Sabbaths. It is a sacred holiday to Hashem, when you shall do no work..." (*Vayikra* 23:3). It

May the Compassionate One reign over us to all eternity. May the Compassionate One be blessed in heaven and on earth. May the Compassionate One be praised from generation to generation, glorified through us for all eternity, and garbed in majesty through us for everlasting. May the Compassionate One grant us an honorable livelihood. May the Compassionate One break our yoke from off our neck and lead us upright to our land. May the Compassionate One send abundant blessing into this house, and upon this table at which we have eaten. May the Compassionate One send us Eliyahu the Prophet, may he be remembered for good, to bring us good news of salvation and consolation.

הָרַחֲמָן הוּא יִמְלוֹךְ עָלֵינוּ לְעוֹלָם וָעֶד. הָרַחֲמָן הוּא יִתְבָּרַךְ בַּשָּׁמַיִם וּבָאָרֶץ. הָרַחֲמָן הוּא יִשְׁתַּבַּח לְדוֹר דּוֹרִים וְיִתְפָּאַר בָּנוּ לָעַד וּלְנֵצַח נְצָחִים וְיִתְהַדַּר בָּנוּ לָעַד וּלְעוֹלְמֵי עוֹלָמִים. הָרַחֲמָן הוּא יְפַרְנְסֵנוּ בְּכָבוֹד. הָרַחֲמָן הוּא יִשְׁבּוֹר עֻלֵּנוּ מֵעַל צַוָּארֵנוּ וְהוּא יוֹלִיכֵנוּ קוֹמְמִיּוּת לְאַרְצֵנוּ. הָרַחֲמָן הוּא יִשְׁלַח לָנוּ בְּרָכָה מְרֻבָּה בַּבַּיִת הַזֶּה וְעַל שֻׁלְחָן זֶה שֶׁאָכַלְנוּ עָלָיו. הָרַחֲמָן הוּא יִשְׁלַח לָנוּ אֶת אֵלִיָּהוּ הַנָּבִיא זָכוּר לַטּוֹב וִיבַשֶּׂר לָנוּ בְּשׂוֹרוֹת טוֹבוֹת יְשׁוּעוֹת וְנֶחָמוֹת.

May the Compassionate One bless ([my father, my teacher] the master of this house, and [my mother, my teacher] the mistress of this house) me, (my wife/husband and children) and all that is mine, and all that sit here, both them, their household, their children and all that belongs to them, also us and all that is ours, even as our fathers, Avraham, Yitzchak, and Yaakov were blessed in everything, from everything and with everything, so may He bless all of us together with a perfect blessing and let us say, Amen.

הָרַחֲמָן הוּא יְבָרֵךְ (אֶת [אָבִי מוֹרִי] בַּעַל הַבַּיִת הַזֶּה וְאֶת [אִמִּי מוֹרָתִי] בַּעֲלַת הַבַּיִת הַזֶּה). אוֹתִי (וְאֶת אִשְׁתִּי / בַּעְלִי וְאֶת זַרְעִי) וְאֶת כָּל אֲשֶׁר לִי וְאֶת כָּל הַמְסוּבִּין כַּאן. אוֹתָם וְאֶת בֵּיתָם וְאֶת זַרְעָם וְאֶת כָּל אֲשֶׁר לָהֶם אוֹתָנוּ וְאֶת כָּל אֲשֶׁר לָנוּ כְּמוֹ שֶׁנִּתְבָּרְכוּ אֲבוֹתֵינוּ אַבְרָהָם יִצְחָק וְיַעֲקֹב בַּכֹּל מִכֹּל כֹּל כֵּן יְבָרֵךְ אוֹתָנוּ כֻּלָּנוּ יַחַד בִּבְרָכָה שְׁלֵמָה וְנֹאמַר אָמֵן:

May their and our merits be pleaded on High so that it may contribute to enduring peace, and that we may receive a blessing from Hashem and kindness from the God of our salvation, and obtain worthiness of favor and understanding of the good in the sight of God and man.

בַּמָּרוֹם יְלַמְּדוּ עֲלֵיהֶם וְעָלֵינוּ זְכוּת שֶׁתְּהֵא לְמִשְׁמֶרֶת שָׁלוֹם. וְנִשָּׂא בְרָכָה מֵאֵת יהוה וּצְדָקָה מֵאֱלֹהֵי יִשְׁעֵנוּ וְנִמְצָא חֵן וְשֵׂכֶל טוֹב בְּעֵינֵי אֱלֹהִים וְאָדָם:

On Shabbos add:

May the Compassionate One let us inherit that day which shall be all Shabbos and rest for life everlasting.

הָרַחֲמָן הוּא יַנְחִילֵנוּ יוֹם שֶׁכֻּלּוֹ שַׁבָּת וּמְנוּחָה לְחַיֵּי הָעוֹלָמִים:

May the Compassionate One let us inherit that day which is altogether good. That everlasting day, the day when the righteous sit with crowns upon their heads, enjoying the radiance of the Divine Presence — and may our portion be among them.

הָרַחֲמָן הוּא יַנְחִילֵנוּ יוֹם שֶׁכֻּלּוֹ טוֹב. יוֹם שֶׁכֻּלּוֹ אָרוּךְ. יוֹם שֶׁהַצַּדִּיקִים יוֹשְׁבִים וְעַטְרוֹתֵיהֶם בְּרָאשֵׁיהֶם וְנֶהֱנִים מִזִּיו הַשְּׁכִינָה וִיהִיֶה חֶלְקֵנוּ עִמָּהֶם:

is a day of repose and tranquillity for the soul, a day on which we get a taste of eternity. It is a day to cease our worldly activities, to sanctify ourselves to Hashem....It is not a day to sleep away!

Ohel Yaakov, *Vayak'hel*

May our portion be among them.

On Pesach, we add the following request in Birkas Ha-Mazon: "May the

Compassionate One let us inherit that day which is altogether good. That everlasting day, the day when the righteous sit with crowns upon their heads, enjoying the radiance of the Divine Presence — and may our portion be among them."

"May our portion be among them." What are we asking for here? If we are praying to be tzaddikim, is that in Hashem's hands? Isn't it well known that, "All is in the hands of Heaven except the fear of Heaven" (*Berachos* 33b)? How can we ask God to give us a portion along with the righteous if our own actions are wanting?

On the other hand, if we truly work on ourselves and become more virtuous and righteous, how can we even ask for compensation for such work? Besides the fact that Hashem would certainly not withhold reward from us if we were deserving, this attitude of asking to be reimbursed for our services runs directly counter to the injunction, "Do not be like employees who serve their master in order to receive reward" (*Pirkei Avos* 1:3).

Rabbi Chayim Elazar, the holy Munkatcher, answered these questions with the following parable:

A king hired hundreds of local townsmen to build a large dam. After a month of hard labor, payday arrived. As the day came to an end, the king drove up in his carriage, accompanied by his royal guard. He sat behind a desk and began calling out the names of each worker. Each one approached the king, bowed down, and stretched forth his hand to receive his salary. The king smiled and willingly paid them all what was coming to them. To the townsmen, this day was no cause for extra joy. It was just payday.

When the king stood up to make an announcement, however, there was a hush in the air. "While paying your well-earned salaries today, I wish to take this opportunity to announce a special bonus. Know that all of your parents worked for me when I first became king. They were my first loyal servants. In their memory, I therefore hereby notify you, their children, that I wish to honor the kindness they showed me by giving you an extra bonus for your work!"

Everyone present was very surprised. The king had given no indication of this when he had hired them. It was the last thing they expected. And yet, here it was happening. Their eyes lit up, their mouths were full of song and laughter. They stretched forth their hands and received their gifts with great joy. The king, too, was visibly moved to joy upon seeing his subjects' appreciation. There was great rejoicing throughout the kingdom.

It will be like this, the rebbe concluded, in the Ultimate Future. The righteous

May the Compassionate One make us worthy of reaching the days of the Mashiach and life everlasting; He Who is a tower of salvation to His King and shows lovingkindness to His Anointed, to David and his descendants forever. May He Who makes peace in His High places, make peace for us and for all of Yisrael, and let us say, Amen.

הָרַחֲמָן הוּא יְזַכֵּנוּ לִימוֹת הַמָּשִׁיחַ וּלְחַיֵּי הָעוֹלָם הַבָּא. מִגְדּוֹל יְשׁוּעוֹת מַלְכּוֹ וְעוֹשֶׂה חֶסֶד לִמְשִׁיחוֹ לְדָוִד וּלְזַרְעוֹ עַד עוֹלָם. עֹשֶׂה שָׁלוֹם בִּמְרוֹמָיו הוּא יַעֲשֶׂה שָׁלוֹם עָלֵינוּ וְעַל כָּל יִשְׂרָאֵל וְאִמְרוּ אָמֵן:

will come to receive their rewards — what they earned by selflessly serving Hashem with all their hearts and souls. According to our sacred tradition (*Ta'anis* 31a), the righteous will then gather around the Divine Presence in the Garden of Eden. They will form a circle and slowly begin to dance around Him, as it were. Each one will then point towards the center of the circle. Together they will sing, "Behold, this is our God. We hoped in Him, and [waited] for His salvation. This is the Eternal God. We hoped in Him. Let us rejoice eternally and delight in His salvation" (*Yeshayahu* 25:9).

But think of the joy when Hashem invites us to join them as well. Who are we and what place do we have with such great individuals? We are poor in mitzvos and lacking in good deeds. And yet, in memory of our ancestors' self-sacrifice, in memory of their total devotion to their Creator, He will also let "our portion be among them."

What great joy will be felt in heaven and on earth! It will rise higher and higher, higher than any joy ever experienced, as the Psalmist wrote, "Sing a new song to Hashem! His praise is reflected in the assembly of His devoted servants. Let Yisrael rejoice in its Maker. Let the inhabitants of Tzion delight in their King. Let them praise His Name in circular dance. Let them play a chant song for Him with drum and harp. For Hashem desires His people. He will crown the humble with salvation" (*Tehillim* 149:1-4).

Hashem's joy will also be great, as the Psalmist wrote, "[When] Hashem's Glory will be revealed to the world, Hashem Himself will rejoice in all that He has made" (*Tehillim* 104:31).[1]

based on **Sha'ar Yissachar**, *Aggadeta D'Pischa* 103

---

[1] Yeshayahu referred specifically to the joy of the righteous when he said, "Let us rejoice eternally and delight in His salvation!" David Ha-Melech extended this to include those who are not so worthy when he said, "For Hashem desires His people. He will crown the humble with salvation!" Hashem's own joy will not be complete, as it were, until this Ultimate Future. This is the meaning of the future tense in "Hashem Himself will rejoice" — as the Midrash comments, "It is not written 'samach' (rejoiced) but 'yismach' (will rejoice)"; see *Pesikta d'Rav Kahana, Acharei Mos*, p. 171a; *Vayikra Rabbah* 20:2.

He Who is a tower of salvation...

The Maggid of Dubno expressed surprise: Our holy ancestors underwent so many trials and tribulations! Without a shadow of a doubt, based on their actions alone, they should be have been worthy of dwelling in peace and security during their lifetimes. Why did they have to undergo so much privation? Why couldn't they have a moment's respite?

The answer will become clear from the following parable.

A wealthy man had a son who contracted a mild illness. The father called a doctor in to treat his son. In addition to the fact that the treatment lasted quite a bit longer than he expected, his son's condition only worsened. The father complained to the doctor, "I delivered my beloved son into your hands with a mild illness — he could stand at the time. Now he lies there, unable to move, without any strength. What is going on here?"

"The explanation is as follows," the doctor replied. "You may rest assured that I cured that first condition on the spot. That was no problem. In the process of examining your son, however, I discovered another, more serious ailment which would not have emerged for a number of years. I decided to speed up its development (appearance) and treat it now while your son is young and has the strength to fully recover from it. In years to come, however, who knows what would have happened?"

Hashem "called forth the generations from the beginning" (*Yeshayahu* 41:4). He knew that later generations would be weak in their faith and perhaps unable to withstand certain trials and tribulations. Perhaps they would snap if stretched beyond their limit, God forbid. He therefore brought about certain events before their time, during the lives of our ancestors. With their great faith and courage, they withstood those trials in our stead![2] When Hashem then delivered them, He was showing them that He would deliver us, their descendants, as well. This is the meaning of, "You have been our ancestors' support and assistance from the beginning. [For this reason] You have continually protected and delivered them...and their children, generation after generation" (*Shacharis*). This is also the meaning of, "He is a tower of salvation to His king and shows lovingkindness to His anointed, to David and to his descendants forever."

Kochav Mi'Yaakov, *Haftarah of Ha'azinu*

---

2 This is a unique way of expressing this concept, one not found anywhere else. It is usually said that former generations set certain precedents for future generations, not that they underwent trials in place of their descendants. Thus, the generation of the Exodus remained in the

יְראוּ אֶת יהוה קְדֹשָׁיו כִּי אֵין מַחְסוֹר לִירֵאָיו. כְּפִירִים רָשׁוּ וְרָעֵבוּ וְדֹרְשֵׁי יהוה לֹא יַחְסְרוּ כָל טוֹב. הוֹדוּ לַיהוה כִּי טוֹב כִּי לְעוֹלָם חַסְדּוֹ. פּוֹתֵחַ אֶת יָדֶךָ וּמַשְׂבִּיעַ לְכָל חַי רָצוֹן. בָּרוּךְ הַגֶּבֶר אֲשֶׁר יִבְטַח בַּיהוה וְהָיָה יהוה מִבְטַחוֹ. נַעַר הָיִיתִי גַּם זָקַנְתִּי וְלֹא רָאִיתִי צַדִּיק נֶעֱזָב וְזַרְעוֹ מְבַקֶּשׁ לָחֶם. יהוה עֹז לְעַמּוֹ יִתֵּן יהוה יְבָרֵךְ אֶת עַמּוֹ בַשָּׁלוֹם:

O' fear Hashem, you who are sanctified to Him, for there is no want for them that fear Him. Young lions have become poor and suffered hunger, but they who seek Hashem shall never want for any good thing. Avow it to Hashem that He is good, that His lovingkindness endures forever. You open Your hand and satisfy the desire of every living thing. Blessed is the man who trusts in Hashem, and to whom Hashem is also the source of His trust. I was young and I have grown old, but I have never seen a righteous man forsaken whose progeny was forced to beg for bread. May Hashem grant to His people the power to be victorious over all; may Hashem bless His people with peace.

They who seek Hashem shall never want for any good thing.

David Ha-Melech wrote, "O' fear Hashem, you are sanctified to Him, there is no want for them that fear Him. Young lions have become poor and suffered hunger but they who seek Hashem shall never want for any good thing" (*Tehillim* 34:10-11), and "I was young and I have grown old, but I have never seen a righteous man forsaken whose progeny was forced to beg for bread [alone]" (ibid. 37:25).

Said Rabbi Eliyahu Lopian: These verses contain an apparent difficulty. Haven't many righteous and upright individuals suffered want? Haven't the children of many a righteous person been forced to beg for their bread? Who was greater than Rabbi Chanina ben Dosa, in whose merit the whole world was sustained, and yet, who subsisted on little more than a pound of carob seeds for an entire week? (*Berachos* 17b).

The answer lies, Rabbi Lopian continued, in the exact wording of the verse. It is not guaranteed that those who seek Hashem will have every good thing in the world. This is not the way of the Torah, concerning which it was taught, "Eat bread with salt, drink water by the measure, sleep on the ground, live a life of hardship, and toil in the Torah. If you do this, you will be happy in this world, and it will be good for you in the World-to-Come!" (*Pirkei Avos* 6:4). Rather, they "shall never want for any good thing" — they will not equate their lack of physical comforts with a lack of goodness. Let us clarify this with the following parable.

---

wilderness for forty years and was constantly tried under difficult test conditions. They did not undergo these trials instead of their descendants. On the contrary, by undergoing them, they empowered future generations to undergo them as well. Even their apparent failures impressed something very deep into the Jewish psyche — that the Jewish People can and will always return to Hashem, no matter how far they stray.

Chayim once visited his friend Yaakov. He opened the medicine cabinet in the bathroom and found it empty. He later he mentioned this to Yaakov, "I feel sorry for you. You should come to my house and see how a real medicine cabinet looks. I have pills for headaches, backaches, high and low blood pressure, dizziness, fainting...you name it, I have it!"

Chayim laughed, "I feel sorry for you! You need all those medicines because of your many ailments. We are healthy, thank God, so we have no use for such things!"

All the "good things" of this world — the ephemeral wealth we spend our lives trying to amass, all the various luxuries, even the "necessities" that we convince ourselves we cannot live without — are like so many different medicines for our ailing souls. In our delirium, we think that these comforts will bring us true happiness, so we spend half our lives and all our money chasing after and stocking up on them. But do we ever attain even half of our desires? Aren't we like the fellow who has ten thousand dollars, but who needs twenty; who has twenty, but who needs forty? Do we ever feel we have enough? Or is it that the more we have, the more we want and feel we need?

On the other hand, when we become "seekers of Hashem" — not seekers of riches and honor, but of closeness to the One who provides for our every need, we no longer require all sorts of intermediaries. For now we begin to taste true and lasting happiness. By learning Torah and performing its commands, we attach ourselves to our Provider, and this is our greatest joy. As the Psalmist wrote, "The precepts of Hashem are upright, gladdening the heart; the commandments of Hashem are radiant, enlightening the eyes" (*Tehillim* 19:9).

In summary, those who seek Hashem are not enticed by all the "good things" of this world; they do not suffer from deprivation and want. Even when they or their children lack some of the "basics," even when their sustenance depends on the good graces of others, they never request physical sustenance alone. Closeness with Hashem is their first priority. When they then enjoy physical pleasures, they are not distanced from Hashem by them. On the contrary, they use them to elevate themselves closer to Hashem.

Shevivei Lev II 1:47-48

They who seek Hashem shall never want for any good thing.

Rabbi Elimelech of Lizensk illustrated the difference between those who delight

in riches and those who delight in Hashem with the following:

It is written in our sacred books that all the tzaddikim will gather around the Mashiach when he comes. This gathering will be comprised both of those tzaddikim, whose only desire was spiritual elevation and closeness to Hashem, as well as those who fulfilled every one of the Torah's precepts and were meticulous never to transgress even a minor infraction, but who also desired material prosperity [something which is not wrong in and of itself but which betrays an ulterior motive lurking behind their observance].

In order to expose this motive in the second group, the Mashiach will accompany them all to the shores of the Atlantic Ocean. He will split the sea before them and reveal all its treasures — diamonds and pearls and treasure chests in the bowels of sunken ships. Beholding such wealth, the second group will immediately step onto the dried sea bed and fill their pockets with gold and jewels. Then they will return to the shore where the Mashiach will be waiting with the other tzaddikim.

With the power of his awesome holiness, the Mashiach will then fly up to the Garden of Eden. The entire first group of tzaddikim will follow him. The second group will endeavor to join them, but their pockets, filled with gold and jewels, will weigh them down and prevent them from rising.

This might sound unfair. If these individuals were tzaddikim during their lifetimes, why should they be left behind now? What the holy Rabbi Elimelech was teaching us, however, was that even at that level of holiness, there are still many gradations. When they see that the others have remained standing on the shore with the Mashiach, they should then think twice about what they want to do. By not thinking twice, they will reveal retroactively that their righteousness was not as pure as it could have been. They will realize that they still need to purify themselves. Casting the physical jewels of this world back into the sea would be a good way to start.

Noam Elimelech, Kedoshim

You open Your hand and satisfy the desire of every living thing.

The Maggid of Lublin explained this verse with a parable.

There was once a rich and generous man who distributed charity at every opportunity. He welcomed everyone into his home, fed them, and sent them away with some spending money.

A poor man once came to him and requested charity.

"In a moment I will give you some money," the rich man replied. "In the meantime, are you hungry? Why don't you wash your hands and sit down for a meal?"

The poor man declined, "No thank you, I'm not hungry. I had a meal just an hour ago and am quite full. If you will give me a shot of whiskey, however, my appetite might return, and I would be glad to take you up on your offer."

The rich man laughed, "It is my custom to feed people who are hungry. Why should I arouse your appetite just so you can stuff yourself?"

Hashem could reply to all of our requests for more of a livelihood in the same way, saying, "It would not be to your benefit if I granted your request. True, you now lack something, and you consider it important for your existence. When you receive it, however, will your appetite be satisfied, or will you want more and more and more? Will you ever be satisfied with what I give you?"

What does He do? When, in His goodness, He satisfies a person's desires, He grants him a double portion. That is, He not only fulfills the person's request, but He also grants him the ability to be satisfied and thankful for what he has.

This is the meaning of "You open Your hand and satisfy the desire of every living thing." Not only does Hashem freely open His hand (channels of Divine sustenance), but He also enables us to feel satisfied and happy with what we receive. This is the greatest gift He can give us. For, "Who is rich? Only one who is happy with his portion" (*Pirkei Avos* 4:1).

Yeriyos Ha-Ohel, *Beha'aloscha*

And satisfy the desire of every living thing.

The Alter of Kelm said: To what can a man's heart be likened? To the soil.

A man sees a beautiful orchard of different kinds of fruit trees. On what does the orchard grow? On the soil. He sees a vacant field filled with weeds and wild undergrowth. On what do these things grow? On the soil. He cannot withhold his surprise, "How can the same soil produce such opposites? This soil, does it grow things that are good, or bad ?"

The answer is: It depends on what you plant and how you cultivate it. If you plant trees after cleaning away the weeds and rocks, the soil will yield luscious fruits. If you do not clean up the field, the weeds will strangle the fruit trees.

This is the meaning of the verse, "You open Your hand and satisfy the desire of every living thing." But what does He give to satisfy? It depends on what

kind of a "desire" a person has planted and cultivated in his heart. If he has cultivated faith and trust in God, in sanctity, and purity, they will grow and produce more of the same. If he has planted and cultivated other desires, they will grow wild.

Chochmah U'Mussar 2:40

Blessed is the man who trusts in Hashem...

It is written, "Cast your load upon Hashem, and He will sustain you" (*Tehillim* 55:23). The Alter of Navaradok commented: A person normally is hesitant to place all his trust and reliance on Hashem. "Will my livelihood descend from the heavens?" he asks. "See, I work and I make a living. If I stop, from where will my livelihood come?"

This attitude, the Alter continued, reminded him of a story. There was once a man who sold coal. He worked long hours in his store, breathing in black soot and dust all day, and returning home each night blackened from head to foot.

An old childhood friend couldn't help but feel pity for the poor fellow. "I remember when you were young," he said, "you were a promising artist. Why didn't you choose a cleaner vocation, something more appropriate to your talents? Why didn't you become a goldsmith or a jeweler? You could cut diamonds! In a few moments, you could manufacture beautiful rings that would bring in more money than you earn for an entire weeks's work!"

The coal man laughed and answered, "You must be kidding! I am lucky I didn't become a diamond merchant. Now, at least I make enough to buy a loaf of bread each day, whereas if I were a diamond merchant, I would surely die of starvation! Look, as it is, my livelihood comes from customers who come into my store to buy a few pennies' worth of coal to keep warm in the winter. Nobody ever came in here looking for a diamond! I'm telling you, I'd starve!"

"You foolish man!" his friend exclaimed. "Of course nobody comes into a coal store looking for diamonds. If you would decide to become a jeweler, on the other hand, you could make certain changes. You could wash that black powder off your face and empty your store of every piece of coal. You could then buy the tools of a diamond cutter and hang a sign outside your door that you've changed businesses. Your work would then be cleaner and easier, and you would make a much better living !"

Like this coal man, our trust in Hashem is sorely lacking. Because we rely totally on our own skills and talents, Hashem is willing to leave us to our

own resources. But this is a curse. We become so involved in our businesses, in making a living, that the bread we earn is in exchange for our souls. Not trusting in a Higher Power who takes care of us not only takes a tremendous toll on how well we live but on how long we survive under the strain of modern-day pressures.

If we could only stand back and clear away the soot from our eyes, we might see all kinds of opportunities that were there all the time! And because the quality of trusting Hashem primarily involves a change in attitude, this does not necessarily entail changing our job. On the contrary, we might discover an entirely new range of opportunities right where we are. Even a coal seller might find a diamond that was there all the time! This is the meaning of, "Blessed is the man who trusts in Hashem, and to whom Hashem is also the source of his trust" (*Yirmeyahu* 17:7).

Madregas Ha-Adam 1:23

Hashem is also the source of his trust.

The Alter of Navaradok told another story about the power of bitachon (trusting in Hashem).

Following Shacharis one morning, the great Kabbalist, the holy Rabbi Moshe Alshich of Tzefas, spoke to his students in praise of the quality of bitachon. The local clay digger who extracted lime from the mountains surrounding Tzefas was present at the time.

After listening to the rabbi's words, he said to himself, "Am I crazy? The holy Alshich says that a person who trusts in Hashem is given everything he needs from Above. If this is true, why should I work so hard at my backbreaking job every day? As it is I have no rest. I rise early in the morning, drive my wagon to dig up clay, work for hours loading the wagon, and then drive from street to street selling clay for pennies. In the meantime, I could be making more money by just trusting in Hashem. I must be crazy to continue working!"

No sooner said than done. He decided he would sit near the heater in the beis midrash and recite Tehillim all day. When he did not return home from davening that morning, his wife went looking for him.

When she found him, she asked, "What's with you this morning? Get up and drive the wagon!"

"Do you think I'm crazy?" he asked, raising his head up from his recitations. "I just heard very clearly from the holy Alshich's mouth that if a person trusts in Hashem, Hashem Himself will be his trust! His livelihood will come to him without toil and without the slightest exertion!"

His wife tried to convince him he was wrong, that it wasn't so simple, but he wouldn't budge. Certain that he had gone mad, she went out to look for someone to drive her husband's wagon. She found an Arab in the marketplace who needed work. She offered him a good deal: He would take the mule and the wagon, as well as all of her husband's work tools, his shovel and his pail; he would dig up clay and sell it, and they would split the profits equally.

The Arab accepted, and immediately drove the wagon out of town to find a good location. He began digging and loading clay onto the wagon. The more he dug, the deeper the pit grew. All of a sudden he saw something shiny. He went down into the pit, dug some more, and discovered a hidden treasure! He worked hard to extricate the entire box filled with gold coins, and finally succeeded in loading it onto the wagon. He then carefully covered it with more clay. Going down into the pit one last time to see if any more coins could be found, without warning the walls collapsed. Before the Arab knew it, he was covered with clay. He cried out, but it was too late. More clay fell on him and he was buried alive.

The mule remained there until sundown. It then headed home, as it was accustomed to doing, and found its way to its master's house. Hearing the mule bray, the clay digger's wife and children went out to meet the wagon. The Arab was nowhere to be found, so they unhitched the wagon and led the mule to its trough. Then they examined the wagon and found the gold! One of the older children ran to tell their father that his bitachon in Hashem has borne fruit. He was now rich. He could devote the rest of his life to reciting Tehillim in the holy Alshich's beis midrash.

The story spread all over Tzefas. The Alshich's students came complaining to their master.

"What is so special about this simple Jew?" they asked. "For years we have had the privilege of listening to your Torah every day. We have drunk in every word you have taught us, and cried at hearing the deepest secrets of life ever uttered since the holy Rabbi Shimon bar Yochai walked these very mountains. Now, based on one discussion about bitachon, this clay digger decides to cast his fate into Hashem's keeping, and before the day is over he is the richest man in Tzefas!"

The Alshich replied: "You want to know the difference between you and the clay digger? I will tell you a parable, and you will understand.

"It is analogous to a man who works very hard pounding tent pins into hard earth with a sledgehammer. The tent pins must be wedged into the ground solidly in order to support the entire tent. In the same way I work hard to imbue you, my students, with the teachings of the Living God, so that they

One should have in mind that it is his intention to fulfill the requirement of drinking the third of the four cups of wine.

BLESSED be You, Hashem our God, King of the universe, Who creates the fruit of the vine.

בָּרוּךְ אַתָּה יהוה אֱלֹהֵינוּ מֶלֶךְ הָעוֹלָם בּוֹרֵא פְּרִי הַגָּפֶן:

The required amount of the third cup is drunk, within the required period of time, while reclining to the left.

Hallel

הַלֵּל

A special cup for Eliyahu Hanavi is now poured and the door is opened to indicate that it is leil shimurim, "a night which enjoys the protection of Hashem." In some homes, the fourth cup for everyone is poured now, too, but some wait until before the recitation of the Hallel. Some follow the custom of standing when they open the door.

Pour out Your wrath toward the nations that do not know You and on the kingdoms that have not proclaimed Your Name. For he has devoured Yaakov, and they have laid waste his habitation (*Tehillim* 79:6-7). Pour out Your perceptible wrath over them, and let the fire of Your anger overtake them (*ibid.* 69:25). Pursue them with anger and destroy them from under the Heavens of Hashem (*Eychah* 3:66).

שְׁפוֹךְ חֲמָתְךָ אֶל הַגּוֹיִם אֲשֶׁר לֹא יְדָעוּךָ וְעַל מַמְלָכוֹת אֲשֶׁר בְּשִׁמְךָ לֹא קָרָאוּ: כִּי אָכַל אֶת יַעֲקֹב וְאֶת נָוֵהוּ הֵשַׁמּוּ: שְׁפָךְ עֲלֵיהֶם זַעְמֶךָ וַחֲרוֹן אַפְּךָ יַשִּׂיגֵם: תִּרְדֹּף בְּאַף וְתַשְׁמִידֵם מִתַּחַת שְׁמֵי יהוה:

will remain firmly in your hearts.

"Over the years, your hearts have become so softened by my words, however, that they no longer resemble hard rocks, but sand on the seashore. For this reason, my words have no trouble entering your hearts; and just as they enter easily, they also move you easily. My words have made a deep impression on your hearts and you have been deeply moved — yet still you wonder and you question, 'Is it really possible to rely solely on bitachon without doing anything practical?'

"The simple clay digger, on the other hand, his heart is a heart of stone. He doesn't possess anywhere near your degree of knowledge. Still, or perhaps for this very reason, the tent pin entered directly into his heart and became firmly embedded there. He heard what I said and decided on the spot not to leave the beis midrash. With such bitachon, there is an immediate answer from Heaven. This is the meaning of, 'Blessed is the man who trusts in Hashem, and to whom Hashem is also the source of his trust'" (*Yirmeyahu* 17:7).

Madregas Ha-Adam, Darchei Ha-Bitachon 5

Pour out your wrath.

Following Birkas Ha-Mazon, the third cup of wine is drunk while reclining. The door is opened, and all sing out, "Pour out Your wrath toward the nations that do not know You and on the kingdoms that have not proclaimed Your Name. For He has devoured Yaakov, and they have laid waste his habitation" (*Tehillim* 79:6-7).

"For He [singular] has devoured Yaakov, and they [plural] have laid waste his habitation" (*Tehillim* 79:7). Rabbi Shimshon Rafael Hirsch explains: The subject of "devoured" is the "Your Name" of the preceding verse. We were no longer worthy of bearing His Name, hence it was Hashem, not our foes, who devoured Yaakov. Of course, they were completely unaware of this. They couldn't help thinking that it was they who had succeeded in destroying his habitation (Hirsch ad loc.).

The source for this idea is in the Midrash (*Eichah Rabbah* 1:43):

> An accuser leaped up in front of the Throne of Glory and said: "Shall a wicked man (Nevuchadnetzar) boast that he has destroyed the House of God and burned His Sanctuary? May a fire from heaven descend immediately and burn it [before he does]." This is the meaning of the verse, "From above, He has sent fire to burn my insides" (*Eichah* 1:13). Rabbi Yehoshua said: This is what the prophet meant when he said, "Take the millstones and grind flour" (*Yeshayahu* 47:2). People do not grind flour; they grind wheat into flour! How can you grind flour? However, Yerushalayim said to the Daughter of Babylon, "If fire had not been sent to burn me from above, you never could have overcome me. A dead lion you have killed; ground flour you have ground; a burnt city you have burned...."

Rabbi Chayim of Volozhin explains: How did "nations defile the Abode of Your Holiness" (*Tehillim* 79:1) and "destroy your habitation" (ibid. 79:7)? It was because Yisrael had already weakened and damaged the power of holiness in the world. Only then was Nevuchadnetzar able to destroy the First Temple and Titus the Second. They only destroyed "below" what had already been destroyed "above." This is what our Sages meant when they said, "ground flour you have ground." For only when our sins had damaged the Supernal Universe, which is none other than the Beis Ha-Mikdash above, were our enemies able to destroy the Sanctuary below.

Nefesh Ha-Chayim 1:4

Pour out Your wrath toward the nations that do not know You....For he has devoured Yaakov.

The Maggid of Dubno asked: Why do we call on Hashem to exact revenge

against the nations who have harmed us because they "do not know You and...have not proclaimed Your Name"? What difference does it make whether they have acknowledged Hashem or proclaimed His Name? And if they have, would they be exempted from punishment for their harsh and unrelenting treatment of us? He answered with the following parable.

A well-to-do merchant would purchase goods from a large wholesaler and sell them at a good profit. One year, due to a bad business deal, he lost everything and was left owing a large sum to the wholesaler. He went to inform him that he was unable to pay off his debts.

The wholesaler considered the situation: What can I do with this fellow? I can send my men to beat him. I can get him thrown in jail. But why should I go to all that trouble? And what would I stand to gain?

"I see that the wheel of fortune has made another one of its nasty turns," the wholesaler finally answered the merchant. "Don't be upset or embarrassed. I will hire you as my salesman and pay you a decent salary. Half of it shall be yours and half of it I shall withhold in payment for what you owe me. In no time at all, you will be back on your feet!"

The merchant could not find the words to thank his benefactor. He immediately began his job as a salesman, traveling all over to his new company's clients, taking sizable orders, shipping goods, and collecting payment.

One day our salesman arrived in a distant township to collect an outstanding debt from a local merchant.

The merchant excused himself, however, saying, "Due to a bad business deal, I have lost all my money and cannot pay right now. Please, until I get back on my feet, I beg you, give me more merchandise on consignment. I will then reestablish myself and repay your company all that I owe."

The salesman was infuriated. How was he to know that this merchant was the nephew of the wealthy wholesaler, his boss?

"You have a lot of nerve!" he screamed. "Why didn't you worry about paying your debts before you lost all your money? Did you really think you could get out of paying by stalling like this?"

Beside himself, he stood up and hit the merchant. He then went to the police, issued a complaint, and had the merchant thrown in jail. From jail, the merchant wrote a letter to his uncle, the wealthy wholesaler...

When our salesman returned home, the police were waiting for him. He was immediately taken into custody and thrown into jail.

"Why? What's going on here?" he cried out.

"Your boss issued a complaint against you for not repaying him what you owe him," they explained.

The door is closed (and everyone is seated if they stood), and those who have not already done so pour the fourth cup. Although Hallel is usually said standing, on Pesach night we recite it while seated. However, one should not do so in a reclining position but, rather, sit respectfully, as if in the presence of a king. Some are accustomed to hold the cups in their hands throughout the recitation of the Hallel and some do not. One should have in mind that it is his intention to fulfill the requirement of reciting Hallel on Pesach night.

NOT to us, Hashem, not to us, but to Your own Name give honor, for the sake of Your lovingkindness, for the sake of Your truth. Wherefore shall the nations say: "Where now is their God?" But our God is in the

לֹא לָנוּ יהוה לֹא לָנוּ כִּי לְשִׁמְךָ תֵּן כָּבוֹד עַל חַסְדְּךָ עַל אֲמִתֶּךָ: לָמָּה יֹאמְרוּ הַגּוֹיִם אַיֵּה נָא אֱלֹהֵיהֶם: וֵאלֹהֵינוּ

Shocked, the salesman requested to speak with his boss. The next day, as he sat in his cell, he received a visit from the wholesaler.

He fell at his feet and asked, "Why have you turned against me? You know that I have nothing with which to repay you. Didn't we agree that I would work for you and thereby pay you back in installments? Why then have you had me thrown into jail?"

The wholesaler answered, "When you came to me to tell me you couldn't pay, my sentiments were aroused, for I am sympathetic by nature. When it became clear to me, however, that you are incapable of sympathizing with or being merciful towards those under your charge, I decided to act the same way and stifle my own sympathies toward you!"

This is the meaning of the verse, "Pour out Your wrath toward the nations that do not know You and on the kingdoms that have not proclaimed Your Name!" (*Tehillim* 79:6). If the nations among whom we were exiled had had some compassion or sympathy for us, they could justifiably have demanded that Hashem deal compassionately with them. Since, however, "he has devoured Yaakov, and they have laid waste his habitation" (ibid.), they disqualified themselves from deserving Hashem's forbearance. As a result, it was they who disappeared, not us.

Ohel Yaakov, *Beshallach*

Not to us, Hashem, not to us, but to Your own Name...

The Maggid of Dubno asked: Why do we repeat, "Not to us, Hashem, not to

Heavens; everything is as He has willed to bring it about. Their idols of silver and gold are the work of human hands; they have a mouth, but they do not speak; they have eyes, but they do not see; they have ears, but they do not hear; they have a nose, but they do not smell; [they have] their hands, but they cannot touch with them; [they have] their feet, but they do not walk; they can utter no sound

בַשָּׁמָיִם כֹּל אֲשֶׁר חָפֵץ עָשָׂה: עֲצַבֵּיהֶם כֶּסֶף וְזָהָב מַעֲשֵׂה יְדֵי אָדָם: פֶּה לָהֶם וְלֹא יְדַבֵּרוּ עֵינַיִם לָהֶם וְלֹא יִרְאוּ: אָזְנַיִם לָהֶם וְלֹא יִשְׁמָעוּ אַף לָהֶם וְלֹא יְרִיחוּן: יְדֵיהֶם וְלֹא יְמִישׁוּן רַגְלֵיהֶם וְלֹא יְהַלֵּכוּ לֹא יֶהְגּוּ בִּגְרוֹנָם: כְּמוֹהֶם

us, but to Your own Name give honor" (*Tehillim* 115:1)? What is this reiteration meant to teach us? He answered with the following parable.

Two rich men lived in a certain city and were in constant competition with each other. Whenever one of them experienced the slightest success, the other was beside himself with jealousy. Their jealousy was so strong that it finally brought them to hate one another.

One day, one of these gentlemen was walking along in the street minding his own business. All of a sudden, he was struck down by mistake by a youth dashing along the street. The rich man picked himself up from the sidewalk, brushed himself off, and began beating the youth with his stick.

The youth cried out, "Stop, I am Mr. So-and-So's servant!"

The rich man's anger became even more uncontrollable. "So what," he screamed, "if you are his servant? Does that give you the right to run down the street like a madman, smashing into people and knocking them down?" And he continued beating the boy with his stick.

Just wait and see, mister, the youth vowed to himself, I'll get back at you.

He returned to his master's home, bruised and bleeding. The rich man saw him and asked, "What happened to you? Did somebody beat you up?"

"Don't ask," the youth replied. "You wouldn't be able to do anything about it anyway..."

"Who says I can't do something about it?" the rich man exclaimed. "Tell me who hit you!"

"Who else would beat me like this but that other rich fellow you like so much," the youth replied.

"But certainly he did not know that you were my servant!" the rich man exclaimed.

"Oh, he knew very well," the youth replied. "When I told him who I was, he started beating me even harder!"

His master heard this and was enraged. He would not rest until the other fellow was brought to justice. This time he had gone too far! The rich man went to the police and issued a complaint against his enemy in the name of

his servant. The offender would have to pay for damages, pain, loss of time, cost of cure, and shame incurred! And all this because the servant, was clever enough to mention his master's name to the rich man who assaulted him, and thereby arouse his ire; and then later he was able to secure his master's promise to demand compensation for the disgrace he endured.

The Maggid concluded: Hashem is the Master, Moshe Rabbenu was His servant, and the enemy was Pharaoh. This is what Moshe meant when he returned to Hashem and complained, "As soon as I came to Pharaoh to speak in Your Name, he made things worse for this people. Yet You have done nothing to help Your people!" (*Shemos* 5:23). You must now take revenge and punish him for Your Name's sake!

In the same vein, when we were beaten by the nations, we also implored, "Not to us, Hashem, not to us, but to Your own Name give honor."

Ohel Yaakov, *Shemos*

Wherefore shall the nations say: "Where now is their God?"

The Maggid of Lublin explained this verse with a parable.

A father once sent his son to a shoemaker to live with him, serve as his apprentice, and learn the trade. The father gave the shoemaker a handsome sum, and promised him that he would provide all the food the boy needed on a daily basis, such that the yoke of supporting the lad would not fall on the shoemaker's shoulders. More than this, the father was also happy to provide extra portions of delicious foods for the shoemaker's entire family.

The shoemaker agreed and promised the father that he would take care of the boy "like one of his own." When the father left, however, the true meaning of this statement became clear. The shoemaker beat the boy and treated him cruelly. He also withheld all the food that was delivered daily for the boy and confiscated it for his own family. To the boy he gave just dry bread.

Then, pretending to commiserate with the boy, he would say, "Poor lad, your father seems to have abandoned you? This dry bread is all he sent for you!"

These words would pierce the boy's heart like knives, until one day he could no longer stand it, and he ran back to his father's house. Of course, his father received him with open arms. When he saw the boy's appearance, however, he said, "What's happened to you? You have become so gaunt and pale!"

"And what did I have to eat all this time?" the boy cried.

יִהְיוּ עֹשֵׂיהֶם כֹּל אֲשֶׁר בֹּטֵחַ בָּהֶם: יִשְׂרָאֵל בְּטַח בַּיהוה עֶזְרָם וּמָגִנָּם הוּא: בֵּית אַהֲרֹן בִּטְחוּ בַיהוה עֶזְרָם וּמָגִנָּם הוּא: יִרְאֵי יהוה בִּטְחוּ בַיהוה עֶזְרָם וּמָגִנָּם הוּא:

with their throat. They who make them shall become like them; indeed, everyone who trusts in them. O' Yisrael, trust in Hashem; He is their help and their shield. O' house of Aharon, trust in Hashem; He is their help and their shield. O' you who fear Hashem, trust in Hashem; He is their help and their shield (*Tehillim* 115:1-11).

"What do you mean?" the father asked in shock. "I send meat and chicken and all kinds of delicacies to the shoemaker's house every single day!"

"No," the boy replied, "nothing reached me but dry bread, and the shoemaker made fun of me, telling me that you had rejected and abandoned me, that I was no longer beloved in your eyes. Father, Father, let me stay here with you! Do not send me away anymore!"

Our compassionate Father sent us into exile among the nations of the world. While we were in their charge, he sent them everything they needed in abundance, so that they would in turn provide us with everything we needed (*Zohar* II:152b). They, however, took it all for themselves and left us with dry crumbs.

If this wasn't enough, they made fun of us, saying, "Your God abandoned you and wants nothing more to do with you!"

We, in turn, raised our eyes to heaven and cried out, "Wherefore shall the nations say: 'Where now is their God?' — return us to You, Hashem! Let us receive our sustenance directly from You!

Yerios Ha-Ohel, *Beshallach*

O' Yisrael, trust in Hashem; He is their help and their shield.

What is the highest level of bitachon, of trust in Hashem? Shelomo Ha-Melech provided an answer to this when he said, "Trust in Hashem with all your heart, and do not rely on your own understanding" (*Mishlei* 3:5). The Gaon of Vilna explained: Take the quality of bitachon into your heart completely, and not just partially. Do not say: I trust in Hashem, but I feel obligated to do whatever I can and rely on my own rational intelligence. No, when it comes to Hashem's Torah and His commandments, you must not rely on your own logic [to convince you that you know better]. Rather, trust absolutely in Hashem with all your heart (Gaon of Vilna ad loc.).

The Alter of Kelm added: We must trust in Hashem with all our hearts, and know that our very lives and the lives of our children depend upon it.

We must never be misled into thinking that we should alter, amend, revise, or abandon His commandments just because "times have changed" and "we know better." He illustrated this important point with a famous parable.

A king sent one of his ministers as ambassador to represent him in the court of a neighboring monarch. Before he left, the king commanded him not to make a wager under any circumstances. His minister was offended.

"Does his majesty suspect me of being a gambler?" he asked.

"I do not suspect you," the king replied, "but I warn you nevertheless — do not be tempted to make any wagers, come what may!"

The minister arrived and represented his king with honor. The neighboring king received him with pomp and ceremony, and set out a lavish meal in his honor. After a number of cups of royal wine, one of the neighboring king's ministers challenged boisterously, "How great could our neighboring king's wisdom be? He sent us a minister with a disgraceful mark on his body!"

The first minister was offended and protested, "What disgraceful mark have you found on me?"

"Don't be offended," the second minister mollified him. "It is only a hidden mark, despite the fact that everyone knows about it."

The first minister was shocked and called out, "I demand an explanation! I demand an apology!"

But the second minister was not about to let his prey go. "Why apologize?" he asked. "Everyone knows that you have a large and ugly birthmark."

The first minister was beside himself, "That is a lie and a low-handed libel!"

"As you wish," the second minister chided. "Forget the whole thing. Pretend I never said a word about it."

But the first minister was not about to give in so easily. He demanded an immediate apology.

"Well, if you are going to be stubborn, so am I!" the second minister retorted. "To prove that I'm right, I am willing to bet ten thousand gold dinars! Put your money where your mouth is!"

The first minister remembered that his king had prohibited him from making any wagers. "But," he thought to himself, "that is only if I might possibly end up losing. However, this is just an underhanded libel, and my personal honor as well as that of my country is hanging in the balance. I must go through with it. I hereby pledge the entire ten thousand dinars to my king!"

He thereupon stood up and took off his clothes in front of all those assembled, to prove once and for all that he had no unseemly marks anywhere on his body. The second minister then seemed to sober up. He apologized and handed him ten thousand dinars.

Hashem, Who has been mindful of us, He will bless. He will bless the House of Yisrael; He will bless the House of Aharon; He will bless those who fear Hashem, the small together with the great; Hashem will give you increase, to you and to your children.	יהוה זְכָרָנוּ יְבָרֵךְ יְבָרֵךְ אֶת בֵּית יִשְׂרָאֵל יְבָרֵךְ אֶת בֵּית אַהֲרֹן: יְבָרֵךְ יִרְאֵי יהוה הַקְּטַנִּים עִם הַגְּדֹלִים: יֹסֵף יהוה עֲלֵיכֶם עֲלֵיכֶם וְעַל בְּנֵיכֶם:

When the first minister returned from his trip, he told of the great honor that the neighboring king had shown him. He then took out the ten thousand dinars and offered it to the king.

"What is this?" the king asked.

"A modest gift to His Majesty," the minister replied, and he related the entire episode of the alleged birthmark.

"If so, you made a wager," the king surmised, "and I told you not to do so under any circumstances."

"But this was a sure thing," the minister said, trying to vindicate himself.

"You transgressed my explicit command," the king replied. "And now listen to what I have to say. When I spoke to our friend, the neighboring king, about sending a representative to his court, he said to me, 'Send whomever you wish, but not that particular minister...for he is an absolute oaf.' He was referring to you, and of course I protested on your behalf. 'An oaf?' I asked, 'how can you say such a thing?' And he answered, 'Look, I'll prove it to you. I will get him to take off all his clothes in the middle of a royal banquet and in front of all my ministers.' I replied, 'No, impossible!' But he made a wager with me. He bet fifty thousand gold dinars that he could make you do it.

"Of course, I understood that they would try to lay a trap for you, and I therefore warned you a number of times not to be tempted to make any wagers under any circumstances. You, however, decided that you knew better and you decided to act accordingly... Now, you see, you have won ten thousand dinars, but caused me to lose fifty thousand! What have you gained? Not only did you transgress my explicit command, but you also made yourself the laughingstock of the entire kingdom!"

We resemble this minister, concluded the Alter, when we think we are smarter than Hashem and can make little changes in His Torah. It is therefore written, "Trust in Hashem with all your heart, and do not rely on your own understanding" (*Mishlei* 3:5) — even when your logic tells you that a little change couldn't possibly hurt, trust in Hashem and keep His commandments.

Or Ha-Mussar 1:42, 1:82; **Madregas Ha-Adam** 53

Blessed are you for Hashem, the Maker of heaven and earth. The heavens are the heavens of Hashem, but He has given the earth to the children of men. It is not the dead that proclaim God's might, and not all those who go down into silence. But as for us, we will bless the mighty God from this time forth and forever. Halleluyah! (*ibid.*, 12-18).

בְּרוּכִים אַתֶּם לַיהוה עֹשֵׂה שָׁמַיִם וָאָרֶץ: הַשָּׁמַיִם שָׁמַיִם לַיהוה וְהָאָרֶץ נָתַן לִבְנֵי אָדָם: לֹא הַמֵּתִים יְהַלְלוּ־יָהּ וְלֹא כָּל יֹרְדֵי דוּמָה: וַאֲנַחְנוּ נְבָרֵךְ יָהּ מֵעַתָּה וְעַד עוֹלָם הַלְלוּיָהּ:

The heavens are the heavens of Hashem, but He has given the earth to the children of men. It is not the dead that proclaim God's might....

Asked the Maggid of Slotzk: Surely, "The heavens are the heavens of Hashem, but He has given the earth to the children of men." But how is this connected to, "It is not the dead that proclaim God's might," about which the Sages explained (*Berachos* 18b), "These are the wicked who are called dead even while they are alive"?

To understand this, we must first recall another statement of our Sages (*Berachos* 35a): One verse states, "The earth and all that it contains is Hashem's" (*Tehillim* 24:1), while another verse states, "He has given the earth to the children of men" (ibid. 115:16). [How can both statements be true?] However, there is no contradiction. The earth and all it contains is Hashem's — before one recites a blessing, for whoever enjoys the pleasures of this world without blessing and acknowledging the Creator has misappropriated that which is sacred. He has given the earth to the children of men — only after one recites a blessing.

In another place, on the other hand, the Talmud (*Sanhedrin* 103b) relates that King Yehoyakim rebelled against Hashem and said, "Do we really need the Holy One, even for the light of the sun? We have the gold of Parvayim (a place known for its gold mines), which we use for the Beis Ha-Mikdash. Let Him take away His light!"

His contemporaries said to him, "But don't all the gold and silver in the world also belong to Him, as it is written (*Chaggai* 2:8), 'Mine is the gold and Mine is the silver, says the God of hosts'"?

But Yehoyakim replied, "He has already given them to us, as it is written, 'He gave the earth to the children of men.'"

We see from here that the same verse can be used one way by the righteous and one way by the wicked! The righteous will learn their obligation to bless Hashem for all the bounty He provides for them, while those who have hardened their hearts will conclude that the world is theirs to do with as they please.

I love my voice, indeed, my supplications, for Hashem will hear. For He has inclined His ear to me in the past, and I will call [upon Him] in my fateful days. [When] the pains of death oppressed me, when the straits of the grave gained hold of me, when I faced trouble and sorrow, [when] I call upon the Name of Hashem: "I beseech You, o' Hashem, deliver my soul." Then Hashem deals graciously [with me] and is just, and our God takes pity. Hashem protects the unaware; I had been brought low, but He grants me new life. Return again and again, o' my soul, to your resting places, for it is Hashem Who has caused to ripen that which has come over you. But when You have delivered my soul from death, my eye from tears and my foot from stumbling. Then I shall walk on before Hashem in the lands of the living. So firmly convinced was I that I said it, I, who was so greatly afflicted. I said it during my hasty flight: "All mankind is deluded" (*ibid.* 116:1-11).

אָהַבְתִּי כִּי יִשְׁמַע יהוה אֶת קוֹלִי תַּחֲנוּנָי: כִּי הִטָּה אָזְנוֹ לִי וּבְיָמַי אֶקְרָא: אֲפָפוּנִי חֶבְלֵי מָוֶת וּמְצָרֵי שְׁאוֹל מְצָאוּנִי צָרָה וְיָגוֹן אֶמְצָא: וּבְשֵׁם יהוה אֶקְרָא אָנָּא יהוה מַלְּטָה נַפְשִׁי: חַנּוּן יהוה וְצַדִּיק וֵאלֹהֵינוּ מְרַחֵם: שֹׁמֵר פְּתָאִים יהוה דַּלּוֹתִי וְלִי יְהוֹשִׁיעַ: שׁוּבִי נַפְשִׁי לִמְנוּחָיְכִי כִּי יהוה גָּמַל עָלָיְכִי: כִּי חִלַּצְתָּ נַפְשִׁי מִמָּוֶת אֶת עֵינִי מִן דִּמְעָה אֶת רַגְלִי מִדֶּחִי: אֶתְהַלֵּךְ לִפְנֵי יהוה בְּאַרְצוֹת הַחַיִּים: הֶאֱמַנְתִּי כִּי אֲדַבֵּר אֲנִי עָנִיתִי מְאֹד: אֲנִי אָמַרְתִּי בְחָפְזִי כָּל הָאָדָם כֹּזֵב:

The sequence of these verses is now clear: The righteous realize that, "The heavens are the heavens of Hashem," whereas "He has given the earth to the children of men" to bless Him and acknowledge His beneficence. The wicked, on the other hand, are also discussed: "The dead do not praise God, nor can those who sink down into silence." And what about us? Have we learned which course we are to follow? Yes! "We will bless the mighty God from this time forth and forever."

Korban Shabbos 1:4

Hashem protects the unaware; I had been brought low, but He grants me new life.

The Hebrew root "dal" (dales-lamed) has numerous meanings, all of which are interconnected and complementary. "Dal" means "impoverished" or "poor" as in the verse, "Happy is he who cares for the poor ('dal')" (*Tehillim* 41:1), and "brought low," as in our verse, "I had been brought low ('dalosi'), but He grants me new life" (ibid. 116:6). A "dal" is a person who was once rich but who lost his fortune. Like a "d'li," a bucket that is cast down into a well, he too has been cast down. But, just like the bucket, he can be lifted up again, as David Ha-Melech wrote, "I exalt You, Hashem, for You have lifted me up ('dilisani')!" (ibid. 30:2).

Based on this range of meanings, the Sages (*Pesachim* 118a) reread our verse as, "Although I have become impoverished of mitzvos, it is still proper to save me!" This reading requires clarification. If we have become impoverished of mitzvos, what right do we have to ask to be saved? The Maggid of Dubno answered with a parable.

Two beggars were traveling together. One was healthy and strong, while the other was so weak and sickly that he could hardly stand on his feet. The strong beggar would constantly brag about his own physical prowess and make fun of his companion, calling him a frail weakling and other such mocking insults. The weak beggar suffered these insults in silence. Secretly, however, he prayed to Hashem, "Master of the universe, behold and look down upon my disgrace and let this arrogant blockhead have a taste of his own medicine!"

His prayer was accepted in heaven, as it is written, "God will surely take up the cause of the victim" (*Koheles* 3:15; Rashi ad loc.).

In the king's court that day, the king's physician and his mightiest warrior died. The king mourned their passing and was anxious to find suitable replacements. He sent his servants to scout out the kingdom. Days passed and they returned with the two most likely candidates. One was a seasoned warrior, and the other, an experienced physician.

The king spoke to them, saying, "The two men who died were expert in their respective fields. Anyone wishing to fill their shoes must first prove himself worthy. The truth is, I doubt I will ever find worthy successors!"

The physician said, "May it please your majesty, just let me treat one critically sick patient. I will demonstrate my competence by curing his illness and restoring him to perfect health!"

The warrior said, "May it please your majesty, just have the strongest man in the kingdom brought before me, and I will defeat him with my little pinky!"

The king ordered his servants to conduct a search for two such men. They found our two friends at the gate of the city, the strong man together with his weak and frail companion. The king's servants hurried and brought them to the king. The physician took the weak beggar under his care, and the warrior got ready to fight.

In the end, the strength of the strong beggar was his own undoing, while the frailty of the sick beggar led to his complete recovery!

The nations of the world make fun of Yisrael, saying, "Where now is their God?" (*Tehillim* 115:2). They boast of their wealth and their power, "They congratulate themselves, they converse freely and openly [about the evil they plan to do], they talk big, they boast of all their evil doings... They slay the

widow and the stranger, and murder orphans, and they say: God will not see, and the God of Yaakov will not consider" (*Tehillim* 94:4-7).

When Hashem redeems His people, however, He will reveal an inkling of His awesome power to the world, and in this way, "bring the arrogant down to the ground" (*Shacharis*). At that moment, it will be crystal clear that no thing and no one can stand before Him. At the same time, He will also heal and "elevate the lowly to the heights" (ibid.), as the prophet foretold, "On that day, Hashem will bind His people's fracture and heal the sores of their wound" (*Yeshayahu* 30:26).

This salvation and healing will not necessarily be a reward for our piety and excellence. On the contrary, we are told, "Not because of your righteousness and the uprightness of your heart" (*Devarim* 9:5) will Hashem do this. Similarly, in our morning prayers we say, "We do not pretend to rely on our own righteousness when casting our supplications before You, but rather on Your abundant mercies. What are we? What is our life? What is our piety worth? What is our righteousness worth? Can we effect our own salvation? What is our strength? What is our might?" Rather, Hashem will redeem and heal us out of the purest love, as we pray three times each day, "He recalls the loving deeds of the forefathers and will bring a redeemer to their children's children, for the sake of His Name, with love..." (*Shemoneh Esreh*).

"With love" means exactly what it says. "For the sake of His Name" means that He will redeem and heal us in order to reveal His absolute sovereignty over the entire world, as the prophet declared, "Hashem will be [recognized as] King over the entire earth. On that day, Hashem's Oneness and the Oneness of His Name [will be revealed to all mankind]" (*Zecharyah* 14:9). "For the sake of His Name" means, as the prophet put it, "For My own sake, for My own sake I shall do it [redeem you], for how can I allow My honor to be profaned?" (Yeshayahu 48:11).

This then is the meaning of, "Although I have become impoverished of the mitzvos, it is still proper to save me!" Because we are lowly, He chooses to redeem us, and in this way manifest His Oneness to the world.

Ohel Yaakov, *Bo*

So firmly convinced was I that I said it, I, who was so greatly afflicted.

The Gaon, Rabbi Yochanan Berush, read this verse slightly differently: "When will my words of encouragement have the ability to instill faith" in the heart

of a broken and downtrodden person? When "I have also suffered as much as he has." He illustrated this important insight with the following parable.

A poor beggar was sitting at the table of a wealthy businessman. As he ate, he also cried uncontrollably. The businessman tried to comfort him, "Take heart and have faith! Hope in Hashem. A person's mazal is like a wheel that goes round and round. The very fact that your mazal has reached its lowest level is cause enough to hope that it will soon begin making its climb back up! Your sun will surely shine, and Hashem will fill your life with light and happiness."

The poor beggar was not consoled. "You are wealthy and Hashem has blessed you with everything," he sighed. "You don't lack a thing, so it's easy for you to talk."

But the businessman replied, "No, these are not just empty words. I was once like you, even worse off than you. But then, when everything seemed lost, the wheel turned and I was saved! You can expect the same!"

At that moment, the beggar's face lit up, and hope began to come alive in his heart.

This is what David Ha-Melech meant. When will the poor man's eyes light up with hope? When words of encouragement that are offered him are forthcoming from someone who once suffered the same as he, from someone who himself refused to be consoled, who himself said in his panic, "All of man is false." The soothing words of such a person can sow deep and abiding faith in the hearts of his listeners. They must only be spoken from the heart and they will surely have their effect.

Pidyon Shevuyim

But what shall I do for Hashem in return, once all His ripened bounties will have come upon me?

The Maggid of Dubno asked: To what can this be likened? To a man who had a bright and precocious son whom he loved dearly. One day, he turned to his son and announced, "I want you to learn a proper trade, a clean and easy craft. I suggest gem cutting. I have already hired a master craftsman to initiate you into the secrets of the trade. I have paid him handsomely. I only ask that

you listen attentively to everything he teaches you. If you do this, I promise to buy you a special gift when you complete your lessons."

The son began the period of his apprenticeship with great enthusiasm. Under his master's tutelage, it wasn't long before he felt completely at home in the world of precious gems. By the end of his apprenticeship, he was proficient enough to land a job with a large jewelry concern.

In the meantime, his father also kept his promise. He arranged a large family celebration in his son's honor. At one point during the celebration, he presented his son with the gift he had promised.

The young man was moved to tears by his father's kindness. He rose up from his seat to thank him.

"My beloved father, is it you who should be presenting me with such a gift at the conclusion of my apprenticeship? It was you who was concerned for my future. It was you who discovered this wonderful profession for me. It was you who searched and finally found a gem cutter who was truly a master of his trade. It was you who paid him. It was only in the merit of your loving and gracious concern that I have learned so much and have now begun to earn my own living. And now you wish to give me even more?"

In the merit of learning His Torah and keeping His commandments, Hashem promised us wondrous rewards in this world and the next for our eternal good. It is for this great privilege that each one of us is obligated to thank Him with all our hearts, with all our souls, and with all our might: "Hashem, it is not You who owe me something! How can I ever repay You for all the kindness You have shown me?"

Ohel Yaakov, *Ekev*

I shall raise the cup of salvation's many forms and call in the Name of Hashem.

The Maggid of Dubno said: "Kos yeshuos" means literally "a cup of salvations." Why is the plural, "salvations," used? And what is the connection between this and "calling out Hashem's Name" in prayer? He answered with a parable.

A man fell ill and his entire body was racked with pain. His head ached, his limbs were sore, he could not sleep, and he had no appetite. He went to a doctor, who examined him and conducted an entire battery of tests to determine the source of the trouble. After checking the test results, the doctor diagnosed the ailment and counseled surgery. The man was given a date, six

in the Name of Hashem. I will fulfill my vows to Hashem; o' would that it were in the presence of all His people. Precious in the eyes of Hashem is even the ebb of life that has come to his devoted ones. If, Hashem, I am Your servant, I am Your servant only as the son of Your handmaid, o' You Who has now

אֲשַׁלֵּם נֶגְדָה נָּא לְכָל־עַמּוֹ: יָקָר בְּעֵינֵי יהוה הַמָּוְתָה לַחֲסִידָיו: אָנָּא יהוה כִּי אֲנִי עַבְדֶּךָ אֲנִי עַבְדְּךָ בֶּן

months hence, when the surgery was to take place.

"And until then," the man asked, "am I doomed to live with this excruciating pain?"

"Not necessarily," the doctor replied. "After the surgery, your health will be fully restored, and all these symptoms will disappear. In the meantime, I shall prescribe four different medications, one against headaches, one for sore muscles, one to help you sleep, and one to regain your appetite."

When we tell a person that he is healthy, it is assumed that his head does not hurt, that he has a decent appetite, and that his sleep is deep and restorative. By definition, being healthy includes all of the above. Only when his health deteriorates is it necessary to specify particulars.

The same is true of the Jewish People with regard to the Final Redemption. When that day comes, it will be unnecessary to go into detail, for it will be completely wondrous in every way. For this very reason, however, we understood that the Exodus from Egypt was not the Final Redemption when we heard Hashem use four distinct expressions, "I will *bring* you out from under the burden of Egyptian forced labor, *deliver* you from servitude to them, and *redeem* you with an outstretched arm and powerful judgments. I will *take* you to Me for a nation, and I will be your God..." (*Shemos* 6:6-7).

Our Sages therefore instituted four cups of wine on Pesach — firstly, to thank Hashem for that first salvation, and secondly, to pray for the ultimate salvation that is yet to come. This is the meaning of "I will raise the cup of salvation's many forms" — for all the times He has delivered us in the past, "and call in the Name of Hashem" — to hasten the Final Redemption which is yet to come!

Ohel Yaakov, *Va'era*

I will fulfill my vows to Hashem; o' would that it were in the presence of all His people.

The Maggid of Lublin expressed surprise: We have just acknowledged that it is impossible to "repay Hashem for all the kindness He has shown us." How

loosened my bonds. I will bring You offerings to acknowledge my debt of gratitude, and call in the Name of Hashem. I will fulfill my vows to Hashem; o' would that it were in the presence of all His people. In the courts of the House of Hashem, in your midst, o' Yerushalayim, Halleluyah! (*ibid.*, 12-19).	אֱמָתֶךָ פִּתַּחְתָּ לְמוֹסֵרָי: לְךָ אֶזְבַּח זֶבַח תּוֹדָה וּבְשֵׁם יהוה אֶקְרָא: נְדָרַי לַיהוה אֲשַׁלֵּם נֶגְדָה נָּא לְכָל עַמּוֹ: בְּחַצְרוֹת בֵּית יהוה בְּתוֹכֵכִי יְרוּשָׁלָיִם הַלְלוּיָהּ:
O' proclaim the praise of Hashem's mighty acts, all you nations; laud Him, all you tribes of mankind. For His lovingkindness was mighty over us, and the faithfulness of Hashem endures forever, Halleluyah! (*ibid.*, 117).	הַלְלוּ אֶת יהוה כָּל גּוֹיִם שַׁבְּחוּהוּ כָּל הָאֻמִּים: כִּי גָבַר עָלֵינוּ חַסְדּוֹ וֶאֱמֶת יהוה לְעוֹלָם הַלְלוּיָהּ:

then do we turn around and take upon ourselves the extra burden of fulfilling private vows? Have we repaid what we owe already? Have we performed the obligatory mitzvos as perfectly as we can? To what can this be likened?

A young man once returned home from a short trip.

"When will you pay me what you owe me?" his father asked him.

The boy laughed.

"Why do you laugh?" the father asked.

The boy answered, "Show me the son who can repay his parents even a tenth of what he owes them for all the favors they have bestowed upon him! He can't be found! This being the case, there isn't a father in the world who would even ask his son to repay him."

"My dear boy, don't you think I know that?" the father exclaimed. "You could never repay all the loving favors your mother and I have done for you. Did you think for a moment that I was asking you to do something that was impossible? I only meant to remind you that before you left on your trip you promised to bring me a special bottle of old wine. Since you promised me, why shouldn't you fulfill your vow?"

This is what David Ha-Melech meant: True, I will never be able to repay even an infinitesimal part of the kindness that Hashem has bestowed upon me. But at least I can pay back what I myself vowed to pay; I can try to fulfill the specific promises which I voluntarily took upon myself to fulfill!

Rashei Besamim, Eretz Ha-Chadashah 88a

O' proclaim the praise of Hashem's mighty acts, all you nations....For His lovingkindness was mighty over us.

If Hashem's love for us has remained in full force throughout our long exile, it

is certainly proper for *us* to praise Him. The question is, why should the other nations praise Him for this? Rabbi Avraham Adler explained with a parable.

A blind man was accustomed to walk to the marketplace each day to purchase whatever food he needed. Having traveled the same route every day for many years, he knew exactly how many steps to take before turning right at the corner, and how many steps to continue before arriving at his usual food stand.

A gang of ruffians living in the neighborhood decided to play a prank. They placed a large object in the blind man's way and then waited on the side of the road to rejoice at his fall.

The blind man walked out of his front yard and headed for the marketplace, completely unaware of the trap that had been set for him. What did Hashem do? He made the blind man forget his wallet at home. Just as he was approaching the object, he remembered the wallet. At the last moment, he turned around and retraced his steps back home, picked up his wallet, and started off once again for the marketplace. In the meantime, passers-by had seen this intended stumbling block and moved it aside. The blind man arrived at his destination safely, made his purchases, and returned home.

If we would ask the blind man what kind of a day he'd had, he'd probably answer that it had been difficult in view of the fact that he had had to go back home to get his wallet. At the most, he would accept his lot stoically and hope that he would never have to suffer such an inconvenience again.

The ruffians, on the other hand, know that Someone was watching over the blind man, and that that same Someone spoiled their plan! Why else would the blind man have forgotten his wallet just on that day? And why did he remember to return home for it just as he was about to stumble over their trap? He could have remembered a few seconds later. So they realized that Hashem's providence was hovering over that blind man!

Like this blind man, we are unaware of all the schemes and strategies which our enemies have devised against us. And we are totally unaware of all the ways in which Hashem has consistently frustrated and upset these schemes. The nations, on the other hand, the ones who have tried to bring about our downfall, they know very well! They know how their plans have been ruined time and again, and how Hashem has protected us from their evil machinations. They know how "His lovingkindness was mighty over us, and the faithfulness of Hashem endures forever, Halleluyah!" (*Tehillim* 117:2).

Haggadas Chachmei Yerushalayim 147

If there are at least three participants at the Seder, the leader chants each of the following four verses aloud, and the others respond by repeating the first verse each time, followed by the succeeding verse, just as it is recited in shul.

הוֹדוּ לַיהוה כִּי טוֹב כִּי לְעוֹלָם חַסְדּוֹ:
יֹאמַר נָא יִשְׂרָאֵל כִּי לְעוֹלָם חַסְדּוֹ:
יֹאמְרוּ נָא בֵית אַהֲרֹן כִּי לְעוֹלָם חַסְדּוֹ:
יֹאמְרוּ נָא יִרְאֵי יהוה כִּי לְעוֹלָם חַסְדּוֹ:

Avow it to Hashem, that He is good,
that His lovingkindness endures forever.
Say it now, o' Yisrael,
that His lovingkindness endures forever.
Say it now, o' House of Aharon,
that His lovingkindness endures forever.
Say it now, o' those that fear Hashem,
that His lovingkindness endures forever (*ibid.* 118:1-4).

מִן הַמֵּצַר קָרָאתִי יָּהּ עָנָנִי בַמֶּרְחַב יָהּ: יהוה לִי לֹא אִירָא מַה יַּעֲשֶׂה לִי אָדָם: יהוה לִי בְּעֹזְרָי וַאֲנִי אֶרְאֶה בְשֹׂנְאָי: טוֹב לַחֲסוֹת בַּיהוה מִבְּטֹחַ בָּאָדָם: טוֹב לַחֲסוֹת בַּיהוה מִבְּטֹחַ בִּנְדִיבִים: כָּל גּוֹיִם סְבָבוּנִי בְּשֵׁם יהוה כִּי אֲמִילַם: סַבּוּנִי גַם סְבָבוּנִי בְּשֵׁם יהוה כִּי אֲמִילַם: סַבּוּנִי כִדְבוֹרִים דֹּעֲכוּ כְּאֵשׁ קוֹצִים בְּשֵׁם יהוה כִּי אֲמִילַם: דָּחֹה דְחִיתַנִי לִנְפּוֹל וַיהוה עֲזָרָנִי: עָזִּי וְזִמְרָת יָהּ וַיְהִי לִי לִישׁוּעָה: קוֹל רִנָּה וִישׁוּעָה בְּאָהֳלֵי צַדִּיקִים יְמִין יהוה עֹשָׂה חָיִל: יְמִין יהוה רוֹמֵמָה יְמִין יהוה עֹשָׂה חָיִל: לֹא אָמוּת כִּי אֶחְיֶה וַאֲסַפֵּר מַעֲשֵׂי יָהּ: יַסֹּר יִסְּרַנִּי יָּהּ וְלַמָּוֶת לֹא נְתָנָנִי: פִּתְחוּ לִי שַׁעֲרֵי צֶדֶק אָבֹא בָם אוֹדֶה יָהּ: זֶה הַשַּׁעַר לַיהוה צַדִּיקִים יָבֹאוּ בוֹ:

From out of the straits I called upon God; He answered me through the breadth of Divine relief. Hashem was for me; therefore I did not fear; what can man do to me? If Hashem is for me through my helpers, I shall calmly look upon those who hate me. It is better to look to Hashem than to trust in man. It is better to look to Hashem than to trust in noblemen. All the nations surrounded me; it was with the Name of Hashem that I faced them. They surrounded me; indeed, they closed in about me; it was with the Name of Hashem that I faced them. They surrounded me like bees; they were put out as the fire of thorns; it was with the Name of Hashem that I faced them. True, you have struck me again and again that I might fall, but Hashem helped me. God was my strength and song, and this has become my salvation. Therefore let the voice of rejoicing and salvation be in the tents of the righteous: "The right hand of Hashem does valiantly. The right hand of Hashem has ever proven exalted. The right hand of Hashem does valiantly still." I shall not die, but I shall live and recount the works of God. God has chastised me heavily, but He has not turned me over to death. Open for me the gates of righteousness; I will enter into them and avow [my debt to] God. This gate is Hashem's, the righteous shall enter into it.

God has chastised me heavily, but He has not turned me over to death.

The Maggid of Dubno's profound explanation of this verse began with the following parable.

A millionaire's wife gave birth to an only child, a daughter, when her husband was fairly advanced in age. Shortly after giving birth, the mother passed away. Beside himself with grief, the millionaire found no comfort except in his only daughter. He devoted himself exclusively to her upbringing. Nothing was too good or too expensive for his beloved daughter.

One night, the millionaire was thinking about all that had befallen him in his old age. All of a sudden, he began to worry that the very love he had for his daughter might lead him to pamper and spoil her. From that day on, he forced himself to treat her without partiality. He assigned certain chores to her around the house, and she was to perform them, on threat of punishment. Her allowance, as well, was kept to a bare minimum. Every penny had to be accounted for.

Years passed. His daughter was now twelve years old, and the millionaire fell ill. Fearing that her inheritance of millions of dollars might undo his careful upbringing, the millionaire appointed a close friend as guardian over her estate. "Although all that I own will belong to my daughter," the millionaire explained, "I forbid you to give her a penny until she marries. I want her to learn to take care of herself. She has to be independent and self-motivated." When he finished, he closed his eyes and passed away.

Arising from her mourning, the orphaned daughter found herself destitute and without a penny. She had no choice but to hire herself out as a maidservant in exchange for a meager salary. Her relatives approached her guardian and informed him of her dire circumstances. They described how hard she had to work, her gauntness, and her general frailty. He listened, but did nothing.

Winter arrived in full force. The orphan girl was dressed in rags. She did not have enough to buy anything new. The relatives again came and informed the guardian. "Buy her a coat for the winter," they pleaded. But he acted completely oblivious to their pleas.

The forced labor, the cold, and her general frailty all began to take their toll. The orphan girl fell ill. The relatives came to inform the guardian. Still, he remained steadfast. After all, her father had forbidden him to give her anything until she was married.

Her illness became critical. Her whole body began to burn with a high fever and she hovered between life and death. They ran to the guardian and begged him to summon a doctor. He didn't move. This time, however, they began shouting at him, "Insensitive fool! Is this what her father intended? Don't you understand that if she dies now, there won't be anyone left to get married or to receive the inheritance! You must spend some of that money now. Call the doctor!"

The millionaire is Hashem, and the daughter Yisrael, the soul, and mankind. The guardian is the Divine quality of justice. The relatives are the angels of mercy. This parable thus involves the concept of free will which is so central to Hashem's just governing of the universe. As much as Hashem wishes to bestow His love and perfection upon man, His own quality of justice demands

that man earn this reward through his own free will and desire. If he were compelled to choose perfection, he would not be its master and Hashem's purpose would not be fulfilled. It was therefore necessary that man be created with free will (*Derech Hashem* 1:3:1).

Like the millionaire, Hashem forces Himself, as it were, to hold His love back for our own good. Instead of bestowing His love upon us freely, which would be in keeping with His loving nature, He gives us the ability and the obligation to earn His closeness and love. Even when this Divine restraint results in our suffering, it is ultimately for our own benefit. As our Sages said, "Suffering purifies" (*Berachos* 5a), and "Suffering is beloved" (*Sanhedrin* 101a). Similar to an apple on a tree, man must grow slowly, and may not be plucked (i.e., saved) before he has reached full maturity through his own efforts.

But there is a point beyond which the demands of justice must be overruled. Suffering is justified only as long as the apple continues growing, as long as a person continues to be refined by suffering. When suffering threatens to snuff out a man's existence, however, Hashem will hasten to his rescue. David HaMelech referred to this when he prayed: "To the One Who grants victory — a psalm of David. How long, Hashem? Will You forget me forever? How long will You hide Your presence from me? How long must I seek counsel within myself [at night only to be plagued with] grief in my heart by day? How long will my enemy continue to raise himself up high above me? Look down and answer me, Hashem, my God! Enlighten my eyes lest I sleep the sleep of death! Lest my enemy say, 'I have prevailed against him,' and my oppressors rejoice when I stumble. As for me, I have trusted in Your lovingkindness, and my heart will rejoice in Your deliverance. I will sing to Hashem for bestowing [His love] upon me" (*Tehillim* 13). "Answer me quickly, Hashem, for my spirit has become depleted. Do not hide Your presence from me, lest I be like those who descend to the pit" (ibid. 143:7). This is also the meaning of David's thanksgiving prayer in *Hallel*: "God has chastised me heavily, but He has not turned me over to death" (ibid. 118:18).

Ohel Yaakov, *Vayechi*

I will avow [my debt to] You, for You have answered me ...

The key word in our verse is "anisani," from the verb "l'anos," which means

both "to afflict" and "to answer." As we saw above in the Haggadah, matzah is called "lechem oni." Although this is usually translated "bread of affliction," the Talmud (*Pesachim* 36a) also interprets it as "bread over which many answers are given." Thus, although our verse is usually translated, "I will thank You, for You answered me," it is possible to translate it as the Midrash does, "I will thank You, though You afflicted me" (*Shochar Tov, Tehillim* 118:21).

The only problem, the Maggid of Lublin pointed out, is this: We can understand thanking Hashem for answering us, but how are we to understand thanking Him for afflicting us? Wouldn't it be better not to suffer affliction in the first place? He answered with a parable.

A poor homeless beggar arrived in town wearing tattered clothes in the middle of the winter. He immediately set about going from door to door collecting pennies in order to buy some stale bread. At night, he would crouch down in the stairwell of an apartment building, seeking a minimum of shelter. No matter what he did, however, he ended up shivering from the cold. Eventually, the starvation and cold took their toll. He developed a fever and became deathly ill.

One morning, as the occupants of the building were leaving to go to work, they found him unconscious in corner of the stairwell. They immediately called for an ambulance to rush him to the hospital.

In the hospital, the poor beggar was cared for and revived. When he woke up, he found himself in a warm hospital room — wearing clean clothes, lying in a clean bed, and being fed delicious and healthy foods. Realizing his good fortune, he exclaimed, "Had I not fainted, I would still be suffering from cold and hunger!"

The same is true of us. As long as we are healthy, we are faced with numerous difficulties and tests which we must overcome on our own. When all our efforts have brought us to the brink of disaster, however, Hashem saves us with a tremendous outpouring of love and light. This is exactly what happened in Egypt. When we had descended to the forty-ninth level of impurity, Hashem "brought us forth from slavery into freedom, from sorrow into joy, from mourning into festivity, and from darkness into great light, and from subjugation into redemption" (*Haggadah*).

We are also promised that this will be the case in the future. It is thus written, "He that scattered Yisrael will gather them and safeguard them as a shepherd [safeguards] his flock. For Hashem will redeem Yaakov and free him from a mightier power. They will therefore come and sing on the heights of Tzion,

stone which the builders disdained has become the chief cornerstone. The... This is Hashem's doing; it is marvelous in our own eyes. This... Hashem has made this day; we will rejoice in Him and delight. Hashem... (*ibid.*, 5-24).

מָאֲסוּ הַבּוֹנִים הָיְתָה לְרֹאשׁ פִּנָּה: אבן מֵאֵת יהוה הָיְתָה זֹּאת הִיא נִפְלָאת בְּעֵינֵינוּ: מאת זֶה הַיּוֹם עָשָׂה יהוה נָגִילָה וְנִשְׂמְחָה בוֹ: זה

If there are at least three participants at the Seder, the leader chants each of the following four verses aloud, and the others repeat after him:

We beseech You, o' Hashem, grant new life.
We beseech You, o' Hashem, grant new life.
We beseech You, o' Hashem, cause us to prosper.
We beseech You, o' Hashem, cause us to prosper.
(*ibid.*, 25)

אָנָּא יהוה הוֹשִׁיעָה נָּא:
אָנָּא יהוה הוֹשִׁיעָה נָּא:
אָנָּא יהוה הַצְלִיחָה נָּא:
אָנָּא יהוה הַצְלִיחָה נָּא:

Let him who comes be blessed with the Name of Hashem; we have blessed you out of the House of Hashem. Let... Hashem is God when He has given us light; keep the festival offering bound with cords until you reach the high corners of the altar. Hashem... You are my God; I shall acknowledge You; o' my God, I will exalt You. You... Avow it to Hashem, that He is good, that His lovingkindness endures forever Avow...(*ibid.*, 26-29).

בָּרוּךְ הַבָּא בְּשֵׁם יהוה בֵּרַכְנוּכֶם מִבֵּית יהוה: ברוך אֵל יהוה וַיָּאֶר לָנוּ אִסְרוּ חַג בַּעֲבֹתִים עַד קַרְנוֹת הַמִּזְבֵּחַ: אל אֵלִי אַתָּה וְאוֹדֶךָּ אֱלֹהַי אֲרוֹמְמֶךָּ: אלי הוֹדוּ לַיהוה כִּי טוֹב כִּי לְעוֹלָם חַסְדּוֹ: הודו

All Your works shall proclaim Your praise, o' Hashem our God, and let Your devoted ones, the righteous who do Your will, and all Your people, the House of Yisrael, render homage with jubilation and bless and laud and extol and exalt, praise and sanctify and glorify Your Name, o' our King. For it is good to render You homage and it is pleasant to sing to Your Name, for from eternity to eternity You are God.

יְהַלְלוּךָ יהוה אֱלֹהֵינוּ כָּל מַעֲשֶׂיךָ וַחֲסִידֶיךָ צַדִּיקִים עוֹשֵׂי רְצוֹנֶךָ וְכָל עַמְּךָ בֵּית יִשְׂרָאֵל בְּרִנָּה יוֹדוּ וִיבָרְכוּ וִישַׁבְּחוּ וִיפָאֲרוּ וִירוֹמְמוּ וְיַעֲרִיצוּ וְיַקְדִּישׁוּ וְיַמְלִיכוּ אֶת שִׁמְךָ מַלְכֵּנוּ כִּי לְךָ טוֹב לְהוֹדוֹת וּלְשִׁמְךָ נָאֶה לְזַמֵּר כִּי מֵעוֹלָם וְעַד עוֹלָם אַתָּה אֵל:

Avow it to Hashem that He is good,
that His lovingkindness endures forever.
Avow it to the God of gods,
that His lovingkindness endures forever.
Avow it to the Master of masters,
that His lovingkindness endures forever.
To Him Who alone does great wonders,
that His lovingkindness endures forever.
To Him Who shapes the heavens with understanding,
that His lovingkindness endures forever.

הוֹדוּ לַיהוה כִּי טוֹב כִּי לְעוֹלָם חַסְדּוֹ:
הוֹדוּ לֵאלֹהֵי הָאֱלֹהִים כִּי לְעוֹלָם חַסְדּוֹ:
הוֹדוּ לַאֲדוֹנֵי הָאֲדוֹנִים כִּי לְעוֹלָם חַסְדּוֹ:
לְעֹשֵׂה נִפְלָאוֹת גְּדֹלוֹת לְבַדּוֹ כִּי לְעוֹלָם חַסְדּוֹ:
לְעֹשֵׂה הַשָּׁמַיִם בִּתְבוּנָה כִּי לְעוֹלָם חַסְדּוֹ:

and radiate [joy] over Hashem's bounty....Then young maidens will rejoice in dancing; youths and old men will rejoice together. For I [God] will turn their mourning into joy; I will comfort them and bring them happiness after their sorrow..." (*Yirmeyahu* 31:9-12).

Yerios Ha-Ohel, *Bo*

To Him Who firmly establishes the earth upon the waters, that His lovingkindness endures forever.	לְרוֹקַע הָאָרֶץ עַל הַמָּיִם כִּי לְעוֹלָם חַסְדּוֹ:
To Him Who fashions great lights, that His lovingkindness endures forever.	לְעֹשֵׂה אוֹרִים גְּדֹלִים כִּי לְעוֹלָם חַסְדּוֹ:
The sun for dominion by day, that His lovingkindness endures forever.	אֶת הַשֶּׁמֶשׁ לְמֶמְשֶׁלֶת בַּיּוֹם כִּי לְעוֹלָם חַסְדּוֹ:
The moon and the stars for dominions at night, that His lovingkindness endures forever.	אֶת הַיָּרֵחַ וְכוֹכָבִים לְמֶמְשְׁלוֹת בַּלָּיְלָה כִּי לְעוֹלָם חַסְדּוֹ:
To Him Who slays Egypt through their firstborn, that His lovingkindness endures forever.	לְמַכֵּה מִצְרַיִם בִּבְכוֹרֵיהֶם כִּי לְעוֹלָם חַסְדּוֹ:
And brought Yisrael out from their midst, that His lovingkindness endures forever.	וַיּוֹצֵא יִשְׂרָאֵל מִתּוֹכָם כִּי לְעוֹלָם חַסְדּוֹ:
With a strong hand and with an outstretched arm, that His lovingkindness endures forever.	בְּיָד חֲזָקָה וּבִזְרוֹעַ נְטוּיָה כִּי לְעוֹלָם חַסְדּוֹ:
To Him Who divides the Sea of Reeds into parts, that His lovingkindness endures forever.	לְגֹזֵר יַם סוּף לִגְזָרִים כִּי לְעוֹלָם חַסְדּוֹ:
And made Yisrael pass through the midst of it, that His lovingkindness endures forever.	וְהֶעֱבִיר יִשְׂרָאֵל בְּתוֹכוֹ כִּי לְעוֹלָם חַסְדּוֹ:
And poured out Pharaoh and his host into the Sea of Reeds, that His lovingkindness endures forever.	וְנִעֵר פַּרְעֹה וְחֵילוֹ בְיַם סוּף כִּי לְעוֹלָם חַסְדּוֹ:
To Him Who leads His people through the wilderness, that His lovingkindness endures forever.	לְמוֹלִיךְ עַמּוֹ בַּמִּדְבָּר כִּי לְעוֹלָם חַסְדּוֹ:
To Him Who smites great kings, that His lovingkindness endures forever.	לְמַכֵּה מְלָכִים גְּדֹלִים כִּי לְעוֹלָם חַסְדּוֹ:
And killed mighty kings, that His lovingkindness endures forever.	וַיַּהֲרֹג מְלָכִים אַדִּירִים כִּי לְעוֹלָם חַסְדּוֹ:
For Sichon, the king of the Amorites, that His lovingkindness endures forever.	לְסִיחוֹן מֶלֶךְ הָאֱמֹרִי כִּי לְעוֹלָם חַסְדּוֹ:
And for Og, the king of Bashan, that His lovingkindness endures forever.	וּלְעוֹג מֶלֶךְ הַבָּשָׁן כִּי לְעוֹלָם חַסְדּוֹ:

And poured out Pharoah and his host into the Sea of Reeds.

Said the Maggid of Dubno: Hashem's ways are not like those of human beings. A man who wishes to upset his opponent's schemes thinks of ways to prevent him from bringing them to fruition. Hashem, on the other hand, allows a person to bring his plans to fruition, and in doing so, falls into his own trap.

For instance, Pharaoh, after begging Moshe to take his people and leave on Pesach night, regretted sending them away and chased after them — only to meet his end at the Red Sea. The same occurred with Haman. He prepared a set of gallows for Mordechai, only to be hanged on it himself. In each case, Hashem used the person's own sinister schemes to set up the mechanism whereby he received his just punishment.

Shelomo Ha-Melech thus said, "A wicked man's sins shall ensnare him; he shall be bound with the cords of his own wrongdoing" (*Mishlei* 5:22). David Ha-Melech also wrote, "Nations have sunk into pits which they themselves have dug; their feet have been trapped in the same nets they so craftily hid for others...the wicked one is snared in the work of his own hands" (*Tehillim* 9:16-17). He therefore prayed, "O' let them be caught in the plots they themselves

have conceived" (ibid. 10:2).

The Maggid illustrated this principle with the following parable.

A burglar once succeeded in breaking into a wealthy man's mansion. Unable to crack the lock of the wall safe, filled with the wealthy man's silver, gold, diamonds, and other precious gems, he was forced to steal the entire thing. He carried it downstairs to the wealthy man's stables, placed it in the wealthy man's carriage, harnessed up four steeds, and drove off.

Before the burglar could get very far, one of the wealthy man's servants recognized his master's carriage with a stranger driving it. He realized at once that the carriage was being stolen. What did he do? He hailed the driver and signaled to him to stop, saying, "I see that you are a wealthy gentleman, and it is therefore not proper for you to drive your own coach. Since I am traveling in same direction, allow me to be your driver while you sit inside and enjoy the ride."

The burglar concurred, and the servant climbed into the driver's seat. As they drove away, the burglar congratulated himself on a job well done. Now he could relax and enjoy the trip, knowing that every second brought him closer to his destination. As the hours passed and they continued traveling, he fell soundly asleep. Having waited for this moment, the servant now began circling in order to return to his master's estate. Finally, at the right moment, the servant announced that they had arrived at their destination. The burglar roused with a smile on his lips, certain that they had indeed made it to the next city...

It is written, "[Hashem] will recompense a man for his deeds; He will bring about a man's downfall in accord with the way [he has chosen]" (*Iyov* 34:11). The first half of this verse teaches us that a person cannot escape Divine justice. In the end, he will have to pay for what he has done. The second half of this verse teaches us that, in addition to this, Hashem will arrange things so that the person's choice, in the end, will be used to undo him. Truly, this is the meaning of, "And poured out Pharaoh and his host into the Sea of Reeds, that His lovingkindness endures forever" (*Tehillim* 136:15).

Kol Rinah Vi'Yeshuah 60b

To Him Who leads His people through the wilderness, that His lovingkindness endures forever.

The Maggid of Dubno asked: What is the great kindness in leading us through

the desert? Wouldn't it have been better to forego the entire forty-year trek and enter directly into Eretz Yisrael on the wings of eagles? He answered with the following parable.

A master watchmaker was busy at his work, joining miniature flywheels, gears, and springs together with the help of extremely delicate and tiny screwdrivers. All of a sudden, a troop of gendarmes entered his workshop, arrested him on spurious charges, and threw him into jail. A group of detectives then went about conducting their search by callously tossing his precious tools every which way, turning his entire workshop into a scrap heap. In search of certain incriminating documents, when they found one of the watchmaker's drawers locked shut, they pried it open with his delicate tools, completely bending them out of shape. Not finding what they were looking for, they left the room in a shambles.

The watchmaker had been struck a double blow. His freedom had been denied him, and hostile hands had overtaken his workshop. There is, however, a difference between the two. As long as the watchmaker was in jail, he certainly suffered from being imprisoned. When he was taken for interrogation and tortured with agonizing torments to force him to admit to the crime he had never committed, his suffering knew no end. Still, at that time, he knew nothing and suspected nothing about the state of affairs he would later find in his workshop.

When the libel was refuted and revoked, he was released from jail and welcomed the end of his long imprisonment. The moment he returned to his workshop, however, his world turned black. He saw precious watches strewn all over the floor, tiny screws which had been carefully placed in special drawers lay everywhere, and delicate screwdrivers were bent and broken. He tried to make order out of chaos, gathering all the pieces together, but to no avail. He tried fixing one watch, but the screwdriver was bent, the screw did not fit, and the flywheel was warped. In total frustration, he broke down and cried bitterly. Months would pass until he was able to restore his workshop. Even then, he still would come across a misplaced screw, or a tool which could never be used again.

Clearly, each day that passed helped the memory of his suffering in jail to fade more and more, while the grief that confronted him daily in his workshop grew...

It is written, "The Egyptians ill-treated us, and they afflicted us" (*Devarim* 26:6). This verse includes both types of suffering endured by the watchmaker — spiritual and physical. "The Egyptians ill-treated us" can also be read,

And gave their land as an inheritance,
that His lovingkindness endures forever.
As an inheritance to Yisrael His servant,
that His lovingkindness endures forever.
Who remembered us in our lowly state,
because His lovingkindness endures forever.
And freed us from our oppressors,
because His lovingkindness endures forever.
Who gives food to all flesh,
since His lovingkindness endures forever.
Avow it to the God of Heaven,
that His lovingkindness endures forever (*ibid.*, 136).

וְנָתַן אַרְצָם לְנַחֲלָה כִּי לְעוֹלָם חַסְדּוֹ:
נַחֲלָה לְיִשְׂרָאֵל עַבְדּוֹ כִּי לְעוֹלָם חַסְדּוֹ:
שֶׁבְּשִׁפְלֵנוּ זָכַר לָנוּ כִּי לְעוֹלָם חַסְדּוֹ:
וַיִּפְרְקֵנוּ מִצָּרֵינוּ כִּי לְעוֹלָם חַסְדּוֹ:
נֹתֵן לֶחֶם לְכָל בָּשָׂר כִּי לְעוֹלָם חַסְדּוֹ:
הוֹדוּ לְאֵל הַשָּׁמָיִם כִּי לְעוֹלָם חַסְדּוֹ:

"they made us evil," causing us to descend to the forty-ninth level of spiritual impurity. "They afflicted us" physically as well, forcing us to engage in slave labor and backbreaking work.

During the entire time we spent in Egypt, we did not notice the spiritual ruin that we suffered. Only when we left Egypt and desired to elevate ourselves did we confront the extent of our own degradation. Only then did we encounter stumbling blocks everywhere we turned, for all of our spiritual tools had been warped by centuries of slavery, damaged by the Egyptian culture whose values we had internalized.

We can now understand the great kindness Hashem showed us by making us tarry in the desert for forty years. There, under the direct supervision of Moshe, surrounded by clouds of Divine glory, and constant witnesses to the miraculous providence that accompanied us everywhere we went, we slowly began to regain our spiritual health and vitality.

This is the meaning of the verse, "I will deliver you from your forced labor in Egypt, and free you from their slavery. I will liberate you with My outstretched arm, and with great acts of judgment. I will take you to Myself as a nation, and I will be your sole God. You will then know that I, the Eternal God, am your Lord, the One who has brought you out from under Egyptian servitude" (*Shemos* 6:6). That is, after redemption from physical oppression and forced labor, a long process of spiritual improvement and cleansing took place which culminated in complete spiritual liberation. It is for this that we thank the One "Who leads His people through the wilderness, that His lovingkindness endures forever" (*Tehillim* 136:16).

Ohel Yaakov, *Beshallach*

THE soul of every living thing shall bless Your Name, o' Hashem our God, and the spirit of all flesh shall ever glorify and exalt Your remembrance, o' our King. From the remotest past to the most distant future, You are God, and beside You we have no King, Who redeems, and saves, delivers and rescues, sustains and has compassion; in all times of trouble and distress we have no King but You. God of the first and of the last, God of all creatures, Master of all that is begotten, proclaimed in an abundance of praises, Who guides His world with lovingkindness and His creatures with compassion. And Hashem neither slumbers nor sleeps; it is He, rather, Who awakens those who sleep, Who rouses those that are stunned, Who gives speech to the mute, Who sets free those that are bound, supports the falling and raises up those that are bowed down. To You and to You alone do we avow thanks. Though our mouths were filled with song as the sea, and our tongues with joy's outpouring as the swell of its waves, and our lips with praise as the expanse of heaven, and though our eyes were brilliant like the sun and moon, our hands spread out like the eagles of the heavens, and our feet as light as the deer — we would still be unable to thank You, Hashem our God and God of our fathers, and to bless Your Name for even one thousandth of the myriad favors which You have bestowed upon our fathers and upon us. You have redeemed us from Egypt, o' Hashem our God, and freed us from the house of slavery; You have fed us in famine and satisfied us in plenty. You have delivered us from the sword, freed us from pestilence, and relieved us from severe and lasting diseases. Until now Your compassion has helped us, and Your kindnesses have not forsaken us, so Hashem our God, forsake us never. Therefore the limbs which You have apportioned for us, the spirit and soul which You have breathed into our nostrils and the tongue which You have put into our mouth, shall all render homage, bless, praise, glorify, exalt and declare the power, the holiness and dominion of Your Name, o' our King. For every mouth shall render You homage, every tongue shall swear You allegiance, every knee shall bend before You, and all that stands upright shall fall down before You; all hearts shall fear You, and all the inmost passions shall sing praises to Your Name, even as it is written, "All my limbs shall say, 'O' Hashem, who is like You,

נִשְׁמַת כָּל חַי תְּבָרֵךְ אֶת שִׁמְךָ יהוה אֱלֹהֵינוּ וְרוּחַ כָּל בָּשָׂר תְּפָאֵר וּתְרוֹמֵם זִכְרְךָ מַלְכֵּנוּ תָּמִיד. מִן הָעוֹלָם וְעַד הָעוֹלָם אַתָּה אֵל וּמִבַּלְעָדֶיךָ אֵין לָנוּ מֶלֶךְ גּוֹאֵל וּמוֹשִׁיעַ פּוֹדֶה וּמַצִּיל וּמְפַרְנֵס וּמְרַחֵם. בְּכָל עֵת צָרָה וְצוּקָה אֵין לָנוּ מֶלֶךְ אֶלָּא אָתָּה. אֱלֹהֵי הָרִאשׁוֹנִים וְהָאַחֲרוֹנִים אֱלוֹהַּ כָּל בְּרִיּוֹת אֲדוֹן כָּל תּוֹלָדוֹת הַמְּהֻלָּל בְּרוֹב הַתִּשְׁבָּחוֹת הַמְנַהֵג עוֹלָמוֹ בְּחֶסֶד וּבְרִיּוֹתָיו בְּרַחֲמִים. וַיהוה לֹא יָנוּם וְלֹא יִישָׁן הַמְעוֹרֵר יְשֵׁנִים וְהַמֵּקִיץ נִרְדָּמִים וְהַמֵּשִׂיחַ אִלְּמִים וְהַמַּתִּיר אֲסוּרִים וְהַסּוֹמֵךְ נוֹפְלִים וְהַזּוֹקֵף כְּפוּפִים. לְךָ לְבַדְּךָ אֲנַחְנוּ מוֹדִים. אִלּוּ פִינוּ מָלֵא שִׁירָה כַּיָּם וּלְשׁוֹנֵנוּ רִנָּה כַּהֲמוֹן גַּלָּיו וְשִׂפְתוֹתֵינוּ שֶׁבַח כְּמֶרְחֲבֵי רָקִיעַ וְעֵינֵינוּ מְאִירוֹת כַּשֶּׁמֶשׁ וְכַיָּרֵחַ וְיָדֵינוּ פְרוּשׂוֹת כְּנִשְׁרֵי שָׁמָיִם וְרַגְלֵינוּ קַלּוֹת כָּאַיָּלוֹת אֵין אֲנַחְנוּ מַסְפִּיקִים לְהוֹדוֹת לְךָ יהוה אֱלֹהֵינוּ וֵאלֹהֵי אֲבוֹתֵינוּ וּלְבָרֵךְ אֶת שְׁמֶךָ עַל אַחַת מֵאָלֶף אֶלֶף אַלְפֵי אֲלָפִים וְרִבֵּי רְבָבוֹת פְּעָמִים הַטּוֹבוֹת שֶׁעָשִׂיתָ עִם אֲבוֹתֵינוּ וְעִמָּנוּ. מִמִּצְרַיִם גְּאַלְתָּנוּ יהוה אֱלֹהֵינוּ וּמִבֵּית עֲבָדִים פְּדִיתָנוּ בְּרָעָב זַנְתָּנוּ וּבְשָׂבָע כִּלְכַּלְתָּנוּ מֵחֶרֶב הִצַּלְתָּנוּ וּמִדֶּבֶר מִלַּטְתָּנוּ וּמֵחֳלָיִם רָעִים וְנֶאֱמָנִים דִּלִּיתָנוּ. עַד הֵנָּה עֲזָרוּנוּ רַחֲמֶיךָ וְלֹא עֲזָבוּנוּ חֲסָדֶיךָ וְאַל תִּטְּשֵׁנוּ יהוה אֱלֹהֵינוּ לָנֶצַח. עַל כֵּן אֵבָרִים שֶׁפִּלַּגְתָּ בָּנוּ וְרוּחַ וּנְשָׁמָה שֶׁנָּפַחְתָּ בְּאַפֵּינוּ וְלָשׁוֹן אֲשֶׁר שַׂמְתָּ בְּפִינוּ הֵן הֵם יוֹדוּ וִיבָרְכוּ וִישַׁבְּחוּ וִיפָאֲרוּ וִירוֹמְמוּ וְיַעֲרִיצוּ וְיַקְדִּישׁוּ וְיַמְלִיכוּ אֶת שִׁמְךָ מַלְכֵּנוּ. כִּי כָל פֶּה לְךָ יוֹדֶה וְכָל לָשׁוֹן לְךָ תִשָּׁבַע וְכָל בֶּרֶךְ לְךָ תִכְרַע וְכָל קוֹמָה לְפָנֶיךָ תִשְׁתַּחֲוֶה. וְכָל לְבָבוֹת יִירָאוּךָ וְכָל קֶרֶב וּכְלָיוֹת יְזַמְּרוּ לִשְׁמֶךָ. כַּדָּבָר שֶׁכָּתוּב כָּל עַצְמֹתַי תֹּאמַרְנָה יהוה מִי כָמוֹךָ

מַצִּיל עָנִי מֵחָזָק מִמֶּנּוּ וְעָנִי וְאֶבְיוֹן מִגּוֹזְלוֹ. מִי יִדְמֶה לָּךְ וּמִי יִשְׁוֶה לָּךְ וּמִי יַעֲרָךְ לָךְ הָאֵל הַגָּדוֹל הַגִּבּוֹר וְהַנּוֹרָא אֵל עֶלְיוֹן קוֹנֵה שָׁמַיִם וָאָרֶץ. נְהַלֶּלְךָ וּנְשַׁבֵּחֲךָ וּנְפָאֶרְךָ וּנְבָרֵךְ אֶת שֵׁם קָדְשֶׁךָ כָּאָמוּר לְדָוִד בָּרְכִי נַפְשִׁי אֶת יהוה וְכָל קְרָבַי אֶת שֵׁם קָדְשׁוֹ:

Who delivers the poor from one that is stronger than him, the poor and the defenseless from one who would rob him?'" Who is like You, who is equal to You, and who can be compared to You, o' great, strong, and awesome God, the Most High God, the Owner of heaven and earth? We shall proclaim Your praise, laud You, glorify You and bless Your Holy Name, even as it is said: "By David. Bless Hashem, o' my soul, and all that is within me, bless His holy Name."

Great, strong, and awesome God.

The Anshei Knesses Ha-Gedolah (Men of the Great Assembly) were a body of 120 great prophets and Sages who flourished at the onset of the Second Temple era. Led by Ezra and Nechemyah, they not only rebuilt the Second Temple but the entire Jewish nation at a very crucial time in our history.

Under Ezra and Nechemyah's leadership, the Anshei Knesses Ha-Gedolah enacted a number of important decrees in order to nurture and preserve the Jewish People with a powerful awareness of Hashem's providence in their communal and personal lives. They knew that the time would come when the Jewish People would be scattered to every corner of the globe. They therefore saw their task as one of assuring the spiritual survival of the Jewish People until the coming of the Mashiach. Besides building for the present, therefore, by rebuilding Yerushalayim and the Second Temple, they insured the future by finalizing the text of the Tanach and by composing the *Shemoneh Esreh*. In fact, they were named after a specific phrase which appears once in the book of *Nechemyah* and once in the *Shemoneh Esreh*. They were called the Anshei Knesses Ha-Gedolah, "the Assembly that restored the honor of God's greatness" because they addressed Hashem as the "great, strong, and awesome God" (*Nechemyah* 9:32; *Shemoneh Esreh*).

Our tradition (*Yoma* 69b) thus records:

> Why were they called the Anshei Knesses Ha-Gedolah? Because they restored the crown to its original splendor. How? Moshe said, "[Hashem] is the great, the mighty, and the awesome God" (*Devarim* 10:17). Yirmeyahu came and said: Strangers are dancing in His Sanctuary! Where is His awesomeness? [If Hashem's awesomeness had been so concealed that strangers could enter and not die on the spot,] he would delete this attribute and say, "O' great and mighty God!" (*Yirmeyahu* 32:18). Daniel came and said: Strangers are subjugating His children in exile! Where is His might? He therefore deleted this attribute when he said, "O' great and awesome God!" (*Daniel* 9:4). But they [the Anshei Knesses Ha-Gedolah] came and said: On the contrary, this itself attests to His awesomeness, this itself

attests to His might! If it were not for the awe of the Blessed Holy One, how could this tiny nation survive! [Thus, they reinstated what Moshe had said; they taught us to address Hashem as the "great, the strong, and awesome God."]

The Maggid of Dubno explained this tradition with the following parable: A man once sent his son to learn in a yeshivah in a neighboring town. He made all the necessary arrangements and asked his son's host to provide the boy with food and lodging. Within a short time of his arrival, however, the boy fell ill and lost his appetite. For two months, his host continued caring for him in this condition, and finally sent a message to his father to bring him home.

The father came to take his son, and the host asked for the money that was coming to him.

"What makes you think that you have any payment coming to you?" asked the father. "After all, my son was ill for the majority of the time that he spent here. He hardly ate a thing!"

"The truth is," the host replied, "you should pay me double the original sum. Your son is not the first yeshivah student to stay with us. In the past, our boys have spent the majority of the day learning Torah, only returning once or twice a day to rest and eat. They eat from the same pot and drink from the same pitcher as the members of my family. When your son fell ill, he became a burden for all of us. He spent the entire day at home, requiring the attendance of doctors and the purchase of expensive medicines. My wife worked hard cooking especially healthy foods for him. One of our servants spent a good part of his working day attending to your son's needs. If you would take all this into account, you would pay me double the original amount we agreed upon!"

When we lived in our beloved land, Hashem performed open and revealed miracles for us. Many ancient nations witnessed and/or knew of Hashem's greatness, His invincible might, and His awesome wonders — all aspects of the providence with which He supervises the history of the Jewish People, and by extension, all of creation.

Something changed when we were exiled from our land. The fact that we were ruled by foreign nations made it seem like Hashem had withdrawn His special providence from us. It is for this reason that Yirmeyahu and Daniel, who lived at the end of the First Temple period and saw their people taken into captivity by Nevuchadnetzar, deleted mention of Hashem's greatness and awesomeness.

Seventy years after the destruction of the First Temple, Hashem "remem-

O' God, in the abundance of Your might, great in the glory of Your Name, almighty in eternity and feared for Your awesome acts, the King Who, highly exalted, is seated upon a throne.

Dwelling in eternity, His Name is exalted and holy. And it is written: "Exult, o' righteous ones, in beholding Hashem; it behooves the upright to sing praises of the acts that reveal His might." By the mouth of the upright there is song in Your praise, by the words of the righteous You are blessed, by the tongue of Your devoted ones You are extolled, and in the midst of the holy You are sanctified.

And in the assemblies of the tens of thousands of Your people Yisrael, Your Name, o' our King, is glorified in every generation with fervent emotion. For it is the duty of all creatures to avow thanks before You, o' Hashem our God and God of our fathers, and to praise Your mighty acts, to laud, glorify, exalt and

הָאֵל בְּתַעֲצֻמוֹת עֻזֶּךָ הַגָּדוֹל בִּכְבוֹד שְׁמֶךָ הַגִּבּוֹר לָנֶצַח וְהַנּוֹרָא בְּנוֹרְאוֹתֶיךָ הַמֶּלֶךְ הַיּוֹשֵׁב עַל כִּסֵּא רָם וְנִשָּׂא:

שׁוֹכֵן עַד מָרוֹם וְקָדוֹשׁ שְׁמוֹ. וְכָתוּב רַנְּנוּ צַדִּיקִים בַּיהוה לַיְשָׁרִים נָאוָה תְהִלָּה: בְּפִי יְשָׁרִים תִּתְהַלָּל וּבְדִבְרֵי צַדִּיקִים תִּתְבָּרַךְ וּבִלְשׁוֹן חֲסִידִים תִּתְרוֹמָם וּבְקֶרֶב קְדוֹשִׁים תִּתְקַדָּשׁ:

וּבְמַקְהֲלוֹת רִבְבוֹת עַמְּךָ בֵּית יִשְׂרָאֵל בְּרִנָּה יִתְפָּאַר שִׁמְךָ מַלְכֵּנוּ בְּכָל דּוֹר וָדוֹר. שֶׁכֵּן חוֹבַת כָּל הַיְצוּרִים לְפָנֶיךָ יהוה אֱלֹהֵינוּ וֵאלֹהֵי אֲבוֹתֵינוּ לְהוֹדוֹת לְהַלֵּל לְשַׁבֵּחַ לְפָאֵר לְרוֹמֵם לְהַדֵּר לְבָרֵךְ

bered" His people and allowed them to return to their beloved land under the leadership of Ezra and Nechemyah. Looking back at the exile, they realized that Hashem had never abandoned them. On the contrary, they taught, Hashem's greatness and awesomeness are magnified seventy times over when one contemplates the magnitude of Divine Providence needed to protect the Jewish People in their exile!

This, then, is the meaning of the verse, "For I am Hashem, I do not change; therefore, O' children of Yaakov, you will never be destroyed!" (*Malachi* 3:6). That is, Hashem does not change. Despite all appearances to the contrary, He remains infinitely great, supremely mighty and wondrously awesome at all times. How can we be sure? The proof is clear: While all the great ancient civilizations have disappeared and been forgotten, the people of Yisrael remains eternally alive!

True, Yisrael is likened to a single defenseless sheep surrounded by seventy bloodthirsty wolves (*Pesikta Rabbasi* 9:2). True, the author of the Haggadah has already told us, "For not just one has risen up against us to destroy us, but in every single generation they rise up against us to destroy us!" But if, despite this, the children of Yaakov have never been and can never be destroyed...if, despite this, the Blessed Holy One has saved us and will continue to save us from their clutches, then the great miracle of Jewish existence becomes ever more obvious, and Hashem's mastery and supervision over nature and history is greater than ever. This is the meaning of the host's statement, "If you would take all this extra care and providence into account, you would pay me double, i.e., double the original amount of honor due My Name!"

Kochav Mi'Yaakov, *Haftarah of Shabbos Ha-Gadol*

לְעַלֵּה וּלְקַלֵּס עַל כָּל דִּבְרֵי שִׁירוֹת וְתִשְׁבְּחוֹת דָּוִד בֶּן יִשַׁי עַבְדְּךָ מְשִׁיחֶךָ:

proclaim Your might, to bless, to extol You and to celebrate You in keeping with all the words and songs of praise by Your servant David, the son of Yishai, Your Anointed.

יִשְׁתַּבַּח שִׁמְךָ לָעַד מַלְכֵּנוּ הָאֵל הַמֶּלֶךְ הַגָּדוֹל וְהַקָּדוֹשׁ בַּשָּׁמַיִם וּבָאָרֶץ כִּי לְךָ נָאֶה יהוה אֱלֹהֵינוּ וֵאלֹהֵי אֲבוֹתֵינוּ שִׁיר וּשְׁבָחָה הַלֵּל וְזִמְרָה עֹז וּמֶמְשָׁלָה נֶצַח גְּדֻלָּה וּגְבוּרָה תְּהִלָּה וְתִפְאֶרֶת קְדֻשָּׁה וּמַלְכוּת בְּרָכוֹת וְהוֹדָאוֹת מֵעַתָּה וְעַד־עוֹלָם. בָּרוּךְ אַתָּה יהוה אֵל מֶלֶךְ גָּדוֹל בַּתִּשְׁבָּחוֹת אֵל הַהוֹדָאוֹת אֲדוֹן הַנִּפְלָאוֹת הַבּוֹחֵר בְּשִׁירֵי זִמְרָה מֶלֶךְ אֵל חֵי הָעוֹלָמִים:

Praised be Your Name forever, o' our King, God, the King Who is great and holy in Heaven and on earth. For to You, o' Hashem our God and God of our fathers, pertain song and laud, praise and hymn, strength and dominion, victory, greatness, and might, renown and glory, holiness and kingship, blessings and [utterances of] thanksgiving henceforth and unto eternity. Blessed be You Hashem, God and King, great in hymns of praise, God of thanksgivings, Master of wonders, Who takes pleasure in hymns, King, God, the Life of all times.

In most homes the fourth cup is drunk immediately after Hallel, followed by nirtzah and then, the Hadgadah songs. In some Ashkenazic communities, however, the songs are now sung until after ki lo naeh, (pages 250-51) and then the wine is drunk, followed by nirtzah and the remainder of the songs.

One should have in mind that it is his intention to fulfill the requirement of drinking the fourth of the four cups of wine.

בָּרוּךְ אַתָּה יהוה אֱלֹהֵינוּ מֶלֶךְ הָעוֹלָם בּוֹרֵא פְּרִי הַגָּפֶן:

Blessed be you, Hashem our God, King of the universe, Who creates the fruit of the vine.

The entire amount of the fourth cup is drunk (to enable one to recite the berachah after drinking wine), within the required period of time, while reclining to the left.

בָּרוּךְ אַתָּה יהוה אֱלֹהֵינוּ מֶלֶךְ הָעוֹלָם עַל הַגֶּפֶן וְעַל פְּרִי הַגֶּפֶן וְעַל תְּנוּבַת הַשָּׂדֶה וְעַל אֶרֶץ חֶמְדָּה טוֹבָה וּרְחָבָה שֶׁרָצִיתָ וְהִנְחַלְתָּ לַאֲבוֹתֵינוּ לֶאֱכוֹל מִפִּרְיָהּ וְלִשְׂבּוֹעַ מִטּוּבָהּ. רַחֵם נָא יהוה אֱלֹהֵינוּ עַל יִשְׂרָאֵל עַמֶּךָ וְעַל יְרוּשָׁלַיִם עִירֶךָ וְעַל צִיּוֹן מִשְׁכַּן כְּבוֹדֶךָ וְעַל מִזְבְּחֶךָ וְעַל הֵיכָלֶךָ וּבְנֵה יְרוּשָׁלַיִם עִיר הַקּוֹדֶשׁ בִּמְהֵרָה בְיָמֵינוּ וְהַעֲלֵנוּ לְתוֹכָהּ וְשַׂמְּחֵנוּ בְּבִנְיָנָהּ וְנֹאכַל מִפִּרְיָהּ וְנִשְׂבַּע מִטּוּבָהּ וּנְבָרֶכְךָ עָלֶיהָ בִּקְדֻשָּׁה וּבְטָהֳרָה (בשבת וּרְצֵה וְהַחֲלִיצֵנוּ בְּיוֹם הַשַּׁבָּת הַזֶּה) וְשַׂמְּחֵנוּ בְּיוֹם חַג הַמַּצּוֹת הַזֶּה כִּי אַתָּה יהוה טוֹב וּמֵטִיב לַכֹּל וְנוֹדֶה לְּךָ עַל הָאָרֶץ וְעַל פְּרִי הַגָּפֶן:* בָּרוּךְ אַתָּה יהוה עַל הָאָרֶץ וְעַל פְּרִי הַגָּפֶן:*

Blessed be You, Hashem our God, King of the universe, for the vine and the fruit of the vine; for the produce of the field and for the desirable, good and spacious land which You have given to our fathers as an inheritance in favor, that they might eat of its fruit and be satisfied with its goodness. Have compassion, Hashem our God, upon Your people Yisrael, upon Yerushalayim, Your City, and upon Tzion, the Abode of Your glory, upon Your altar and upon Your Temple, and rebuild Yerushalayim, the city of holiness,* speedily in our days; bring us up into it and make us rejoice in its rebuilding. May we eat of its fruit and be satisfied with its goodness so that we may bless You for it in holiness and purity. (*On Shabbos add: And be pleased to fortify us on this Shabbos day.*) And gladden us on this day of the Festival of Unleavened Bread, for You, Hashem, are good and do good to all. To You we give thanks for the land and for the fruit of the vine.* Blessed be You, Hashem, for the land and for the fruit of the vine.*

*For wine or grape juice from Eretz Yisrael substitute: fruit of *her* vine.

*For wine or grape juice from Eretz Yisrael substitute: וְעַל פְּרִי גַפְנָהּ

Nirtzah

נִרְצָה

חֲסַל סִדּוּר פֶּסַח כְּהִלְכָתוֹ. כְּכָל מִשְׁפָּטוֹ וְחֻקָּתוֹ. כַּאֲשֶׁר זָכִינוּ לְסַדֵּר אוֹתוֹ. כֵּן נִזְכֶּה לַעֲשׂוֹתוֹ: זָךְ שׁוֹכֵן מְעוֹנָה. קוֹמֵם קְהַל עֲדַת מִי מָנָה. בְּקָרוֹב נַהֵל נִטְעֵי כַנָּה. פְּדוּיִם לְצִיּוֹן בְּרִנָּה:

THE order of the Pesach is complete, according to its laws, all of its ordinances and statutes. Just as we merited to perform it, so may we merit to offer the sacrifice in deed. O' Pure One, Who abides on high, uplift the assembly of the community who cannot be counted (Yisrael). Soon, and in joy, may You lead the offshoots of the stock which You have planted, redeemed, to Tzion.

לַשָּׁנָה הַבָּאָה בִּירוּשָׁלָיִם:

Next Year May We Be in Yerushalayim!

וּבְכֵן וַיְהִי בַּחֲצִי הַלַּיְלָה

Vayehi Bachatzi Halaylah

And It Came To Pass at Midnight

אָז רוֹב נִסִּים הִפְלֵאתָ בַּלַּיְלָה.
בְּרֹאשׁ אַשְׁמוֹרֶת זֶה הַלַּיְלָה.
גֵּר צֶדֶק נִצַּחְתּוֹ כְּנֶחֱלַק לוֹ לַיְלָה.
וַיְהִי בַּחֲצִי הַלַּיְלָה:

Of old You worked so many miracles at night;
At the start of the watches, this very night;
To the righteous convert [Avraham] You gave victory when [his army] divided for him in the night;
And it came to pass at midnight.

דַּנְתָּ מֶלֶךְ גְּרָר בַּחֲלוֹם הַלַּיְלָה.
הִפְחַדְתָּ אֲרַמִּי בְּאֶמֶשׁ לַיְלָה.
וַיָּשַׂר יִשְׂרָאֵל לְמַלְאָךְ וַיּוּכַל לוֹ לַיְלָה.
וַיְהִי בַּחֲצִי הַלַּיְלָה:

You judged the King of Gerar in a dream in the night;
Frightened [Laban] the Aramean the preceding night;
And Yisrael [Yaakov] fought an angel and overcame him in the night;
And it came to pass at midnight.

זֶרַע בְּכוֹרֵי פַתְרוֹס מָחַצְתָּ בַּחֲצִי הַלַּיְלָה.
חֵילָם לֹא מָצְאוּ בְּקוּמָם בַּלַּיְלָה.
טִיסַת נְגִיד חֲרוֹשֶׁת סִלִּיתָ בְכוֹכְבֵי לַיְלָה.
וַיְהִי בַּחֲצִי הַלַּיְלָה:

The firstborn sons of Pasros [Egypt] You crushed at midnight;
Their host they never found as they arose in the night;
The soaring flight of [Sisra] the prince of Charoshes You trampled by the stars of night;
And it came to pass at midnight.

יָעַץ מְחָרֵף לְנוֹפֵף אִוּוּי הוֹבַשְׁתָּ פְגָרָיו בַּלַּיְלָה.
כָּרַע בֵּל וּמַצָּבוֹ בְּאִישׁוֹן לַיְלָה.
לְאִישׁ חֲמוּדוֹת נִגְלָה רָז חֲזוֹת לַיְלָה.
וַיְהִי בַּחֲצִי הַלַּיְלָה:

Blaspheming [Sancheriv] schemed to raise his hand against [Yerushalayim] the cherished Abode;
You let his [soldiers'] carcasses rot in the night;
Bel [Babylon's god] and its pedestal fell prostrate in the dark of the night;
To [Daniel] the man of [Your] delight was revealed the secret of the [king's] vision of night;
And it came to pass at midnight.

מִשְׁתַּכֵּר בִּכְלֵי קֹדֶשׁ נֶהֱרַג בּוֹ בַּלַּיְלָה.
נוֹשַׁע מִבּוֹר אֲרָיוֹת פּוֹתֵר בִּעֲתוּתֵי לַיְלָה.
שִׂנְאָה נָטַר אֲגָגִי וְכָתַב סְפָרִים בַּלַּיְלָה.
וַיְהִי בַּחֲצִי הַלַּיְלָה:

[Belshatzar] drank himself drunk with the sacred [Temple] vessels, was slain that very night;
[Daniel] saved from the lion's den, interpreted the fearful phantasms of night;
[Haman] the Agagi nursed hatred in his heart and wrote [lethal] edicts in the night;
And it came to pass at midnight.

You aroused Your victory over him by disturbing [Achashverosh's] sleep	at night;	לַיְלָה.	עוֹרַרְתָּ נִצְחֲךָ עָלָיו בְּנֶדֶד שְׁנַת
The wine-press [of our enemies' destruction] You will tread for [Jewry that asks]		מִלַּיְלָה.	פּוּרָה תִדְרוֹךְ לְשׁוֹמֵר מַה
"Watchman! What will be	of the night?"	לַיְלָה.	צָרַח כַּשּׁוֹמֵר וְשָׂח אָתָא בֹקֶר וְגַם
[God] will exclaim like the watchman and say, "Morning has come [for Jewry] and also [for Esav]	the night";		
And it came to pass at midnight.			וַיְהִי בַּחֲצִי הַלַּיְלָה:

[God] will exclaim like the watchman and say, "Morning has come [for Jewry] and also [for Esav] the night."

The Maggid of Dubno likened the Jewish People's lengthy exile to a king's minister who had been unjustly imprisoned. Some of the king's advisors had slandered the minister, falsely accusing him of not having fulfilled his duties. The king agreed to conduct an inquiry. He began by ordering the minister to be placed in administrative detention. Soldiers were sent in the pre-dawn hours to arrest him. They found the minister sleeping soundly on his bed. They attempted to arouse him, but to no avail. They then carried him that way to the royal prison, and locked him in a dark dungeon.

A number of hours passed and the minister opened his eyes. All he saw was darkness. "It must still be nighttime," he muttered to himself, "I'll simply fall back asleep until dawn." He fell back asleep and woke up again at approximately noon. "What is going on here? This is the second time I've woken up tonight, and it is still dark!" He closed his eyes again and tried to fall back asleep...

The king, meanwhile, was waiting in his palace for the minister to request a meeting with him in order to disprove the accusations that had been leveled against him. The minister, however, was still sleeping...

The king could wait no longer. He thought to himself: Why doesn't the minister ask to be released? Why doesn't he shake heaven and earth? Could this be an admission of guilt?"

The king finally went to the prison. Placing his ear against the door of the dungeon, he overheard the minister saying to himself, "This night is unending! When will morning finally come?"

The king could hold back no longer. "Fool!" he shouted, entering the dungeon. "Do you really think you are still lying in your comfortable bedroom? Do you imagine that the sun is late in shining through your window? Don't you understand that you have been cast into a dark dungeon, and that not only has the morning light already dawned, but it is already noontime? Are you going to continue to lie here? Stand up and beg to have your case brought

O' bring the [Mashiach's] day [of Redemption] which is neither day nor night;	לַיְלָה.	קָרֵב יוֹם אֲשֶׁר הוּא לֹא יוֹם וְלֹא
Make it known, exalted God, that Yours is the day, and even Yours the night;	הַלַּיְלָה	רָם הוֹדַע כִּי לְךָ הַיּוֹם אַף לְךָ
Appoint sentries for Your city, for all the day and all the night;	הַלַּיְלָה.	שׁוֹמְרִים הַפְקֵד לְעִירְךָ כָּל הַיּוֹם וְכָל
Brighten as with the light of day the darkness of night;	לַיְלָה.	תָּאִיר כְּאוֹר יוֹם חֶשְׁכַּת
And it came to pass at midnight.		וַיְהִי בַּחֲצִי הַלַּיְלָה:

before me, so that you can prove your innocence and I can restore you to your post!"

Whereas redemption is likened to the dawn, our long and bitter exile is likened to nighttime, as it is written, "It is good to thank You, Hashem...to declare Your love in the morning, and Your faithfulness by night" (*Tehillim* 92:3), and to a dungeon, as it is written, "He has laid me down in dark places, like those who have been dead for ages" (*Eichah* 3:6). This being the case, we could justifiably ask, "Watchman! What of the night, and what of the morning?" (*Yeshayahu* 21:11), that is, "Hashem, why has our night exile lasted so long? Why doesn't the morning dawn and redemption come?" The Watchman answers, "Morning redemption is imminent [for the upright]; so is the punishment of the night [for the wicked]. If you will request, request! Return, come!" (ibid. 21:12; Rashi ibid.).

Like the king's minister, we must know that many special hours have come and gone, especially auspicious moments during which the redemption could and might have come. Because we were asleep, unaware of the gravity of the moment, oblivious to the ways of Divine Providence, we did not pray enough. We did not realize that redemption depends on our awakening, and on how much we want the exile to end.

Kochav Mi'Yaakov, *Haftarah of Ki Sissa*

O' bring the [Mashiach's] day [of Redemption] which is neither day nor night.

We ask here that Hashem accelerate history and hasten the dawn of redemption. This is based on His promise to us through His prophet, "In its due time, I, Hashem, will hasten it" (*Yeshayahu* 60:22).

The Maggid of Dubno commented: Hashem made us take an oath, saying, "You shall not arouse the desire [for redemption] until the time is right" (*Shir Ha-Shirim* 2:7; *Kesuvos* 110a). If this means that we are to wait patiently until the end of the exile, doesn't this contradict our request that Hashem hasten it? How are we to distinguish between the two? He answered with the following parable.

A small town merchant arrived in the big city to purchase merchandise. He stayed at an inn where the custom was to serve meals at preset times during the day. One morning, the merchant left the inn early and returned before lunchtime. He turned to the innkeeper and asked to be served lunch a little earlier in order to be on time for his noon appointment.

"It's early," replied the innkeeper. "I have just put the food in the oven to cook. It's still raw."

"Serve it to me as it is," the merchant insisted, "for I cannot be late for my appointment."

He did as he was asked, setting the table and serving the meal. The merchant tasted the food, but it was almost completely inedible.

"He was right," he grumbled to himself, "the food is hard, cold, and tasteless." He got up from his table, hungry and disappointed. On the way out, he couldn't help commenting to the cook, "I am accustomed to eating tasty foods..."

"I told you it would have been better to wait," he replied. "Then you wouldn't say such things about my food!"

The next day, the merchant had no other appointments. While he was relaxing under a tree just outside the inn, the innkeeper came up to him and asked him if he would like to eat right then. The merchant glanced at his watch. It was exactly the same hour as the day before!

"Would I like to eat? Certainly not!" he blurted out. "I shall never again subject myself to eating one of your uncooked meals!"

"You needn't worry about a thing," the innkeeper replied. "This time, the food will be superb!" He then went about setting the table.

The merchant washed his hands, broke bread, carefully tasted each dish and exclaimed, "Well, he was right, this is excellent!"

"What makes today different from yesterday?" he asked his host. "The hour is the same, and yet the food is ready..."

He answered, "I will explain. Yesterday, I planned on serving lunch at the normal hour. When you asked to eat early, it was still not sufficiently cooked. Today, I must be somewhere else at noon, so I was forced to prepare everything earlier..."

The Sages (*Sanhedrin* 98a) explain: "If Yisrael is worthy, God will accelerate the redemption. If Yisrael is not worthy, redemption will still come, but only in its due time." There are three ways in which the redemption can come.

The first way, if Yisrael is worthy, involves open miracles that completely bypass the slow incremental process of history. The second way, if Yisrael is not worthy, involves a Divine concealment that is fraught with trials and tribulations. There is a third way. Even if Yisrael is not worthy, and redemption must therefore be postposed to the last possible moment or due date, the due date itself will be brought closer by accelerating the events leading up to it. In this way, the quantum leap of "I will hasten it" will be subtly hidden in the incremental development of "in its due time." The third way is a synthesis of the first and the second.

Exile is a long and drawn out process intended to prepare Yisrael and the world for redemption. To what can redemption be likened? To a fruit which can only reach maturity while still attached to the tree. If the fruit is picked prematurely, it will be inedible and indigestible. It is for this reason that we may not force things by asking, as the merchant did, to eat early, for the food will simply be inedible.

It is different, however, when the Innkeeper Himself lights the fire of redemption in His people's hearts — if He wishes to accelerate the entire process. This is why we ask that He "hasten the day which will be neither day nor night!"

Ohel Yaakov, *Bo*

Appoint sentries for Your city [Yerushalayim], for all the day and all the night.

Hashem said through His prophet, "O' Yerushalayim, I have set watchmen on your walls who shall not hold their peace by day or by night. [They cry out:] Those who remember Hashem, do not rest..." (*Yeshayahu* 62:6). David Ha-Melech sang, "My soul yearns for God more than watchmen [of the night yearn] for the morning, more than those who watch [throughout the night vigil of this world yearn] for the morning [of redemption]" (*Tehillim* 130:6).

The Maggid of Dubno asked: Why are those who yearn and pray for the redemption likened to watchmen on a wall? Because watchmen on a wall call out, "All is quiet, all is well," every hour on the hour throughout the night. Why do they do this? It is not to wake up the town's inhabitants. On the contrary, they want all the townsfolk to sleep peacefully. They call out in order to demonstrate that they themselves are awake, alert, and on duty; they call out to assure the townsfolk that they have not fallen asleep on the job.

The same is true of those who pray for the redemption. Their intention

is not to remind Hashem or even to arouse His mercies. They know that "the Guardian of Yisrael neither sleeps nor slumbers" (ibid. 121:4). They pray to keep themselves from falling asleep, in order not to sink into complete oblivion.

The Talmud (*Menachos* 87a) states that these watchmen are angels who lament the destruction of the Temple, never resting by day or by night. The Maggid asked: What good does their crying do? Why hasn't it helped until now?

The answer, he said, is given by Rabbi Yitzchak Luria, the holy Ari. He commented on the statement of the Sages (*Pirkei Avos* 6:2): "Every single day a prophetic echo emanates from Mount Chorev and declares, 'Woe to mankind for the disgrace of the Torah!'" The Ari asked: Who hears this prophetic echo? And if no one hears it, of what benefit is it? Rather, this announcement issues forth from heaven and reverberates in our souls to arouse us to honor the Torah.

The same is true about the crying of the angels. It arouses in all Jewish souls a deep yearning for the redemption. This is the meaning of the verse, "O' Yerushalayim, I have set watchmen on your walls who shall not hold their peace, not by day or by night" — these are the angels set up over the walls of the heavenly Yerushalayim. When they cry, they remind the souls "who remember Hashem, do not rest...."

This is the meaning of the verse, "A voice is heard in the heights, lamentation and bitter weeping, [the voice of] Rachel crying for her children... (*Yirmeyahu* 31:14). She is crying in order to arouse her children to pray for the redemption. But the verse continues, "She refuses to be comforted for her children, because they are not..." (ibid.). She refuses to be comforted when it becomes all too evident that her weeping is in vain, and that no one seems to pay any attention....She is then likened to a mother whose only son fell ill. As his illness worsened daily, she never moved from his side. When his temperature soared, and he was on fire with fever, she washed him with an ice cold wet cloth.

One night, the boy seemed to stop breathing. It was dark, so she could not be sure. Quickly, she thought of something. Knowing that children cry when they hear someone else crying, she began to cry. There was no response. She cried louder. Silence. She cried more, but the boy was still. It began to dawn on her that her son was no longer alive. She then broke down and cried bitterly.

"A voice is heard in the heights" — our mother Rachel cries in heaven to awaken our souls, to feel the pain of exile, and to pray for the redemption. When she sees that we have become desensitized to the point that we cannot even hear her weeping, she raises her voice in "lamentation and bitter weeping."

When we still do not respond, she comes to the bitter realization that we have become completely inured to the exile and perfectly at home with the destruction. She then breaks down and "refuses to be comforted for her children, because they are not" — because they have become incapable of responding to her cry.

Kochav Mi'Yaakov, *Haftarah of Nitzavim*

Brighten as with the light of day the darkness of night.

The Maggid of Dubno said: Woe to us! Look how sunken we are in our exile! If we are so far away from the greatness of former generations, how will future generations fare? Is the course of history inevitably downhill? Are our children's children bound to sink even further?

Woe to us! We are so far away! Even with great tzaddikim among us, we are not worthy of being redeemed. What must the future hold in store? How will we ever merit to see the son of David?

But wait, we are not only moving away from the redemption, we are also moving towards it. And the son of David, our anointed Mashiach, whom our ancestors were not worthy of seeing — we shall be worthy of witnessing his emergence out of hiding! How can this be? The following parable will explain.

A man, let us call him Reuven, realized one day that he was losing his eyesight. He went to the doctor, who recommended immediate surgery to remove cataracts. The doctor performed the surgery, but when Reuven woke up and opened his eyes, he couldn't see a thing! He panicked and screamed out, "What have you done to me? Before the surgery, at least I could see shapes. Now I'm completely blind!"

But soon he heard the reassuring voice of the doctor, "Relax, calm down, and don't worry about a thing. The surgery was successful, and your eyesight has been restored. It is just that your eyes are bandaged right now, and that is why you cannot see. Just wait until the bandages are removed, and you will enjoy perfect eyesight!"

Like Reuven, we must have faith that the afflictions we have suffered have cleansed and refined our souls. We must recognize that everything we have undergone has been for our benefit and the benefit of our children. This is what Hashem meant when He said, "I know the thoughts that I think regarding you, says Hashem; they are thoughts of peace, and not evil, to give you a future and a hope" (*Yirmeyahu* 29:11). This prophetic message was delivered

Va'amartem Zevach Pesach
Say Then: It Is the Feast of Pesach

וּבְכֵן וַאֲמַרְתֶּם זֶבַח פֶּסַח

The power of Your mighty deeds You wondrously displayed	on Pesach;	בַּפֶּסַח.	אֹמֶץ גְּבוּרוֹתֶיךָ הִפְלֵאתָ
Above all festivals did You elevate	Pesach;	פֶּסַח.	בְּרֹאשׁ כָּל מוֹעֲדוֹת נִשֵּׂאתָ
To the oriental [Avraham] You revealed the [miraculous exodus at] midnight	of Pesach;	פֶּסַח.	גִּלִּיתָ לְאֶזְרָחִי חֲצוֹת לֵיל
Say then: It is the feast of Pesach.			וַאֲמַרְתֶּם זֶבַח פֶּסַח
At his door You knocked in the heat of midday	on Pesach;	בַּפֶּסַח.	דְּלָתָיו דָּפַקְתָּ כְּחוֹם הַיּוֹם
He served the sparkling angels cakes of matzah	on Pesach;	בַּפֶּסַח.	הִסְעִיד נוֹצְצִים עֻגוֹת מַצּוֹת
And ran to the cattle, a harbinger of the ox, [the festive offering] related	to Pesach;	פֶּסַח.	וְאֶל הַבָּקָר רָץ זֵכֶר לְשׁוֹר עֵרֶךְ
Say then: It is the feast of Pesach.			וַאֲמַרְתֶּם זֶבַח פֶּסַח

to the Jewish People on the eve of their being exiled to Babylonia. Now, as we approach the end of the exile, we need to remember this message.

Yes, the exile is likened to nighttime and darkness (*Pesachim* 2b), but redemption is likened to the dawn. And when the light of dawn begins to shine, all that is needed is to remove the bandages from our eyes. Then, that light, together with the suffering we underwent while in exile, will purify us and refine us. Then our night will be turned into day, as the author of *Vayehi Bachatzi Halaylah* wrote: "[Hashem,] brighten as with the light of day the darkness of [our long exile] night!"

Kol Yeshorer 7a

He served the sparkling angels cakes of matzah on Pesach.

The Maggid of Dubno said: Our teachers revealed to us that when Moshe ascended to heaven to receive the Torah, the ministering angels sought to harm him. What did the Holy One do? He changed Moshe's facial features and made him resemble Avraham Avinu! He then said to the angels, "Aren't you ashamed? Isn't this the one whom you visited and at whose table you ate?" (*Shemos Rabbah* 28:1).

We must try to understand, the Maggid continued. When Hashem was about to give the Torah to Moshe on Mount Sinai, it was these very angels who protested, saying, "O God, our master, Your Name is too powerful to rule on the earth. Establish Your splendor in the heavens above....What is mortal man that You think of him, and the finest human that You even consider him?" (*Tehillim* 8:2, 5). If the angels objected so strongly to lowering the Divine Torah down to the level of human beings, what possible difference could it make to remind them of their meal with Avraham? Why should this convince them to retract their objection?

The Maggid answered with a parable: A king had a son who loved playing in his father's room. At all hours of the day, the boy could be seen engrossed in playing with his toy soldiers, fighting his father's battles, and claiming victory for the crown.

The king also had a chief minister who was more distinguished than all the other ministers in the kingdom. The king sought his advice on every matter of royal importance. There wasn't a day that the chief minister wasn't seen entering the king's private quarters on urgent business.

At times, during his meetings with the chief minister, the king would find it necessary to send his son away. Only thus could the king be assured of complete privacy when discussing highly confidential matters of state with the minister.

One day, the chief minister was in a particularly good mood after having had a few too many drinks. He began to brag to his fellow ministers, "See how beloved and important I am to the king? He even sends his darling little boy out of the room when he speaks with me!"

Words have wings, and news of the minister's boasting reached the king's son's ears.

With malicious intent, certain palace informants said to the boy, "Can't you see now that the chief minister is far more important to your father than you are?" Their words pierced his heart like daggers.

When he was again sent away from the king's quarters that day and the next, the pain of rejection was too great to bear. He fell ill.

The king summoned the best doctors to his son's bedside. They could not find anything wrong with the boy, except that he was depressed and dejected. Unable to think of anything better, they prescribed doing everything possible to make the boy laugh and be happy. The king immediately called for a circus band. They played and danced, but the king's son did not laugh.

The king sought his royal physician's advice. "His majesty's son must be shown something new and wondrous, something that will force him to laugh and forget himself. I suggest, therefore, that one of his majesty's ministers dress up like a clown each day and act silly in front of the boy. Seeing the minister of the royal army or the minister of the treasury acting like a fool, the prince will not be able to contain himself," he said.

The suggestion seemed worthwhile to the king. Orders were given, and on the first day, the minister of the treasury danced and tumbled, sang and chirped, and generally made a fool of himself before the prince. Nothing seemed to help, however, for the boy didn't even crack a smile.

On the second day, the minister of the army dressed up like a bear, but the prince remained unmoved.

On the third day, it was the chief minister's turn. He dressed up like a clown. He stood on his hands and tumbled forwards and backwards. He struck a large gong, blew a funny trumpet, waved a toy flag, and clapped his hands — and the prince clapped too! He broke out in uncontrollable laughter!

And we know why. Now he was sure that his father loved him much more than the chief minister. Hadn't he commanded the chief minister to act like a clown just to make him happy?

The ministering angels had complained, "What is mortal man that You think of him, and the finest human that You even consider him?" (*Tehillim* 8:5). "We are better than human beings," they maintained. "We are holy and infinitely more important!"

What did the Holy One do? He reminded them that when his beloved Avraham was in pain on the hottest day in history, and there were no human beings capable of visiting him in the heat, Hashem ordered his ministering angels to dress up as Arab nomads in order to reveal themselves to Avraham and bring him good tidings. With this they understood that, despite their great importance, the King's beloved son, Avraham, was far more important. They understood and were silent.

Ohel Yaakov, *Yisro*

He served the sparkling angels cakes of matzah on Pesach.

Our Sages (*Bava Metzia* 86a) point out that Avraham and Sarah's angelic visitors did not really eat the meal they were served. Rather, they followed the ancient rule: A person should always conduct himself in accordance with the local customs. Since part of Avraham's hospitality was serving a scrumptious meal of calf's tongue, they understood that while visiting Avraham, they should at least act like they were eating!

The Sages learned the same lesson in reverse from Moshe Rabbenu. When Moshe ascended to the spiritual dimension, he followed the same rule, conducting himself according to the local custom. It is thus written, "He remained there with Hashem for forty days and forty nights without eating bread or drinking water" (*Shemos* 34:28).

The Maggid of Dubno asked: Why did the Torah and the Sages emphasize the fact that Moshe did not eat and drink in order to teach us this lesson? Wouldn't it have been more impressive to inform us that he did not sleep

for forty nights? Doesn't the Talmud (*Nedarim* 15a) state that a man can go without food for one week, but not without sleep for more than three days?

The Maggid answered with a true story about himself. Once he was traveling from city to city and from town to town in order to warm Jewish hearts to their Father in heaven with his spellbinding parables. While on his way from one town to the next, the sun began to set, and he was forced to knock on the door of a poor villager who did not recognize him. The villager and his family invited the distinguished rabbi into their humble abode.

The Maggid first recited the evening prayer, and then asked his host for a bite to eat before retiring for the night. He was informed that there was no food in the house. The Maggid regretted not having brought enough food along with him. He was terribly hungry after the long journey. He asked if there wasn't something left over from the day before. No, he was told. There was no bread or any other kind of food in the house. Nothing.

Seeing that he had no choice, he asked to lie down for the night. A bed was prepared for him in a far corner of the hut. He lay down and tried to fall asleep. He was unable to, however, due to the terrible hunger pangs that gnawed at him.

An hour later, when the villager and his family were certain that the Maggid was sound asleep, they opened the oven and proceeded to feast on a meal fit for a king! From his corner bed, the Maggid saw bread, vegetables, fish, meat, wine... He couldn't believe his eyes, his ears, and more than anything, his nose! The smell of the food was overwhelming.

All of a sudden, the Maggid sat up and blurted out, "The Sages (*Pirkei Avos* 3:4) told us that eating a meal without speaking words of Torah at the table is tantamount to eating sacrifices offered to the dead idols!" He walked across the room, and continued, "I can tell you some wonderful Torah so that your meal will taste even better!"

His hosts were embarrassed, to say the least. Their faces turned pale, but the Maggid wasn't finished with them yet.

He sat down and continued, "The Sages learn from Moshe Rabbenu that a person must never act contrary to the local customs of the place he is visiting..." The Maggid paused and looked at the food on the table. "They learn this from the fact that he was in heaven and did not eat. Of course, the question has already been asked: Why didn't they learn this from the fact that he did not sleep?" The Maggid looked around. "Only now has the answer become clear to me!

"The very fact that Moshe conducted himself like an angel by not eating proves that he did not sleep as well! For if he had slept, how would he have

זֹעֲמוּ סְדוֹמִים וְלוֹהֲטוּ בָּאֵשׁ בַּפֶּסַח.
חֻלַּץ לוֹט מֵהֶם וּמַצּוֹת אָפָה בְּקֵץ פֶּסַח.
טִאטֵאתָ אַדְמַת מוֹף וְנוֹף בְּעָבְרְךָ בַּפֶּסַח.
וַאֲמַרְתֶּם זֶבַח פֶּסַח

The men of Sedom kindled Your wrath,
and were set aflame with fire on Pesach;
Lot was saved from their midst,
and baked matzos at the close of Pesach;
You swept clean the ground of Moph and
Noph [Egypt] When You passed through on Pesach;
Say then: It is the feast of Pesach.

יָהּ רֹאשׁ כָּל אוֹן מָחַצְתָּ בְּלֵיל שִׁמּוּר פֶּסַח.
כַּבִּיר עַל בֵּן בְּכוֹר פָּסַחְתָּ בְּדַם פֶּסַח.
לְבִלְתִּי תֵּת מַשְׁחִית לָבֹא בִּפְתָחַי בַּפֶּסַח.
וַאֲמַרְתֶּם זֶבַח פֶּסַח

God, You crushed every firstborn's head on
the watchnight of Pesach;
O' Great One, yet over Your firstborn You skipped
by [to spare him] because of
the blood [marking the doors] of the Pesach;
So as not to let the destroyer enter my doorways on Pesach;
Say then: It is the feast of Pesach.

מְסֻגֶּרֶת סֻגָּרָה בְּעִתּוֹתֵי פֶּסַח.
נִשְׁמְדָה מִדְיָן בִּצְלִיל שְׂעוֹרֵי עֹמֶר פֶּסַח.
שׂוֹרְפוּ מִשְׁמַנֵּי פּוּל וְלוּד בִּיקַד יְקוֹד פֶּסַח.
וַאֲמַרְתֶּם זֶבַח פֶּסַח

The locked shut [city of Yericho] fell at the time of Pesach;
Midyan was wiped out through a barley cake,
the omer offering of Pesach;
The stalwart men of Pul and Lud [Ashur]
were burned in a great blaze on Pesach;
Say then: It is the feast of Pesach.

עוֹד הַיּוֹם בְּנֹב לַעֲמוֹד עַד גָּעָה עוֹנַת פֶּסַח.
פַּס יַד כָּתְבָה לְקַעֲקֵעַ צוּל בַּפֶּסַח.
צָפֹה הַצָּפִית עָרוֹךְ הַשֻּׁלְחָן בַּפֶּסַח.
וַאֲמַרְתֶּם זֶבַח פֶּסַח

"Yet today" [Sancheriv planned] to arrive at Nov
[and besiege Yerushalayim] till [he had his
downfall when] came the time of Pesach;
An unseen hand wrote to prophesy the
destruction of Tzul [Babylon] on Pesach;
While they set the watch, prepared the table, on Pesach;
Say then: It is the feast of Pesach.

קָהָל כִּנְּסָה הֲדַסָּה צוֹם לְשַׁלֵּשׁ בַּפֶּסַח.
רֹאשׁ מִבֵּית רָשָׁע מָחַצְתָּ בְּעֵץ חֲמִשִּׁים בַּפֶּסַח.
שְׁתֵּי אֵלֶּה רֶגַע תָּבִיא לְעוּצִית בַּפֶּסַח.
תָּעֹז יָדְךָ וְתָרוּם יְמִינְךָ כְּלֵיל הִתְקַדֵּשׁ חַג פֶּסַח.
וַאֲמַרְתֶּם זֶבַח פֶּסַח

Hadassah [Esther] assembled the [Jewish] community
for a three-day fast on Pesach;
The head of the wicked house [Haman] You
destroyed on a fifty-foot gallows on Pesach;
Double misfortune o' bring instantly on Utzis [Edom] on Pesach;
May Your Hand be strengthened, and Your right
Hand exalted, as on that night
when You sanctified the Festival of Pesach;
Say then: It is the feast of Pesach.

discovered that angels do not eat, in order for him to act like them? After all, the angels could have waited for him to fall asleep in order to satisfy their stomachs. Rather, we are forced to say that he did not sleep for forty days and nights. Seeing that they truly did not eat, he was forced to act like them!"

It goes without saying that the Maggid continued delighting his hosts with his wonderful words of wisdom. But you can be sure that he ate something first — according to local custom, of course!

Sefas Ha-Yeriyah, *Pinchas*

May Your Hand be strengthened, and Your right Hand exalted, as on that night when You sanctified the Festival of Pesach.

The Maggid of Dubno explained: When singing this line, we should have in mind Hashem's promise to His prophet, "As in the days of your exodus from Egypt, I will show them wonders" (*Michah* 7:15) — that is, the supernatural

wonders of the future redemption will resemble those of our exodus from Egypt. But, the Maggid added, why should this be so? Wouldn't it be better for Hashem to perform new and unheard of miracles? Why make the future redemption a repeat performance of the Exodus? He answered with the following parable.

A wealthy entrepreneur ran a manufacturing plant. He employed hundreds of workers, all of whom wore special uniforms according to their different jobs in the plant.

One day, a young man came looking for work. The entrepreneur hired him for a short period of time and saw that he was very competent, sharp, and devoted. The entrepreneur decided that he was capable of running the entire plant, ordering raw materials, overseeing all major jobs — in short, of becoming his right-hand man. His only shortcoming was his youth and his lack of experience. So what did the entrepreneur do? He fired him!

The young man was stunned. What should he do now? he asked his former employer. "Don't worry," the entrepreneur replied, "I have gotten you a position in another plant. I have already spoken to your new employers, and they are ready to hire you."

And so it was; the young man went there and was hired. The pay was considerably less and the conditions worse, but he had no choice, so he remained at his new job.

In the meantime, the entrepreneur hired another man to be his manager and fired him after a year. He hired another man, and fired him as well. During this entire period, he inquired regarding the young man's progress, and kept tabs on him. He was satisfied with what he heard, knowing that his original assessment of his capabilities was correct. He received confirmation of the young man's astuteness and the experience he was accumulating. When he felt that he had acquired enough experience, he called him to his office.

The young man came and stood before him. The entrepreneur offered him a seat. Surprised at the honor he was being shown, he sat down. The entrepreneur then spoke to him, "I wish to appoint you as supervising manager over my plant. You will be responsible for the entire work force, for production, pricing of goods, sales — in short, everything. No business will be conducted without your signature. And the pay will be commensurate."

The young man was speechless. If he hadn't already been sitting, he surely would have fallen off his feet. "But," he stammered, "you fired me a few years ago..."

"I fired you," the entrepreneur answered, "so that you could get the experience you needed for this job somewhere else — so that you could come into this job as a seasoned worker."

The young man couldn't believe what he was hearing. It was too good to be true. And then, a creeping suspicion stole into his heart. He said, "What will happen if I leave my present job and come to work for you? Won't you fire me after a short while, just like you fired all the others who preceded me? Won't my fate be like theirs, and won't I then find myself out in the cold with nothing to show for all my efforts?"

The entrepreneur set the young man's suspicions to rest. "I fired them for one reason and for one reason only. I had already reserved the job for you, and I didn't want anybody else to become well-established in your place."

But the young man had one more reservation. It was hard for him to digest the fact that the whole thing was planned out from the beginning — that the entrepreneur had already had his eye on him from the moment he first came to work for him, and had been pulling strings behind the scenes ever since to bring his true purpose to fruition.

The entrepreneur saw his hesitancy and understood what was bothering him. With a smile on his lips, he asked, "Tell me, do you remember that when you first got here we sent you to a tailor to fit you for a uniform like the other workers?"

"Certainly," the young man replied. "But I wasn't here long enough to receive the uniform before you fired me!" he added with a sigh.

"That wasn't the reason," the entrepreneur assured him. "Please go over to that closet there and open it. The uniform inside is waiting for you!"

He went over to the closet and found a beautiful suit fit for a manager, tailor-made for him!

The entrepreneur explained, "I had this suit made for you then and it has been waiting here for you ever since."

The young man was speechless.

True, Hashem redeemed us from Egypt, but shortly afterwards we were cast out of our land and exiled to the four corners of the world. Many nations ruled over us, and many empires rose in power and influence while we descended to the depths of pain, grief, and degradation.

When Hashem brings the Final Redemption to end our long and bitter exile, our first response will be, "When You exiled us, we thought that You had abandoned us altogether! Look at all the other empires You appointed to rule the world, while You sent us away into darkness and anonymity." As veterans of so much bitterness and suffering, we will find it hard to believe that our millennia-old dream has finally come true.

But Hashem will answer, "No, My children, the exile was solely for your

Ki Lo Na'eh, Ki Lo Ya'eh

For To Him It Is Becoming; For To Him It Is Fitting

Mighty in majesty, truly supreme, His companies [of angels] say to Him: To You, again to You; to You, for to You; to You, indeed to You; to You, Hashem, belongs all sovereignty. For to Him it is becoming; for to Him it is fitting.

Excelling in majesty, truly resplendent, His faithful [in Jewry] say to Him: *To You etc.*

Pristine in majesty, truly powerful, His [angelic] princes say to Him: *To You etc.*

Unique in majesty, truly omnipotent, His disciples [in Jewry] say to Him: *To You etc.*

Ruling in majesty, truly held in awe, His surrounding [Heavenly] companions say to Him: *To You etc.*

Humble in majesty, truly a Redeemer, His righteous ones [in Jewry] say to Him: *To You etc.*

Holy in majesty, truly compassionate, His chorus of angels say to Him: *To You etc.*

Forceful in majesty, truly all-sustaining, His perfect ones say to Him: *To You etc.*

כִּי לוֹ נָאֶה. כִּי לוֹ יָאֶה:

אַדִּיר בִּמְלוּכָה. בָּחוּר כַּהֲלָכָה. גְּדוּדָיו יֹאמְרוּ לוֹ. לְךָ וּלְךָ. לְךָ כִּי לְךָ. לְךָ אַף לְךָ. לְךָ יהוה הַמַּמְלָכָה. כִּי לוֹ נָאֶה. כִּי לוֹ יָאֶה:

דָּגוּל בִּמְלוּכָה. הָדוּר כַּהֲלָכָה. וָתִיקָיו יֹאמְרוּ לוֹ. לך ולך וכו'.

זַכַּאי בִּמְלוּכָה חָסִין כַּהֲלָכָה טַפְסְרָיו יֹאמְרוּ לוֹ לך ולך וכו'.

יָחִיד בִּמְלוּכָה כַּבִּיר כַּהֲלָכָה לִמּוּדָיו יֹאמְרוּ לוֹ לך ולך וכו'.

מֶלֶךְ בִּמְלוּכָה נוֹרָא כַּהֲלָכָה סְבִיבָיו יֹאמְרוּ לוֹ לך ולך וכו'.

עָנָו בִּמְלוּכָה פּוֹדֶה כַּהֲלָכָה צַדִּיקָיו יֹאמְרוּ לוֹ לך ולך וכו'.

קָדוֹשׁ בִּמְלוּכָה רַחוּם כַּהֲלָכָה שִׁנְאַנָּיו יֹאמְרוּ לוֹ לך ולך וכו'.

תַּקִּיף בִּמְלוּכָה תּוֹמֵךְ כַּהֲלָכָה תְּמִימָיו יֹאמְרוּ לוֹ לך ולך וכו'.

Those who do not drink the fourth cup until this point, do so now.
They then say the berachah after drinking wine and continue to recite "The order of the Pesach service," etc., until "Next year in Yerushalayim!" and then continue from here.

Adir Hu

Mighty Is He

May He build His House soon! Speedily, yes speedily, in our days, soon! Build, o' God; build, o' God; build Your House soon!

Foremost is He, great is He, supreme is He *May He build...*

Resplendent is He, faithful is He, worthy is He, kindly is He *May He build...*

אַדִּיר הוּא

אַדִּיר הוּא יִבְנֶה בֵיתוֹ בְּקָרוֹב בִּמְהֵרָה בִּמְהֵרָה בְּיָמֵנוּ בְּקָרוֹב אֵל בְּנֵה אֵל בְּנֵה בְּנֵה בֵיתְךָ בְּקָרוֹב.

בָּחוּר הוּא גָּדוֹל הוּא דָּגוּל הוּא הָדוּר הוּא וָתִיק הוּא זַכַּאי הוּא חָסִיד הוּא יִבְנֶה בֵיתוֹ בְּקָרוֹב. בִּמְהֵרָה בִּמְהֵרָה בְּיָמֵינוּ בְּקָרוֹב. אֵל בְּנֵה אֵל בְּנֵה. בְּנֵה בֵיתְךָ בְּקָרוֹב:

benefit, to cleanse you and refine you!" Seeing our consternation, He will then add, "As a proof that I had only you in mind, I will perform miracles and wonders for you like those I performed in Egypt! The truth is that those miracles were not only for then. They were the suit I prepared, My sign to you that I never once abandoned you, and that all the heartache you suffered since then was in preparation for the great day." May it come soon!

Ohel Yaakov, *Bo*

Build Your House soon.

The Maggid of Dubno told a parable about an aristocrat who sought an appropriate match for his son. The daughter of a respected community member was offered. The aristocrat decided to look into the matter. He showed up at the girl's family's mansion and was pleased to see that they were well-to-

טָהוֹר הוּא יָחִיד הוּא כַּבִּיר הוּא לָמוּד הוּא מֶלֶךְ הוּא נוֹרָא הוּא
סַגִּיב הוּא עִזּוּז הוּא פּוֹדֶה הוּא צַדִּיק הוּא יִבְנֶה בֵּיתוֹ בְּקָרוֹב.
בִּמְהֵרָה בִּמְהֵרָה בְּיָמֵינוּ בְּקָרוֹב. אֵל בְּנֵה אֵל בְּנֵה. בְּנֵה בֵיתְךָ
בְּקָרוֹב.

קָדוֹשׁ הוּא רַחוּם הוּא שַׁדַּי הוּא תַּקִּיף הוּא יִבְנֶה בֵּיתוֹ בְּקָרוֹב.
בִּמְהֵרָה בִּמְהֵרָה בְּיָמֵינוּ בְּקָרוֹב. אֵל בְּנֵה אֵל בְּנֵה. בְּנֵה בֵיתְךָ
בְּקָרוֹב:

Pure is He, unique is He, omnipotent is He, learned is He, sovereign is He, awesome is He, sublime is He, powerful is He, the Redeemer is He, righteous is He

May He build...

Holy is He, compassionate is He, the Almighty is He, puissant is He

May He build...

do. He was served with the finest crystal, silver, and gold. Everywhere he turned, he saw signs of great wealth. As far as he was concerned the matter was settled. The bride's family agreed, and the match was made.

A few weeks passed and the groom's father again decided to visit his future in-laws in order to set a date for the wedding and finalize certain details. The moment he entered their home and looked around, however, his eyes darkened. All the valuable belongings had disappeared. The parlor was empty, with no trace of ever having housed expensive gold, silver, or crystal. Even the drink he received was served in a modest cup and saucer. He also noticed that the owner of the house was troubled and absentminded.

Unable to hold himself back, he asked, "Why are you so bothered... and where is all your furniture?"

The owner answered, "That is why I am so ill-at-ease. I was offered a business deal with the promise of tremendous profits. In order to participate in the deal, however, I needed to put up a certain amount of money. I pledged my furniture as collateral, as security for the loan."

The aristocrat breathed a sigh of relief. "If so, you have nothing to be embarrassed about. For a moment I thought that perhaps you had borrowed all the beautiful and expensive things I saw in your home last time I was here in order to appear wealthy. That would have been sufficient grounds for me to annul our agreement. If the furniture is really yours, however, and you have merely offered it as security, I am sure the deal will come through and you will not only redeem your belongings, but add to them!"

Like the owner of this house, we too have been temporarily deprived of what is rightfully ours. Though our Beis Ha-Mikdash was taken from us as a security, we have not lost it altogether. For just as Hashem destroyed the Temple with fire, we are promised that the time will come when He will rebuild it with fire (*Bava Basra* 60b). This is the meaning of our song on Pesach night, "Mighty is He, may He rebuild His House soon! Speedily, yes speedily, in our days, soon! Build o' God; build, o' God; build Your House soon!"

Kochav Mi'Yaakov, *Haftarah of Shemini*

Those who live in chutz la'aretz and have not yet counted the Omer after maariv on the second night of Pesach do so now.

בָּרוּךְ אַתָּה יהוה אֱלֹהֵינוּ מֶלֶךְ הָעוֹלָם אֲשֶׁר קִדְּשָׁנוּ בְּמִצְוֹתָיו וְצִוָּנוּ עַל סְפִירַת הָעוֹמֶר:
הַיּוֹם יוֹם אֶחָד לָעֹמֶר:

Blessed be You, Hashem our God, King of the universe, Who has sanctified us by His commandments and commanded us concerning the counting of the Omer.

Today is the first day of the Omer.

יְהִי רָצוֹן מִלְּפָנֶיךָ יְיָ אֱלֹהֵינוּ וֵאלֹהֵי אֲבוֹתֵינוּ שֶׁיִּבָּנֶה בֵּית הַמִּקְדָּשׁ בִּמְהֵרָה בְיָמֵינוּ וְתֵן חֶלְקֵנוּ בְּתוֹרָתֶךָ. וְשָׁם נַעֲבָדְךָ בְּיִרְאָה כִּימֵי עוֹלָם וּכְשָׁנִים קַדְמוֹנִיּוֹת:

May it be Your will, Hashem, our God and God of our fathers, that the Temple be speedily rebuilt in our days, and give us our portion in your Torah, so that we may serve You there with awe as in the days of old and as in former years.

אֶחָד מִי יוֹדֵעַ

אֶחָד מִי יוֹדֵעַ. אֶחָד אֲנִי יוֹדֵעַ. אֶחָד אֱלֹהֵינוּ שֶׁבַּשָּׁמַיִם וּבָאָרֶץ:
שְׁנַיִם מִי יוֹדֵעַ. שְׁנַיִם אֲנִי יוֹדֵעַ. שְׁנֵי לֻחוֹת הַבְּרִית. אֶחָד אֱלֹהֵינוּ שֶׁבַּשָּׁמַיִם וּבָאָרֶץ:
שְׁלֹשָׁה מִי יוֹדֵעַ. שְׁלֹשָׁה אֲנִי יוֹדֵעַ. שְׁלֹשָׁה אָבוֹת. שְׁנֵי לֻחוֹת הַבְּרִית. אֶחָד אֱלֹהֵינוּ שֶׁבַּשָּׁמַיִם וּבָאָרֶץ:
אַרְבַּע מִי יוֹדֵעַ. אַרְבַּע אֲנִי יוֹדֵעַ. אַרְבַּע אִמָּהוֹת. שְׁלֹשָׁה אָבוֹת. שְׁנֵי לֻחוֹת הַבְּרִית. אֶחָד אֱלֹהֵינוּ שֶׁבַּשָּׁמַיִם וּבָאָרֶץ:
חֲמִשָּׁה מִי יוֹדֵעַ. חֲמִשָּׁה אֲנִי יוֹדֵעַ. חֲמִשָּׁה חֻמְשֵׁי תוֹרָה. אַרְבַּע אִמָּהוֹת. שְׁלֹשָׁה אָבוֹת. שְׁנֵי לֻחוֹת הַבְּרִית. אֶחָד אֱלֹהֵינוּ שֶׁבַּשָּׁמַיִם וּבָאָרֶץ:
שִׁשָּׁה מִי יוֹדֵעַ. שִׁשָּׁה אֲנִי יוֹדֵעַ. שִׁשָּׁה סִדְרֵי מִשְׁנָה. חֲמִשָּׁה חֻמְשֵׁי

Echad Mi Yodei'a

Who Knows One?

Who knows one? I know one. Our God is One, in heaven and on the earth.

Who knows two? I know two. The tablets of the covenant are two, our God is One, in heaven and on the earth.

Who knows three? I know three. The Patriarchs are three, the tablets of the covenant are two, our God is One, in heaven and on the earth.

Who knows four? I know four. The Matriarchs are four, the Patriarchs are three, the tablets of the covenant are two, our God is One, in heaven and on the earth.

Who knows five? I know five. The books of the Torah are five, the Matriarchs are four, the Patriarchs are three, the tablets of the covenant are two, our God is One, in heaven and on the earth.

Who knows six? I know six. The Mishnah sections are six, the books

Who knows one? I know one.

The Maggid of Lublin asked: Who doesn't know? Who is the song coming to exclude? It is coming to exclude the ministering angels! With all their brilliance, they do not grasp the awesome fact of Hashem's Oneness as we do.

And if you ask why this is so, the answer is that each and every angel was created to embody one particular attribute, to serve one specific function, and to fulfill one definite task. The Midrash (*Bereishis Rabbah* 50:2) thus states, "One angel cannot have two missions. Neither can two angels share the same mission." Angels can be differentiated only by their mission. Two angels therefore cannot share the same mission. It is only their different missions that make two angels different entities. If they both had the same mission, there would be no difference between them, and they would be one! Similarly, one angel cannot have two missions. If an angel had two missions, then by definition he would be two angels!

For example, Micha'el is the angel that embodies Hashem's quality of

lovingkindness, while Gavriel is the angelic embodiment of Hashem's justice. Like a defending attorney pitted against a prosecuting attorney, Micha'el is the polar opposite of Gavriel. Micha'el defends Yisrael — even when they are not apparently worthy, and Gavriel demands justice — even when they are! Each of them is limited to his particular function and attribute, and it is simply beyond their ability to grasp the fact that Hashem comprehends and includes all of His attributes within Himself as one.

There is one creature, however, who can grasp this. Man was created as a miniature reflection of the Divine, meaning that he possesses all of Hashem's attributes. It is for this reason that man can contemplate the entire creation and perceive the awesome unity of the Creator that lies concealed behind its apparent diversity and multiplicity. He can perceive the hidden Hand that guides all things and can affirm, "One is our God in heaven and on earth!"

This is alluded to by our Sages in the *Zohar* (3:207b) and Midrash (*Bereishis Rabbah* 17:4):

> We have learned that when the Holy One decided to create Adam, He called various groups of angels in and sat them down before Him. He announced to them, "I wish to create Adam." The angels responded, "With all his honor, if Man will not understand, he is likened to the dumb beasts" (*Tehillim* 49:21). The Holy One stretched forth His finger and burned them up! He seated other groups before Him and said, "I wish to create Adam." They responded, "What is mortal man that You think of him, and the finest human that You even consider him?" (*Tehillim* 8:5) — "What is the nature of this Man?" He replied to them: "His wisdom will exceed yours." To prove His point, He brought all the various animals and birds before them one at a time and asked them, "What is this? What is its name?" They could not answer. He brought them all before Adam. He contemplated and said, "This is a shor (ox), this is a chamor (donkey)..."

Our commentators have explained the connection between angels and animals, and the difference between them and man. Like angels, each animal represents a particular quality and is designed and programmed to fulfill a certain limited function. Because of this one-to-one relationship, the most that an angel can do is to know the name of its corresponding animal. Only man, who possesses all the different qualities within himself, is able to identify the essence of each one and name it according to that essence.

The Maggid continued: Having ascertained that our song begins by referring to the angels, we can now understand the next phrase: "Who knows two? I know two. The tablets of the covenant are two, our God is One, in heaven and on the earth." Our Sages (*Shabbos* 88b) remind us that when Moshe ascended to the heavens to receive the Torah, the angels again countered:

"O God, our Master, Your Name is too powerful to rule on the earth. Establish Your splendor in the heavens above....What is mortal man that You think of him, and the finest human that You even consider him?" (*Tehillim* 8:2, 5).

The Holy One then said to Moshe, "You answer them!"

Moshe replied, "Master of the world, I fear lest they consume me with the breath of their mouths!"

He answered him, "Grab onto My Throne of Glory and you will be able to give them an answer!"...

Now Moshe said before Him, "Master of the world, what is written in the Torah that You are giving me, but: 'I am Hashem your God who brought you out of Egypt' (*Shemos* 20:2)." He turned to the angels and said, "Did you descend to Egypt, were you subjugated by Pharaoh? Why should the Torah remain with you? And again, what is written in it, but 'Do not have any other gods before Me' (ibid. 20:3). Do you dwell among idolatrous nations? Again, what is written in it, but 'Remember the Shabbos to set it aside and sanctify it' (ibid. 20:8). Do you do any work that you should need to rest? Again, what is written in it, but 'Do not take the Name of Hashem your God in vain' (ibid. 20:7). Do you conduct business with each other [that you might come to take an oath in vain]? Again, what is written in it, but 'Honor your father and your mother,' (ibid. 20:12). Do you have parents? Again, what is written in it, but 'Do not commit murder; do not commit adultery; do not steal' (ibid. 20:13). Is there jealousy among you? Do you possess an evil inclination?" With this, they conceded.

How did Moshe prevail? It is known that the five commandments written on the first tablet all involve the relationship between God and man. To some extent, angels have a connection with this tablet. All the commandments on the second tablet, on the other hand, involve the relationship between man and man. Angels have no connection to such laws. For this reason, we now say to them, "Who knows two? I know two." I know, not you. "The tablets of the covenant are two, our God is One, in heaven and on the earth!"

We can now understand the next phrase: "Who knows three? I know three. The patriarchs are three." It is known that the holy patriarchs embodied all of Hashem's qualities, but emphasized one in particular. Avraham emphasized Hashem's quality of lovingkindness, Yitzchak emphasized His quality of justice, and Yaakov emphasized the quality of truth. Similarly, every Jew inherited these qualities from the patriarchs, and possesses all of them within himself. As mentioned, angels are limited in this respect. We learn this from Avraham. After his circumcision at the age of 100, three angels were sent to him. Micha'el was sent to save Lot, Gavriel was sent to overturn Sodom, and Rapha'el was sent to heal Sarah's barrenness. The reason, as the Midrash quoted above states, is: "One angel cannot have two missions. Neither can two angels share the same mission."

This can be illustrated by the following parable: The owner of a large manufacturing company had a foreman to whom he paid a rather modest salary. A young man showed up one day who showed managerial potential. Shortly after beginning his work, the owner promoted him to a supervisory position in the company and gave him a hefty raise in salary.

The foreman complained to the owner, "Why is this young man getting special treatment? Why did he get a raise so soon? Why have you underrated my experience and longstanding service to the company and shown him preference?"

The owner did not answer. He stood with his back to the foreman, looking out of his office window. Suddenly he said, "Look, there's a wagon driving by. Go quickly and see what it is carrying!"

The foreman ran outside, caught up to the wagon, spoke with the driver, and returned. "It's some kind of goods," he reported.

"Go and find out if the entire stock is for sale," the owner replied.

The foreman ran to stop the wagon again, spoke with the driver, returned out of breath, and reported, "Yes, the stock is for sale."

"If so," the owner ordered, "go and find out how much he wants for it."

The wagon had continued on its way and was already out of sight, but the faithful foreman ran until he caught up with it. He asked the driver to quote a price for the entire stock. The foreman returned and reported the driver's price back to the owner.

"Fine, thank you," the owner replied. Then he called over the young supervisor and said, "A few minutes ago, a wagon full of goods passed by here. Go and find out what it was carrying."

The young man left the office, and mounted a horse to chase after the wagon. A few minutes later, he was back with the following report. "The wagon is carrying a certain kind of merchandise belonging to a certain well-known manufacturer. The quality of the merchandise is such-and-such, and we could put it to a number of important uses. The owner of the merchandise is asking for such-and-such a price for the entire stock, but he is willing to go down to such-and-such a price, since he bought it for such-and-such a price. My feeling is that we could bargain him down to such-and-such a price. I asked him to wait until I returned with an answer."

The owner authorized the purchase, and turned to the foreman. "Do you understand now what the difference is between the two of you? I sent you out three times, and each time you came back with a specific answer. I sent him out once, and he brought back a complete report. The reason why his salary is double that of yours is because he does the work of three of you, and more."

of the Torah are five, the Matriarchs are four, the Patriarchs are three, the tablets of the covenant are two, our God is One, in heaven and on the earth.

Who knows seven? I know seven. The days of the week are seven, the Mishnah sections are six, the books of the Torah are five, the Matriarchs are four, the Patriarchs are three, the tablets of the covenant are two, our God is One, in heaven and on the earth.

Who knows eight? I know eight. The days of circumcision are eight, the days of the week are seven, the Mishnah sections are six, the books of the Torah are five, the Matriarchs are four, the Patriarchs are three, the tablets of the covenant are two, our God is One, in heaven and on the earth.

Who knows nine? I know nine. The months of childbirth are nine, the days of circumcision are eight, the days of the week are seven, the Mishnah sections are six, the books of the Torah are five, the Matriarchs are four, the Patriarchs are three, the tablets of the covenant are two, our God is One, in heaven and on the earth.

Who knows ten? I know ten. The Ten Commandments are ten, the months of childbirth are nine, the days of circumcision are eight, the days of the week are seven, the Mishnah sections are six, the books of the Torah are five, the Matriarchs are four, the Patriarchs are three, the tablets of the covenant are two, our God is One, in heaven and on the earth.

Who knows eleven? I know eleven. The stars [in Joseph's dream] are eleven, the Ten Commandments are ten, the months of childbirth are nine, the days of circumcision are eight, the days of the week are seven, the Mishnah sections are six, the books of the Torah are five, the Matriarchs are four, the Patriarchs are three, the tablets of the covenant are two, our God is One, in heaven and on the earth.

Who knows twelve? I know twelve. Twelve are the tribes of Yisrael, the stars are eleven, the Ten Commandments are ten, the months of childbirth are nine, the days of circumcision are eight, the days of the week are seven, the Mishnah sections are six, the books of the Torah are five, the Matriarchs are four, the Patriarchs are three, the tablets of the covenant are two, our God is One, in heaven and on the earth.

Who knows thirteen? I know thirteen. God's attributes are thirteen, the tribes of Yisrael are twelve, the stars are eleven, the Ten Commandments are ten, the months of childbirth are nine, the days of circumcision are eight, the days of the week are seven, the Mishnah sections are six, the books of the Torah are five, the Matriarchs are four, the Patriarchs are three, the tablets of the covenant are two, our God is One, in heaven and on the earth.

תּוֹרָה. אַרְבַּע אִמָּהוֹת. שְׁלֹשָׁה אָבוֹת. שְׁנֵי לֻחוֹת הַבְּרִית. אֶחָד אֱלֹהֵינוּ שֶׁבַּשָּׁמַיִם וּבָאָרֶץ:

שִׁבְעָה מִי יוֹדֵעַ. שִׁבְעָה אֲנִי יוֹדֵעַ. שִׁבְעָה יְמֵי שַׁבַּתָּא. שִׁשָּׁה סִדְרֵי מִשְׁנָה. חֲמִשָּׁה חֻמְשֵׁי תוֹרָה. אַרְבַּע אִמָּהוֹת. שְׁלֹשָׁה אָבוֹת. שְׁנֵי לֻחוֹת הַבְּרִית. אֶחָד אֱלֹהֵינוּ שֶׁבַּשָּׁמַיִם וּבָאָרֶץ:

שְׁמוֹנָה מִי יוֹדֵעַ. שְׁמוֹנָה אֲנִי יוֹדֵעַ. שְׁמוֹנָה יְמֵי מִילָה. שִׁבְעָה יְמֵי שַׁבַּתָּא. שִׁשָּׁה סִדְרֵי מִשְׁנָה. חֲמִשָּׁה חֻמְשֵׁי תוֹרָה. אַרְבַּע אִמָּהוֹת. שְׁלֹשָׁה אָבוֹת. שְׁנֵי לֻחוֹת הַבְּרִית. אֶחָד אֱלֹהֵינוּ שֶׁבַּשָּׁמַיִם וּבָאָרֶץ:

תִּשְׁעָה מִי יוֹדֵעַ. תִּשְׁעָה אֲנִי יוֹדֵעַ. תִּשְׁעָה יַרְחֵי לֵדָה. שְׁמוֹנָה יְמֵי מִילָה. שִׁבְעָה יְמֵי שַׁבַּתָּא. שִׁשָּׁה סִדְרֵי מִשְׁנָה. חֲמִשָּׁה חֻמְשֵׁי תוֹרָה. אַרְבַּע אִמָּהוֹת. שְׁלֹשָׁה אָבוֹת. שְׁנֵי לֻחוֹת הַבְּרִית. אֶחָד אֱלֹהֵינוּ שֶׁבַּשָּׁמַיִם וּבָאָרֶץ:

עֲשָׂרָה מִי יוֹדֵעַ. עֲשָׂרָה אֲנִי יוֹדֵעַ. עֲשָׂרָה דִבְּרַיָּא. תִּשְׁעָה יַרְחֵי לֵדָה. שְׁמוֹנָה יְמֵי מִילָה. שִׁבְעָה יְמֵי שַׁבַּתָּא. שִׁשָּׁה סִדְרֵי מִשְׁנָה. חֲמִשָּׁה חֻמְשֵׁי תוֹרָה. אַרְבַּע אִמָּהוֹת. שְׁלֹשָׁה אָבוֹת. שְׁנֵי לֻחוֹת הַבְּרִית. אֶחָד אֱלֹהֵינוּ שֶׁבַּשָּׁמַיִם וּבָאָרֶץ:

אַחַד עָשָׂר מִי יוֹדֵעַ. אַחַד עָשָׂר אֲנִי יוֹדֵעַ. אַחַד עָשָׂר כּוֹכְבַיָּא. עֲשָׂרָה דִבְּרַיָּא. תִּשְׁעָה יַרְחֵי לֵדָה. שְׁמוֹנָה יְמֵי מִילָה. שִׁבְעָה יְמֵי שַׁבַּתָּא. שִׁשָּׁה סִדְרֵי מִשְׁנָה. חֲמִשָּׁה חֻמְשֵׁי תוֹרָה. אַרְבַּע אִמָּהוֹת. שְׁלֹשָׁה אָבוֹת. שְׁנֵי לֻחוֹת הַבְּרִית. אֶחָד אֱלֹהֵינוּ שֶׁבַּשָּׁמַיִם וּבָאָרֶץ:

שְׁנֵים עָשָׂר מִי יוֹדֵעַ. שְׁנֵים עָשָׂר אֲנִי יוֹדֵעַ. שְׁנֵים עָשָׂר שִׁבְטַיָּא. אַחַד עָשָׂר כּוֹכְבַיָּא. עֲשָׂרָה דִבְּרַיָּא. תִּשְׁעָה יַרְחֵי לֵדָה. שְׁמוֹנָה יְמֵי מִילָה. שִׁבְעָה יְמֵי שַׁבַּתָּא. שִׁשָּׁה סִדְרֵי מִשְׁנָה. חֲמִשָּׁה חֻמְשֵׁי תוֹרָה. אַרְבַּע אִמָּהוֹת. שְׁלֹשָׁה אָבוֹת. שְׁנֵי לֻחוֹת הַבְּרִית. אֶחָד אֱלֹהֵינוּ שֶׁבַּשָּׁמַיִם וּבָאָרֶץ:

שְׁלֹשָׁה עָשָׂר מִי יוֹדֵעַ. שְׁלֹשָׁה עָשָׂר אֲנִי יוֹדֵעַ. שְׁלֹשָׁה עָשָׂר מִדַּיָּא. שְׁנֵים עָשָׂר שִׁבְטַיָּא. אַחַד עָשָׂר כּוֹכְבַיָּא. עֲשָׂרָה דִבְּרַיָּא. תִּשְׁעָה יַרְחֵי לֵדָה. שְׁמוֹנָה יְמֵי מִילָה. שִׁבְעָה יְמֵי שַׁבַּתָּא. שִׁשָּׁה סִדְרֵי מִשְׁנָה. חֲמִשָּׁה חֻמְשֵׁי תוֹרָה. אַרְבַּע אִמָּהוֹת. שְׁלֹשָׁה אָבוֹת. שְׁנֵי לֻחוֹת הַבְּרִית. אֶחָד אֱלֹהֵינוּ שֶׁבַּשָּׁמַיִם וּבָאָרֶץ:

This is the meaning of "Who knows three? I know three. The patriarchs are three." For only we have within us the comprehensive qualities of all three patriarchs. We are therefore more precious in Hashem's eyes than all the hosts of the heavens!

end of **Ohel Yaakov**

Chad Gadya

An Only Kid

An only kid, an only kid, which my father bought for two zuzim. An only kid, an only kid.

And the cat came, and ate the kid, which my father bought for two zuzim. An only kid, an only kid.

And the dog came, and bit the cat, that ate the kid, which my father bought for two zuzim. An only kid, an only kid.

And the stick came, and beat the dog, that bit the cat, that ate the kid, which my father bought for two zuzim. An only kid, an only kid.

And the fire came, and burned the stick, that beat the dog, that bit the cat, that ate the kid, which my father bought for two zuzim. An only kid, an only kid.

And the water came, and extinguished the fire, that burned the stick, that beat the dog, that bit the cat, that ate the kid, which my father bought for two zuzim. An only kid, an only kid.

And the ox came, and drank the water, that extinguished the fire, that burned the stick, that beat the dog, that bit the cat, that ate the kid, which my father bought for two zuzim. An only kid, an only kid.

And the slaughterer came, and killed the ox, that drank the water, that extinguished the fire, that burned the stick, that beat the dog, that bit the cat, that ate the kid, which my father bought for two zuzim. An only kid, an only kid.

And the Angel of Death came, and slew the slaughterer, who killed the ox, that drank the water, that extinguished the fire, that burned the stick, that beat the dog, that bit the cat, that ate the kid, which my father bought for two zuzim. An only kid, an only kid.

And then came the Holy One, Blessed be He, and smote the Angel of Death, who slew the slaughterer, who killed the ox, that drank the water, that extinguished the fire, that burned the stick, that beat the dog, that bit the cat, that ate the kid, which my father bought for two zuzim. An only kid, an only kid.

חַד גַּדְיָא

חַד גַּדְיָא. חַד גַּדְיָא. דְּזַבִּין אַבָּא בִּתְרֵי זוּזֵי. חַד גַּדְיָא חַד גַּדְיָא:

וְאָתָא שׁוּנְרָא וְאָכְלָא לְגַדְיָא דְּזַבִּין אַבָּא בִּתְרֵי זוּזֵי. חַד גַּדְיָא חַד גַּדְיָא:

וְאָתָא כַלְבָּא וְנָשַׁךְ לְשׁוּנְרָא. דְּאָכְלָא לְגַדְיָא. דְּזַבִּין אַבָּא בִּתְרֵי זוּזֵי. חַד גַּדְיָא חַד גַּדְיָא:

וְאָתָא חוּטְרָא וְהִכָּא לְכַלְבָּא. דְּנָשַׁךְ לְשׁוּנְרָא. דְּאָכְלָא לְגַדְיָא. דְּזַבִּין אַבָּא בִּתְרֵי זוּזֵי. חַד גַּדְיָא חַד גַּדְיָא:

וְאָתָא נוּרָא וְשָׂרַף לְחוּטְרָא. דְּהִכָּה לְכַלְבָּא. דְּנָשַׁךְ לְשׁוּנְרָא. דְּאָכְלָא לְגַדְיָא. דְּזַבִּין אַבָּא בִּתְרֵי זוּזֵי. חַד גַּדְיָא חַד גַּדְיָא:

וְאָתָא מַיָּא וְכָבָה לְנוּרָא. דְּשָׂרַף לְחוּטְרָא. דְּהִכָּה לְכַלְבָּא. דְּנָשַׁךְ לְשׁוּנְרָא. דְּאָכְלָא לְגַדְיָא. דְּזַבִּין אַבָּא בִּתְרֵי זוּזֵי. חַד גַּדְיָא חַד גַּדְיָא:

וְאָתָא תוֹרָא וְשָׁתָה לְמַיָּא. דְּכָבָה לְנוּרָא. דְּשָׂרַף לְחוּטְרָא. דְּהִכָּה לְכַלְבָּא. דְּנָשַׁךְ לְשׁוּנְרָא. דְּאָכְלָא לְגַדְיָא. דְּזַבִּין אַבָּא בִּתְרֵי זוּזֵי. חַד גַּדְיָא חַד גַּדְיָא:

וְאָתָא הַשּׁוֹחֵט וְשָׁחַט לְתוֹרָא. דְּשָׁתָה לְמַיָּא. דְּכָבָה לְנוּרָא. דְּשָׂרַף לְחוּטְרָא. דְּהִכָּה לְכַלְבָּא. דְּנָשַׁךְ לְשׁוּנְרָא. דְּאָכְלָא לְגַדְיָא. דְּזַבִּין אַבָּא בִּתְרֵי זוּזֵי. חַד גַּדְיָא חַד גַּדְיָא:

וְאָתָא מַלְאַךְ הַמָּוֶת וְשָׁחַט לְשׁוֹחֵט. דְּשָׁחַט לְתוֹרָא. דְּשָׁתָה לְמַיָּא. דְּכָבָה לְנוּרָא. דְּשָׂרַף לְחוּטְרָא. דְּהִכָּה לְכַלְבָּא. דְּנָשַׁךְ לְשׁוּנְרָא. דְּאָכְלָא לְגַדְיָא. דְּזַבִּין אַבָּא בִּתְרֵי זוּזֵי. חַד גַּדְיָא חַד גַּדְיָא:

וְאָתָא הַקָּדוֹשׁ בְּרוּךְ הוּא וְשָׁחַט לְמַלְאַךְ הַמָּוֶת. דְּשָׁחַט לְשׁוֹחֵט. דְּשָׁחַט לְתוֹרָא. דְּשָׁתָה לְמַיָּא. דְּכָבָה לְנוּרָא. דְּשָׂרַף לְחוּטְרָא. דְּהִכָּה לְכַלְבָּא. דְּנָשַׁךְ לְשׁוּנְרָא. דְּאָכְלָא לְגַדְיָא. דְּזַבִּין אַבָּא בִּתְרֵי זוּזֵי. חַד גַּדְיָא חַד גַּדְיָא:

One should continue to occupy himself with the story of the Exodus and the laws of Pesach until sleep overtakes him.

Many recite Shir Hashirim which expresses the overwhelming love between Hashem and His chosen people, Yisrael.

שִׁיר הַשִּׁירִים

שִׁיר הַשִּׁירִים אֲשֶׁר לִשְׁלֹמֹה: יִשָּׁקֵנִי מִנְּשִׁיקוֹת פִּיהוּ כִּי־טוֹבִים דֹּדֶיךָ
מִיָּיִן: לְרֵיחַ שְׁמָנֶיךָ טוֹבִים שֶׁמֶן תּוּרַק שְׁמֶךָ עַל־כֵּן עֲלָמוֹת
אֲהֵבוּךָ: מָשְׁכֵנִי אַחֲרֶיךָ נָּרוּצָה הֱבִיאַנִי הַמֶּלֶךְ חֲדָרָיו נָגִילָה וְנִשְׂמְחָה
בָּךְ נַזְכִּירָה דֹדֶיךָ מִיַּיִן מֵישָׁרִים אֲהֵבוּךָ: שְׁחוֹרָה אֲנִי וְנָאוָה בְּנוֹת
יְרוּשָׁלָ‍ִם כְּאָהֳלֵי קֵדָר כִּירִיעוֹת שְׁלֹמֹה: אַל־תִּרְאוּנִי שֶׁאֲנִי שְׁחַרְחֹרֶת
שֶׁשֱּׁזָפַתְנִי הַשָּׁמֶשׁ בְּנֵי אִמִּי נִחֲרוּ־בִי שָׂמֻנִי נֹטֵרָה אֶת־הַכְּרָמִים כַּרְמִי
שֶׁלִּי לֹא נָטָרְתִּי: הַגִּידָה לִּי שֶׁאָהֲבָה נַפְשִׁי אֵיכָה תִרְעֶה אֵיכָה תַּרְבִּיץ
בַּצָּהֳרָיִם שַׁלָּמָה אֶהְיֶה כְּעֹטְיָה עַל עֶדְרֵי חֲבֵרֶיךָ: אִם־לֹא תֵדְעִי לָךְ
הַיָּפָה בַּנָּשִׁים צְאִי־לָךְ בְּעִקְבֵי הַצֹּאן וּרְעִי אֶת־גְּדִיֹּתַיִךְ עַל מִשְׁכְּנוֹת
הָרֹעִים: לְסֻסָתִי בְּרִכְבֵי פַרְעֹה דִּמִּיתִיךְ רַעְיָתִי: נָאווּ לְחָיַיִךְ בַּתֹּרִים
צַוָּארֵךְ בַּחֲרוּזִים: תּוֹרֵי זָהָב נַעֲשֶׂה־לָּךְ עִם נְקֻדּוֹת הַכָּסֶף: עַד־שֶׁהַמֶּלֶךְ
בִּמְסִבּוֹ נִרְדִּי נָתַן רֵיחוֹ: צְרוֹר הַמֹּר דּוֹדִי לִי בֵּין שָׁדַי יָלִין: אֶשְׁכֹּל
הַכֹּפֶר דּוֹדִי לִי בְּכַרְמֵי עֵין גֶּדִי: הִנָּךְ יָפָה רַעְיָתִי הִנָּךְ יָפָה עֵינַיִךְ יוֹנִים:
הִנְּךָ יָפֶה דוֹדִי אַף נָעִים אַף־עַרְשֵׂנוּ רַעֲנָנָה: קֹרוֹת בָּתֵּינוּ אֲרָזִים רָהִיטֵנוּ
בְּרוֹתִים:

מָשְׁכֵנִי אַחֲרֶיךָ נָּרוּצָה

O' draw me [out of my constricted state]! [Open our bonds and] we will run after You!

The Maggid of Dubno said: The first half of the verse speaks of our desire to be drawn to Hashem. The need to be drawn implies a refusal or inability to move on one's own. The second half of the verse speaks of our running to Hashem. Clearly, running implies that a person is motivated to go on his own. How can these two expressions be reconciled?

He explained with the following parable. A man's wife passed away and

left him with their only son. The father loved the boy and brought him up with devotion and self-sacrifice. He then sent him to yeshivah and taught him a trade.

Years passed and the father remarried. His second wife looked upon her stepson with contempt. The boy came to his father and complained, "Father, I don't feel at home here any more. I see that my presence upsets your domestic harmony. Give me enough money to open my own business, earn an honorable livelihood, and live on my own."

The father liked the idea, but what could he do? His new wife was such a miser that he was sure she would never agree to his giving his own son anything. He thought for a moment, however, and came up with a solution. He wrote out a bill of debt in which he promised to pay his son money that he owed him from his mother's dowry. He explained, "Now, when you come and demand this money, I will be forced to give it to you. Everything should work out fine!"

The young man thanked his father. He took the bill of debt, moved out of the house, and opened a business on the basis of the sum his father had promised to give him. When he came to collect the money, however, his stepmother opened the door and asked why he was there and what he wanted. When he showed her the bill of debt, she began shouting, "Forgery, forgery!" and she slammed the door in his face.

The boy returned home depressed. The next day, his father met him and asked him, "Why didn't you come to get the money?"

"I did come," he answered, "but your wife wouldn't let me in!"

"So what?" the father answered. "You have a bill of debt in your hand, signed by me. Summons me to court, and the judges will force me to pay!"

"Oh no, Father," the young man exclaimed, "I could never do that! How could a son ever summons his father to court?"

The father smiled, and said, "Foolish boy, it's nothing of the sort! We have no quarrel with each other. My desire to pay you is no less strong than your desire to receive the money. The whole reason for the summons is to make my wife think that I am being forced to pay you what I owe, and she will not be able to prevent me from doing so! As you know, if it were not for her, I would have run after you to give you the money!"

Our souls are extensions of Hashem's holiness. Deeply implanted in us is the desire to serve our Creator and to please Him in everything we do. It is only the yetzer hara (evil inclination) that makes its home within us and prevents us from doing what is most natural. We therefore ask: Master of the

אֲנִי חֲבַצֶּלֶת הַשָּׁרוֹן שׁוֹשַׁנַּת הָעֲמָקִים: כְּשׁוֹשַׁנָּה בֵּין הַחוֹחִים כֵּן רַעְיָתִי
בֵּין הַבָּנוֹת: כְּתַפּוּחַ בַּעֲצֵי הַיַּעַר כֵּן דּוֹדִי בֵּין הַבָּנִים בְּצִלּוֹ חִמַּדְתִּי
וְיָשַׁבְתִּי וּפִרְיוֹ מָתוֹק לְחִכִּי: הֱבִיאַנִי אֶל־בֵּית הַיָּיִן וְדִגְלוֹ עָלַי אַהֲבָה:
סַמְּכוּנִי בָּאֲשִׁישׁוֹת רַפְּדוּנִי בַּתַּפּוּחִים כִּי־חוֹלַת אַהֲבָה אָנִי: שְׂמֹאלוֹ
תַּחַת לְרֹאשִׁי וִימִינוֹ תְּחַבְּקֵנִי: הִשְׁבַּעְתִּי אֶתְכֶם בְּנוֹת יְרוּשָׁלַםִ בִּצְבָאוֹת
אוֹ בְּאַיְלוֹת הַשָּׂדֶה אִם־תָּעִירוּ וְאִם־תְּעוֹרְרוּ אֶת־הָאַהֲבָה עַד שֶׁתֶּחְפָּץ:
קוֹל דּוֹדִי הִנֵּה־זֶה בָּא מְדַלֵּג עַל־הֶהָרִים מְקַפֵּץ עַל־הַגְּבָעוֹת: דּוֹמֶה
דוֹדִי לִצְבִי אוֹ לְעֹפֶר הָאַיָּלִים הִנֵּה־זֶה עוֹמֵד אַחַר כָּתְלֵנוּ מַשְׁגִּיחַ מִן־
הַחַלֹּנוֹת מֵצִיץ מִן־הַחֲרַכִּים: עָנָה דוֹדִי וְאָמַר לִי קוּמִי לָךְ רַעְיָתִי יָפָתִי
וּלְכִי־לָךְ: כִּי־הִנֵּה הַסְּתָו עָבָר הַגֶּשֶׁם חָלַף הָלַךְ לוֹ: הַנִּצָּנִים נִרְאוּ
בָאָרֶץ עֵת הַזָּמִיר הִגִּיעַ וְקוֹל הַתּוֹר נִשְׁמַע בְּאַרְצֵנוּ: הַתְּאֵנָה חָנְטָה פַגֶּיהָ
וְהַגְּפָנִים סְמָדַר נָתְנוּ רֵיחַ קוּמִי לָךְ רַעְיָתִי יָפָתִי וּלְכִי־לָךְ: יוֹנָתִי בְּחַגְוֵי
הַסֶּלַע בְּסֵתֶר הַמַּדְרֵגָה הַרְאִינִי אֶת־מַרְאַיִךְ הַשְׁמִיעִינִי אֶת־קוֹלֵךְ כִּי־
קוֹלֵךְ עָרֵב וּמַרְאֵיךְ נָאוֶה: אֶחֱזוּ־לָנוּ שׁוּעָלִים שׁוּעָלִים קְטַנִּים מְחַבְּלִים
כְּרָמִים וּכְרָמֵינוּ סְמָדַר: דּוֹדִי לִי וַאֲנִי לוֹ הָרֹעֶה בַּשּׁוֹשַׁנִּים: עַד שֶׁיָּפוּחַ
הַיּוֹם וְנָסוּ הַצְּלָלִים סֹב דְּמֵה־לְךָ דוֹדִי לִצְבִי אוֹ לְעֹפֶר הָאַיָּלִים עַל־הָרֵי
בָתֶר:

world, "draw me," force me to do Your will, and thereby weaken the power of the yetzer. We will then automatically "run after you," of our own will.

Our Sages thus prayed: "Master of the world, it is revealed and known before You that our sole desire is to do Your will. What prevents us? The yeast in the dough (yetzer) and our subjugation to foreign governments. May it be Your will to rescue us from their clutches, so that we may return to You and wholeheartedly perform Your will!" (*Berachos* 17a). We also pray: "Open my heart with Your Torah so that my soul will run to do Your commandments [of its own accord]" (end of *Shemoneh Esreh*; *Berachos* ibid.).

Kol Yeshorer 3b

עַל מִשְׁכָּבִי בַּלֵּילוֹת בִּקַּשְׁתִּי אֵת שֶׁאָהֲבָה נַפְשִׁי בִּקַּשְׁתִּיו וְלֹא מְצָאתִיו׃
אָקוּמָה נָּא וַאֲסוֹבְבָה בָעִיר בַּשְּׁוָקִים וּבָרְחֹבוֹת אֲבַקְשָׁה אֵת שֶׁאָהֲבָה נַפְשִׁי בִּקַּשְׁתִּיו וְלֹא מְצָאתִיו׃ מְצָאוּנִי הַשֹּׁמְרִים הַסֹּבְבִים בָּעִיר אֵת שֶׁאָהֲבָה נַפְשִׁי רְאִיתֶם׃ כִּמְעַט שֶׁעָבַרְתִּי מֵהֶם עַד שֶׁמָּצָאתִי אֵת שֶׁאָהֲבָה נַפְשִׁי אֲחַזְתִּיו וְלֹא אַרְפֶּנּוּ עַד־שֶׁהֲבֵיאתִיו אֶל־בֵּית אִמִּי וְאֶל־חֶדֶר הוֹרָתִי׃ הִשְׁבַּעְתִּי אֶתְכֶם בְּנוֹת יְרוּשָׁלִַם בִּצְבָאוֹת אוֹ בְּאַיְלוֹת הַשָּׂדֶה אִם־תָּעִירוּ וְאִם־תְּעוֹרְרוּ אֶת־הָאַהֲבָה עַד שֶׁתֶּחְפָּץ׃ מִי זֹאת עֹלָה מִן־הַמִּדְבָּר כְּתִימְרוֹת עָשָׁן מְקֻטֶּרֶת מוֹר וּלְבוֹנָה מִכֹּל אַבְקַת רוֹכֵל׃ הִנֵּה מִטָּתוֹ שֶׁלִּשְׁלֹמֹה שִׁשִּׁים גִּבֹּרִים סָבִיב לָהּ מִגִּבֹּרֵי יִשְׂרָאֵל׃ כֻּלָּם אֲחֻזֵי חֶרֶב מְלֻמְּדֵי מִלְחָמָה אִישׁ חַרְבּוֹ עַל־יְרֵכוֹ מִפַּחַד בַּלֵּילוֹת׃ אַפִּרְיוֹן עָשָׂה לוֹ הַמֶּלֶךְ שְׁלֹמֹה מֵעֲצֵי הַלְּבָנוֹן׃ עַמּוּדָיו עָשָׂה כֶסֶף רְפִידָתוֹ זָהָב מֶרְכָּבוֹ אַרְגָּמָן תּוֹכוֹ רָצוּף אַהֲבָה מִבְּנוֹת יְרוּשָׁלִָם׃ צְאֶינָה וּרְאֶינָה בְּנוֹת צִיּוֹן בַּמֶּלֶךְ שְׁלֹמֹה בָּעֲטָרָה שֶׁעִטְּרָה־לּוֹ אִמּוֹ בְּיוֹם חֲתֻנָּתוֹ וּבְיוֹם שִׂמְחַת לִבּוֹ׃

מִי זֹאת עֹלָה מִן הַמִּדְבָּר כְּתִימְרוֹת עָשָׁן

Has there ever been another nation like this...

A midrash on this verse reads: The verse states: "Has there ever been another nation like this that came up from the wilderness like columns of incense?" Who is this nation whose every deed is done with fire, who ascend with fire and descend with fire? The Holy One said: They have the merit of the patriarchs on which to rely, as the verse continues, "perfumed with sweet myrrh" — the merit of Avraham, "and frankincense" — the merit of Yitzchak, "more aromatic than all the powders of the merchant" — the merit of Yaakov.

The Maggid of Dubno explained this midrash with the following parable: Three merchants were discussing which kind of merchandise and what approach to merchandising was better.

The first merchant said to his friends, "I travel the tried and true path. I take no chances. I only buy the quality and quantity of merchandise that I am sure I can sell. My profits are thus almost guaranteed!"

The second merchant broke in and said, "But when you buy only a limited quantity of a popular item, you have to pay a high price for it. Your profits are limited from the start. I, on the other hand, buy an entire boxcar of merchandise at the lowest possible price. When I sell it, I more than double my investment! That is the way to get rich."

The first merchant was not satisfied. "All fine and well if you manage to unload the merchandise. But what happens when you get stuck with the goods? With nobody willing to take it off your hands, you lose everything!"

The third merchant finally spoke up, "You are both right, and both of your approaches have plusses and minuses. The first approach is guaranteed, but limited. The second may bring in quick profits overnight, or may end up in total loss. I wouldn't advise anyone to act so rashly."

Both the first and second merchants spoke together, "But this is exactly the kind of business you do. You are famous for some of the great risks you have taken!"

"True," the third merchant admitted, "but I can afford to allow myself the luxury. I have a rich father who has given me his money with which to conduct my business. I thus can take great risks — and thank God I have been successful until now. However, I am aware of the fact that I may take a great fall one day and lose everything. But so what? I will go back to my father and he will provide another large sum of money for me to start with again. Now you understand why I said that I wouldn't advise others to do what I do. They simply don't have a safety net like I do to catch them if they fall."

The nations of the world were given seven basic commandments. They are not too difficult to keep. But this is called "making do with a little," for, after all, how much of a spiritual fortune can they accumulate in this way? The Jewish People, on the other hand, received 613 commandments. By observing all of them, they can attain infinite spiritual wealth. Of course, they take a risk. The danger exists that they will not be as cautious as they should, and they will be reprimanded for this.

When the nations see this, they ask Yisrael: "Who is this nation whose every deed is done with fire, who ascend with fire and descend with fire?" They have the opportunity to rise up to great heights and envision Hashem's blinding

הִנָּךְ יָפָה רַעְיָתִי הִנָּךְ יָפָה עֵינַיִךְ יוֹנִים מִבַּעַד לְצַמָּתֵךְ שַׂעְרֵךְ כְּעֵדֶר
הָעִזִּים שֶׁגָּלְשׁוּ מֵהַר גִּלְעָד: שִׁנַּיִךְ כְּעֵדֶר הַקְּצוּבוֹת שֶׁעָלוּ מִן־
הָרַחְצָה שֶׁכֻּלָּם מַתְאִימוֹת וְשַׁכֻּלָה אֵין בָּהֶם: כְּחוּט הַשָּׁנִי שִׂפְתֹתַיִךְ
וּמִדְבָּרֵיךְ נָאוֶה כְּפֶלַח הָרִמּוֹן רַקָּתֵךְ מִבַּעַד לְצַמָּתֵךְ: כְּמִגְדַּל דָּוִיד
צַוָּארֵךְ בָּנוּי לְתַלְפִּיּוֹת אֶלֶף הַמָּגֵן תָּלוּי עָלָיו כֹּל שִׁלְטֵי הַגִּבּוֹרִים: שְׁנֵי
שָׁדַיִךְ כִּשְׁנֵי עֳפָרִים תְּאוֹמֵי צְבִיָּה הָרוֹעִים בַּשּׁוֹשַׁנִּים: עַד שֶׁיָּפוּחַ הַיּוֹם
וְנָסוּ הַצְּלָלִים אֵלֶךְ לִי אֶל־הַר הַמּוֹר וְאֶל־גִּבְעַת הַלְּבוֹנָה: כֻּלָּךְ יָפָה
רַעְיָתִי וּמוּם אֵין בָּךְ: אִתִּי מִלְּבָנוֹן כַּלָּה אִתִּי מִלְּבָנוֹן תָּבוֹאִי תָּשׁוּרִי
מֵרֹאשׁ אֲמָנָה מֵרֹאשׁ שְׂנִיר וְחֶרְמוֹן מִמְּעֹנוֹת אֲרָיוֹת מֵהַרְרֵי נְמֵרִים:
לִבַּבְתִּנִי אֲחֹתִי כַלָּה לִבַּבְתִּינִי בְּאַחַת מֵעֵינַיִךְ בְּאַחַד עֲנָק מִצַּוְּרֹנָיִךְ: מַה־
יָּפוּ דֹדַיִךְ אֲחֹתִי כַלָּה מַה־טֹּבוּ דֹדַיִךְ מִיַּיִן וְרֵיחַ שְׁמָנַיִךְ מִכָּל־בְּשָׂמִים:
נֹפֶת תִּטֹּפְנָה שִׂפְתוֹתַיִךְ כַּלָּה דְּבַשׁ וְחָלָב תַּחַת לְשׁוֹנֵךְ וְרֵיחַ שַׂלְמֹתַיִךְ
כְּרֵיחַ לְבָנוֹן: גַּן נָעוּל אֲחֹתִי כַלָּה גַּל נָעוּל מַעְיָן חָתוּם: שְׁלָחַיִךְ פַּרְדֵּס
רִמּוֹנִים עִם פְּרִי מְגָדִים כְּפָרִים עִם־נְרָדִים: נֵרְדְּ וְכַרְכֹּם קָנֶה וְקִנָּמוֹן עִם
כָּל־עֲצֵי לְבוֹנָה מֹר וַאֲהָלוֹת עִם כָּל־רָאשֵׁי בְשָׂמִים: מַעְיַן גַּנִּים בְּאֵר
מַיִם חַיִּים וְנֹזְלִים מִן־לְבָנוֹן: עוּרִי צָפוֹן וּבוֹאִי תֵימָן הָפִיחִי גַנִּי יִזְּלוּ
בְשָׂמָיו יָבֹא דוֹדִי לְגַנּוֹ וְיֹאכַל פְּרִי מְגָדָיו:

glory, but they also run the risk of descending to great depths and thereby arousing Hashem's anger.

And the answer is: Yes, you are right, but don't worry, we have rich forefathers. Whenever anything goes wrong, we rely on their merit! Look how Moshe prayed when we fell by serving the Golden Calf, "Remember Avraham, Yitzchak, and Yisrael, Your servants" (*Shemos* 32:13). At that, "Hashem refrained from enacting the evil that He planned for His people" (ibid. 32:14). It is for this reason that we can afford to take the risk of accepting so many commandments and feel confident that we truly will never lose!

Kol Yeshorer 18a

לִבַּבְתִּנִי בְּאַחַת מֵעֵינַיִךְ

You have captivated My heart with one of your eyes [unquestioning faith], with one link of your necklace [of good deeds]!

The Sages (*Shabbos* 88b) explain: "You have captivated My heart with one of your eyes" — with one of your eyes when you first accepted My commandments and with both eyes after you fulfilled them. The Maggid of Dubno explained their intention with the following parable.

A king called his servant and ordered him to move all of his royal furniture and valuables from the palace to another mansion. The servant hurried to fulfill his king's command. With the sweat of his brow he managed to pack up the precious crystal and china, gold and silver antiques, haul all the heavy china closets, tables, desks, sofas, chairs, and beds, disassemble the large clothes closets, take down the drapes and roll up the carpets, pack up the chandeliers and the priceless wall paintings, and move everything to the second mansion. At the end of the day, he appeared exhausted and proud before the king to inform him of the completion of his job.

"Tell me now," the king asked, "what reward would you like for your work?"

The servant answered, "O mighty king! What can I say? You know full well how hard I labored. I therefore leave it to your majesty to determine my wages."

The king said, "First of all, I want to inform you that the new mansion with all that is in it is yours. Unknown to you, all your labor was for your own benefit! And now, I repeat my question: What would you like as a reward for your labor?"

Hearing this, the servant fell at his master's feet and thanked him for his beneficence. He expressed his gratitude from the bottom of his heart and refused to ask for or accept anything else. When the king continued to insist on giving him an additional reward for his faithful services, the servant began to appreciate an aspect of his master's infinite benevolence which he had never even dreamed existed!

Hashem created this world as a stage, with history serving as the drama and free-willed man the main character. As Rabbi Moshe Chaim Luzzatto explained (*Derech Hashem* 1:2-3), in order for man to become the creator of his own good and the master of his own perfection, an environment of the maximum possible

challenge is required. This in turn will result in the greatest possible pleasure of accomplishment. Such an environment must be one where neither Hashem Himself nor the Divine nature of our deeds is obvious. It must be a world where Hashem is hidden, and where good can only be accomplished with great difficulty. As a result, man will come to resemble his Creator and enjoy the greatest possible degree of closeness with the Divine.

The place where man will receive his reward, on the other hand, must be the exact opposite. In order for man to enjoy the maximum possible pleasure from the good he has done, the true nature of his deeds must be as obvious as possible. The existence of God must also be as apparent as possible in such a world. It must be an environment where man realizes the goodness of his deeds and their relationship to God.

It is for this reason that Hashem created two levels of existence. First there is this world (olam ha-zeh), a place of accomplishment and maximum challenge. Secondly, there is the World-to-Come (Olam Ha-Ba), the world of ultimate reward, where both Hashem's existence and the nature of one's deeds are totally apparent.

The Maggid of Dubno next explained the difference between serving Hashem with one eye or two: As long as the ultimate reasons for the commandments are hidden from us, we do them without knowing why, and hope for their reward in the World-to-Come. As the Sages put it, we have split vision. We keep one eye on the commandments, and the other on the future reward.

In the World-to-Come, however, when our eyes will be opened and we will see the true nature of the commandments — how they refine and illuminate the soul with Godliness — we will appreciate the commandments for their intrinsic value, as rewards in and of themselves. In short, we will focus both our eyes on them at the same time.

This is the meaning of, "Hashem commanded us to observe all these chukkim, to remain in awe of Hashem our God, for our everlasting good, to grant us eternal life as of today" (*Devarim* 6:24). At first, the commandments are called chukkim, laws whose reasons transcend human comprehension, regulations that we observe solely out of respect and obedience to the One Who commanded them, "to remain in awe of Hashem." In the future, however, we will understand that they were "for our everlasting good, to grant us eternal life as of today!"

Kol Yeshorer 24a

נֹפֶת תִּטֹּפְנָה שִׂפְתוֹתַיִךְ כַּלָּה, דְּבַשׁ וְחָלָב תַּחַת לְשׁוֹנֵךְ

My bride, your lips give forth sweet [explanations of My mitzvos]; honey and milk [My secrets] are guarded under your tongue.

The Maggid of Dubno taught: The Sages (*Pesachim* 87a) liken our present relationship with Hashem to that of an engaged couple. Yisrael is presently Hashem's betrothed. This is only in preparation for the future, however, when we will be married.

The Torah as well, the Maggid continued, is presently only our betrothed. This is alluded to in the verse, "Moshe prescribed the Torah to us, a morashah (inheritance) for the congregation of Yaakov" (*Devarim* 33:4), concerning which our Sages state, "Do not only read 'morashah' (inheritance) but 'me'orasah' (betrothed)" (*Pesachim* 49b). Again, in the future, this bond will be infinitely stronger. We will be married to the Torah.

In the meantime, it would be well to consider the differences between a betrothed and a married woman. Traditionally, the betrothed will only meet with her husband-to-be on rare occasions. Even on these occasions, she will act with due restraint in his presence and conduct herself with extreme modesty. She will not bare her heart to him, expose her deepest feelings, share her most intimate joys... Only after they are married will she reveal these things and speak openly to her husband.

Similarly, the Torah only reveals her deepest secrets to rare individuals. Even to them, she reveals herself in enigmatic hints and hidden allusions. They must examine in depth and probe her every word, never resting by day or by night. This is the meaning of the following parable from the *Zohar* (2:99a):

> How confused are the minds of the children of men because they do not truly contemplate the way of the Torah. For the Torah calls out each day with a sigh to the children of men, but they pay no attention....When the Torah is revealed and then immediately pulled back into concealment, this is only done for those who know it and occupy themselves with it.
>
> The Torah can thus be likened to a beautiful and stately woman who conceals herself upstairs in her castle. She has one single beloved whom the children of men do not know, for he is concealed. Out of love for her, however, he constantly passes by the gate of her castle, straining his eyes to catch a glimpse of her, looking every which way. She is aware that her beloved constantly passes by her gate. What does she do? She opens the window of her concealed upper chamber ever so slightly, reveals her face to her beloved for a split second, and immediately withdraws into concealment. Of the others who were with her beloved, none saw,

and none even looked, only he did. And his insides, his heart and his entire being were moved in tremendous longing for her. He knew that it was only because of her love for him that she disclosed herself for that split second, to arouse him [to love her even more].

This is the way of the Torah. She does not reveal herself except to the one who loves her, who knows the Torah, whose wise heart compels him to constantly pass back and forth each day at the gate of her castle. She then reveals her face to him from her upper chamber, giving him a hint [of her presence], and immediatley withdrawing to her place of concealment....In this way, the Torah is revealed and concealed, following the one whom she loves, to arouse him and awaken him.

Come and see the way of the Torah. At first, when she begins to reveal herself to a person [for a split second], she gives him a little hint. If he picks up on it, fine. If he does not understand, she sends her messengers to him saying, "Tell that simpleton to come here so that I may speak with him." This is the meaning of the verse, "O [tell the] simpleton, lacking brains, turn in here" (*Mishlei* 9:4). He is brought close to her. She begins to speak with him from behind a curtain. She speaks in the language of his own thoughts, until he starts to understand little by little. This is the level of derashah. Then she speaks to him from behind a thin veil. She speaks in enigmatic parables. This is the level of aggadah. After he becomes accustomed to her, she reveals herself to him face to face, speaking with him of her most concealed mysteries, all the concealed paths which have been hidden in her bosom from ancient days....She says, "Do you remember the hint I gave you back at the very beginning of your search? Do you see how many secrets were embedded in what I said? Do you see how it all fits together now?"

Hashem is always teaching us. Even before we knew anything about Him and His Torah, He was teaching us. If this is true of the individual, how much more so of the entire nation of Yisrael, who is likened to His betrothed! Thus, although we are simpletons who have misunderstood, Hashem has not given up on us. On the contrary, He created us to give us His Torah. His purpose will not be frustrated. We are thus promised that, in the future, "The earth will be filled with the knowledge of Hashem as the waters cover the sea" (*Yeshayahu* 11:9). Similarly, He promised us that, "I will place My Torah inside of them, and inscribe it upon their hearts....A man will no longer teach his friend and his brother saying, 'Know God!' For all of them will know Me, great and small alike" (*Yirmeyahu* 31:32-33). The Torah will thus be revealed to all, in all its fullness!

The Maggid of Lublin connected the Maggid of Dubno's explanation with our verse in the following way: "My bride, your lips give forth sweet [explanations of My mitzvos]; honey and milk [My secrets] are guarded under your tongue...." The Torah is presently like a bride-to-be. She reveals only the simple explanations of her mitzvos. Her deeper mysteries, which remain

בָּאתִי לְגַנִּי אֲחֹתִי כַלָּה אָרִיתִי מוֹרִי עִם־בְּשָׂמִי אָכַלְתִּי יַעְרִי עִם־דִּבְשִׁי
שָׁתִיתִי יֵינִי עִם־חֲלָבִי אִכְלוּ רֵעִים שְׁתוּ וְשִׁכְרוּ דּוֹדִים: אֲנִי יְשֵׁנָה
וְלִבִּי עֵר קוֹל דּוֹדִי דוֹפֵק פִּתְחִי־לִי אֲחֹתִי רַעְיָתִי יוֹנָתִי תַמָּתִי שֶׁרֹּאשִׁי
נִמְלָא־טָל קְוֻצּוֹתַי רְסִיסֵי לָיְלָה: פָּשַׁטְתִּי אֶת־כֻּתָּנְתִּי אֵיכָכָה אֶלְבָּשֶׁנָּה
רָחַצְתִּי אֶת־רַגְלַי אֵיכָכָה אֲטַנְּפֵם: דּוֹדִי שָׁלַח יָדוֹ מִן־הַחֹר וּמֵעַי הָמוּ
עָלָיו: קַמְתִּי אֲנִי לִפְתֹּחַ לְדוֹדִי וְיָדַי נָטְפוּ־מוֹר וְאֶצְבְּעֹתַי מוֹר עֹבֵר עַל
כַּפּוֹת הַמַּנְעוּל: פָּתַחְתִּי אֲנִי לְדוֹדִי וְדוֹדִי חָמַק עָבָר נַפְשִׁי יָצְאָה בְדַבְּרוֹ
בִּקַּשְׁתִּיהוּ וְלֹא מְצָאתִיהוּ קְרָאתִיו וְלֹא עָנָנִי: מְצָאֻנִי הַשֹּׁמְרִים הַסֹּבְבִים
בָּעִיר הִכּוּנִי פְצָעוּנִי נָשְׂאוּ אֶת־רְדִידִי מֵעָלַי שֹׁמְרֵי הַחֹמוֹת: הִשְׁבַּעְתִּי
אֶתְכֶם בְּנוֹת יְרוּשָׁלָם אִם־תִּמְצְאוּ אֶת־דּוֹדִי מַה־תַּגִּידוּ לוֹ שֶׁחוֹלַת אַהֲבָה
אָנִי: מַה־דּוֹדֵךְ מִדּוֹד הַיָּפָה בַּנָּשִׁים מַה־דּוֹדֵךְ מִדּוֹד שֶׁכָּכָה הִשְׁבַּעְתָּנוּ:
דּוֹדִי צַח וְאָדוֹם דָּגוּל מֵרְבָבָה: רֹאשׁוֹ כֶּתֶם פָּז קְוּצּוֹתָיו תַּלְתַּלִּים
שְׁחֹרוֹת כָּעוֹרֵב: עֵינָיו כְּיוֹנִים עַל־אֲפִיקֵי מָיִם רֹחֲצוֹת בֶּחָלָב יֹשְׁבוֹת
עַל־מִלֵּאת: לְחָיָו כַּעֲרוּגַת הַבֹּשֶׂם מִגְדְּלוֹת מֶרְקָחִים שִׂפְתוֹתָיו שׁוֹשַׁנִּים
נֹטְפוֹת מוֹר עֹבֵר: יָדָיו גְּלִילֵי זָהָב מְמֻלָּאִים בַּתַּרְשִׁישׁ מֵעָיו עֶשֶׁת
שֵׁן מְעֻלֶּפֶת סַפִּירִים: שׁוֹקָיו עַמּוּדֵי שֵׁשׁ מְיֻסָּדִים עַל־אַדְנֵי־פָז מַרְאֵהוּ
כַּלְּבָנוֹן בָּחוּר כָּאֲרָזִים: חִכּוֹ מַמְתַקִּים וְכֻלּוֹ מַחֲמַדִּים זֶה דוֹדִי וְזֶה רֵעִי
בְּנוֹת יְרוּשָׁלָם:

hidden "under her tongue" and "in her bosom," can only be grasped with tremendous effort and self-sacrifice. Only in the future will Hashem reveal all her secrets, as Rashi explains at the beginning of his commentary to *Shir Ha-Shirim* 1:2:

> O' that He would kiss me with the kisses of His mouth. Your spiritual love is far more pleasurable to me than a banquet of wine or any other celebration....[Shelomo Ha-Melech] used this imagery [of kissing, intimate love, and the physical pleasures of wine] to describe how Hashem "spoke to us face to face" (*Devarim* 5:4) when

He gave us His Torah, and how that affection and that love remain infinitely more precious to us than any worldly pleasure. [He also wished to inform us of] Hashem's assurance that He will reveal Himself to us again in the future to elucidate the deeper meanings of the Torah's commandments as well as to reveal her hidden mysteries to us. We therefore beseech Him to fulfill His promise. This is the meaning of "O' that He would kiss me with the kisses of His mouth!"

based on **Kochav Mi'Yaakov,** *Haftarah of Bemidbar*

דּוֹדִי שָׁלַח יָדוֹ מִן הַחוֹר, וּמֵעַי הָמוּ עָלָיו
My Beloved stretched His hand through the portal; my insides longed for Him.

Rabbi Yitzchak Isik of Komarna explained this verse with a parable told by the Ba'al Shem Tov: When a customer enters a grocery store that sells all kinds of sweets and delicacies, the storekeeper is happy to let him browse and taste as he wishes so that he will recognize the quality of the merchandise and want to buy it. If the customer finds a particular candy tasty, and wants to take another one, the storekeeper will stop him and say, "Pay first and eat later! We don't give food away in this store!"

Sweets are a parable for the Godly light. When a person first begins to come close to the Blessed One, he is given a little of this light so that he can recognize its goodness and in this way feel motivated to overcome his baser instincts. In this way, when the light is withheld from him afterwards, he will know what work he has to do to regain it and make it his own.

Otzar Ha-Chayim, *Naso*

פָּתַחְתִּי אֲנִי לְדוֹדִי, וְדוֹדִי חָמַק עָבָר
I opened to my Beloved, but my Beloved had already withdrawn Himself and was gone.

The Ba'al Shem Tov was asked: How is it that a person can elevate himself in the service of the Blessed Name, only to be pushed away without warning? How is it that, at first, a person is drawn near, to the extent that the gates of light begin to open for him, so that he tastes the intoxicating sweetness of being close to Hashem, and then, all of a sudden, he feels distant, rejected, and outcast from Hashem's presence?

The Ba'al Shem Tov compared this to a father teaching his son to walk. Holding the child's hand, the father steps backwards. The more steps the child

אָנָה הָלַךְ דּוֹדֵךְ הַיָּפָה בַּנָּשִׁים אָנָה פָּנָה דוֹדֵךְ וּנְבַקְשֶׁנּוּ עִמָּךְ: דּוֹדִי יָרַד
לְגַנּוֹ לַעֲרוּגוֹת הַבֹּשֶׂם לִרְעוֹת בַּגַּנִּים וְלִלְקֹט שׁוֹשַׁנִּים: אֲנִי לְדוֹדִי
וְדוֹדִי לִי הָרֹעֶה בַּשּׁוֹשַׁנִּים: יָפָה אַתְּ רַעְיָתִי כְּתִרְצָה נָאוָה כִּירוּשָׁלָ͏ִם
אֲיֻמָּה כַּנִּדְגָּלוֹת: הָסֵבִּי עֵינַיִךְ מִנֶּגְדִּי שֶׁהֵם הִרְהִיבֻנִי שַׂעְרֵךְ כְּעֵדֶר הָעִזִּים
שֶׁגָּלְשׁוּ מִן־הַגִּלְעָד: שִׁנַּיִךְ כְּעֵדֶר הָרְחֵלִים שֶׁעָלוּ מִן־הָרַחְצָה שֶׁכֻּלָּם
מַתְאִימוֹת וְשַׁכֻּלָה אֵין בָּהֶם: כְּפֶלַח הָרִמּוֹן רַקָּתֵךְ מִבַּעַד לְצַמָּתֵךְ:
שִׁשִּׁים הֵמָּה מְלָכוֹת וּשְׁמֹנִים פִּילַגְשִׁים וַעֲלָמוֹת אֵין מִסְפָּר: אַחַת הִיא
יוֹנָתִי תַמָּתִי אַחַת הִיא לְאִמָּהּ בָּרָה הִיא לְיוֹלַדְתָּהּ רָאוּהָ בָנוֹת וַיְאַשְּׁרוּהָ
מְלָכוֹת וּפִילַגְשִׁים וַיְהַלְלוּהָ: מִי־זֹאת הַנִּשְׁקָפָה כְּמוֹ־שָׁחַר יָפָה כַלְּבָנָה
בָּרָה כַּחַמָּה אֲיֻמָּה כַּנִּדְגָּלוֹת: אֶל־גִּנַּת אֱגוֹז יָרַדְתִּי לִרְאוֹת בְּאִבֵּי הַנָּחַל
לִרְאוֹת הֲפָרְחָה הַגֶּפֶן הֵנֵצוּ הָרִמֹּנִים: לֹא יָדַעְתִּי נַפְשִׁי שָׂמַתְנִי מַרְכְּבוֹת
עַמִּי־נָדִיב:

is able to take, the more the father pulls back and waits for the child to come to him. Just as the child starts feeling the joy of drawing near to his father, his father again moves backwards, not to be cruel, but to force him to take a few more steps on his own. This is repeated many times until the child learns how to walk by himself.

The Holy One conducts Himself in the same way towards those who wish to come near to Him. Every once in a while, He distances Himself from them, not to reject them or encourage them to give up, but so that they might strengthen themselves in serving Him and draw even closer by their own efforts. This is the meaning of David Ha-Melech's statement, "He shall lead them as young children" (*Tehillim* 48:15), to which Rashi adds, "Like a man who walks slowly with his son; like a father teaching his young child [how to walk]."

This, then, is the meaning of, "I opened to my Beloved, but my Beloved had already withdrawn Himself and was gone" (*Shir Ha-Shirim* 5:6). Even when we feel that He has withdrawn His love from us, we must know that He is waiting for us to make the effort to come towards Him on our own.

Kedushas Levi, *Shemos*

שִׁשִּׁים הֵמָּה מְלָכוֹת וּשְׁמֹנִים פִּילַגְשִׁים וַעֲלָמוֹת אֵין מִסְפָּר

There are sixty queens [philosophies], eighty concubines [sciences], and maidens [nation states] without number.

Rabbi Ovadyah Seforno explains this verse thus: "There are sixty queens" — numerous were the opinions of the ancient philosophers concerning the metaphysical nature of the Divinity. "Eighty concubines" — even more numerous were the opinions concerning the nature of the physical world. "And maidens without number" — countless divergent opinions concerning the proper governing of society [family and government].

The holy Rabbi Yisrael of Rizhin was asked: It goes without saying that the wisdom of the Torah and its Sages far surpasses that of the philosophers and scientists of the nations. How is it, then, that in a dispute over the course of the sun, the Jewish Sages conceded to their non-Jewish counterparts? Could it be that the gentile scientists knew something that our rabbis did not? The rabbi answered with a parable.

A mighty and beloved king built a magnificent palace with numerous rooms and chambers, one within the other, with the king's throne room in the innermost chamber.

When the construction of the palace was completed, the king wished to provide his subjects with a hint of the glory of his kingdom. He decided to invite them into his palace to view his hidden treasures, to feast their eyes on the priceless objects on display, and to enter into his throne room. The day and hour were announced; people came from far and wide to honor their beloved king.

Crowds of people began gathering outside the closed gates from the early morning hours. At the stroke of noon, the gates were opened and the people were ushered into an enormous courtyard in which many costly and enchanting objects were in display. Many stopped to browse, to examine their awesome beauty and detail, and to engage in lengthy discussions about their origins, properties, and respective values.

The more learned among them understood that this was only the beginning, and that incalculably greater treasures awaited them inside the palace itself. They entered chambers within chambers and stood transfixed before masterpieces of art, the likes of which they had never seen before.

The wise among them understood that even here they did not dare tarry. They knew that far greater surprises and far more priceless objects awaited them, and that the most wondrous of all were to be found in the king's own

innermost chamber. It was there, too, that the king himself waited to receive his subjects with joy, to show them the most prized objects in his treasuries, and to enlighten them concerning each and every thing they saw.

The rabbi explained: The laws of the physical world, even those governing the astronomical bodies of our solar system, are like the outer courtyard of Hashem's "palace" compared to the endless spiritual dimensions that lie hidden behind and beyond them. It is for this reason that our Sages devoted only a small part of their time to such studies. They preferred entering into the King's palace and making their way into the King's throne room. This is the intent of the following important statement by Rabbi Moshe Chayim Luzzatto in his *Ma'amar Ha-Aggados* concerning our Sages' approach to the scientific knowledge of their day:

> Our Sages of blessed memory encoded much of the esoteric tradition that they had received in matters relating to nature or astronomy. In other words, they utilized the knowledge of nature and astronomy that was accepted among gentile scholars of their time [in order to transmit hidden knowledge]. Thus, they never intended to teach the "physical" facts concerning these phenomena, but rather to utilize these facts as garments or vehicles for esoteric secrets. One should therefore not think that they were wrong because a particular model which they used is no longer accepted. Their intention was to clothe the hidden tradition in the accepted knowledge of their generation. That very tradition itself could have been clothed in a different garment according to what was accepted [as scientific fact] in other generations. And, in fact, the originator of that particular aggadic statement would have done so himself had he stated it in those other generations.

Ner Yisrael 4:1

שׁוּבִי שׁוּבִי הַשּׁוּלַמִּית שׁוּבִי שׁוּבִי וְנֶחֱזֶה־בָּךְ מַה־תֶּחֱזוּ בַּשּׁוּלַמִּית
כִּמְחֹלַת הַמַּחֲנָיִם: מַה־יָּפוּ פְעָמַיִךְ בַּנְּעָלִים בַּת־נָדִיב חַמּוּקֵי
יְרֵכַיִךְ כְּמוֹ חֲלָאִים מַעֲשֵׂה יְדֵי אָמָּן: שָׁרְרֵךְ אַגַּן הַסַּהַר אַל־יֶחְסַר
הַמָּזֶג בִּטְנֵךְ עֲרֵמַת חִטִּים סוּגָה בַּשּׁוֹשַׁנִּים: שְׁנֵי שָׁדַיִךְ כִּשְׁנֵי עֳפָרִים
תָּאֳמֵי צְבִיָּה: צַוָּארֵךְ כְּמִגְדַּל הַשֵּׁן עֵינַיִךְ בְּרֵכוֹת בְּחֶשְׁבּוֹן עַל־שַׁעַר בַּת־
רַבִּים אַפֵּךְ כְּמִגְדַּל הַלְּבָנוֹן צוֹפֶה פְּנֵי דַמָּשֶׂק: רֹאשֵׁךְ עָלַיִךְ כַּכַּרְמֶל
וְדַלַּת רֹאשֵׁךְ כָּאַרְגָּמָן מֶלֶךְ אָסוּר בָּרְהָטִים: מַה־יָּפִית וּמַה־נָּעַמְתְּ
אַהֲבָה בַּתַּעֲנוּגִים: זֹאת קוֹמָתֵךְ דָּמְתָה לְתָמָר וְשָׁדַיִךְ לְאַשְׁכֹּלוֹת: אָמַרְתִּי
אֶעֱלֶה בְתָמָר אֹחֲזָה בְּסַנְסִנָּיו וְיִהְיוּ־נָא שָׁדַיִךְ כְּאֶשְׁכְּלוֹת הַגֶּפֶן וְרֵיחַ
אַפֵּךְ כַּתַּפּוּחִים: וְחִכֵּךְ כְּיֵין הַטּוֹב הוֹלֵךְ לְדוֹדִי לְמֵישָׁרִים דּוֹבֵב שִׂפְתֵי
יְשֵׁנִים: אֲנִי לְדוֹדִי וְעָלַי תְּשׁוּקָתוֹ: לְכָה דוֹדִי נֵצֵא הַשָּׂדֶה נָלִינָה
בַּכְּפָרִים: נַשְׁכִּימָה לַכְּרָמִים נִרְאֶה אִם פָּרְחָה הַגֶּפֶן פִּתַּח הַסְּמָדַר הֵנֵצוּ
הָרִמּוֹנִים שָׁם אֶתֵּן אֶת־דֹּדַי לָךְ: הַדּוּדָאִים נָתְנוּ־רֵיחַ וְעַל־פְּתָחֵינוּ כָּל־
מְגָדִים חֲדָשִׁים גַּם־יְשָׁנִים דּוֹדִי צָפַנְתִּי לָךְ:

מַה יָּפִית וּמַה נָּעַמְתְּ, אַהֲבָה בַּתַּעֲנוּגִים

How beautiful and how pleasant you are when you attain sublime love [for Your King] even through physical delights.

Rabbi Yaakov Yosef of Polnoy explained this verse with a parable he heard from his master, the holy Ba'al Shem Tov.

A king had a son for whom he hired special tutors to teach him the ways of the kingdom. There was only one problem. The prince had no interest in his studies and paid no attention to his tutors. As a result, one tutor after another came to the same conclusion: The boy was a hopeless case.

Only one tutor was determined to stay. As a master educator, he tried everything to interest the prince in his studies, but nothing he did succeeded. Downcast, he went to the king and admitted his failure. He reported the prince's preoccupation with savory foods and tasty delicacies, that he was a connoisseur of candies, and how, as a result, he could never concentrate on his education.

To his astonishment, however, he saw the king's face light up with a smile, as if he were hearing good tidings. The king noticed the tutor's surprise and explained, "You must understand — as long as I thought there was nothing in the world that interested him, I myself was on the verge of giving up hope. But now that I see that he is interested in something, we can utilize it to our advantage!"

Immediately the king ordered the royal chef to stop cooking the foods that the young prince loved, unless he began taking his lessons seriously. He was not to be given any sweets either, unless he would review what he had learned that day. In this way, the boy advanced in his studies until he looked down upon his former ways and desired knowledge more than any other worldly delight!

By nature, we are far from serving Hashem properly. We are predisposed to physical pleasures as opposed to the delights of the soul. Still, we are intellectually aware that we must serve our Creator with love and awe. The question is, how can this be done?

The secret is to utilize the delights which we desire as springboards to more refined service of the Blessed Provider. If we wish to eat something that we "love," we should elevate that "love" to the One who has given us this delight. When we know that He is the Origin of that delight and all other delights, we can bless and thank Him, and attach ourselves to Him with greater fervor and passion than one who was never drawn to any physical pleasure!

This is the fervor and the passion of the ba'al teshuvah, the one who returns to Hashem out of love. The potency of his return is proportional to the attraction he felt for purely physical delights. As a result, he can attain the highest levels of spiritual love by realizing that the delight he thought he was getting from physical pleasures was not that at all! That physical delight was a disguise for something else. It was only the husk or shell around the precious fruit. Now he transfers all of his previous passion from the husk to the fruit!

Ben Poras Yosef, *Vayechi*

אַהֲבָה בְּתַעֲנוּגִים

Even through physical delights.

The Maggid of Dubno also told a parable about the place of physical pleasure in our service of Hashem:

It is written, "You shall rejoice in your Festivals" (*Devarim* 16:14). We are commanded to rejoice in our Festivals by partaking of festive food and

drink and by donning holiday apparel (*Pesachim* 109a). But are such material pleasures all there is to the observance of our sacred Festivals? And, if not, why does the Torah specifically command us thus to express our rejoicing? Why this emphasis on physical pleasures, when the chief feature of our Festivals is spiritual pleasure, the elevation of the soul? The following parable should clarify matters.

There was once a lame man who greatly resented being unable to leave his home. Now this man had a friend who, though strong and otherwise able, was quite deaf. One day it occurred to the lame man that if he and his friend got together, it would be advantageous to them both, one making up for the shortcomings of the other. And so it was agreed that the deaf man would be at his lame friend's disposal all day and carry him through the town on his shoulders, while the latter would act as his guide.

One day, when they were out together, they passed a wedding hall where the most delightful music could be heard. The lame man was very fond of music and he wanted to stop for a while to enjoy the lovely tunes to which he could not dance. But how could he make his friend, who could not hear a sound, stand still for a few minutes? Suddenly, he had an idea. In his pocket he happened to have a small bottle of gin with a tiny cup. He took the bottle out, filled the little cup, and offered it to his bearer. The latter then stopped long enough to drain the cup. Before he could walk on, however, the lame man offered him a second drink, and then a third. By this time, the deaf man had become somewhat tipsy and began to dance and enjoy himself. The lame man benefitted as well, for not only could he stop at this place to listen to the music, but he even got to dance on the shoulders of his partner. In this way, each of them was happy.

So too, said the Maggid of Dubno, it is with the neshamah (the soul) and the guf (the body). The neshamah, especially the neshamah yeserah — the additional soul that joins us on Sabbaths and Festivals (*Betza* 15a; *Ta'anis* 27b) — seeks spiritual pleasure. But the neshamah can only attain its greatest joy if the guf, too, will cooperate. It is therefore necessary to gladden the guf with Kiddush wine, good food, drink, and clothing to achieve the true and proper harmony of rejoicing which is expected of us on our Festivals.

Ohel Yaakov, *Re'eh*

לְכָה דוֹדִי נֵצֵא הַשָּׂדֶה, נָלִינָה בַּכְּפָרִים

Come, my Beloved, let us go out to the field [exile], let us lodge in the villages [of the nations].

In the Talmud (*Eruvin* 21b) we read:

> Rava said: What is the meaning of the verses, "Come, my Beloved, let us go out to the field, let us lodge in the villages. Let us arise early to the vineyards, let us see if the vine has flowered, if the grape blossoms have opened, if the pomegranates have bloomed. There I will offer my love to You" (*Shir Ha-Shirim* 7:12-13). "Come, my Beloved, let us go out to the field" — the Community of Yisrael spoke before the Holy One: Master of the world, do not judge me like the residents of cities in which there is theft, immorality, vain oaths, and false oaths. "Let us go out to the field" — come and I will show You disciples of the Sages who study the Torah in abject poverty. "Let us lodge in the kefarim (villages) [of the nations]" — do not only read kefarim (villages) but kofrim (nonbelievers). Come and I will show You those to whom You have granted prosperity, and yet who deny Your existence! "Let us arise early to the vineyards" — these are the synagogues and houses of study. "Let us see if the vine has flowered" — these are the masters of the Torah. "If the grape blossoms have opened" — these are the masters of Mishnah. "If the pomegranates have bloomed" — these are the masters of the Gemara. "There I will offer my love to You" — I will show You my true glory and greatness, the praiseworthiness of my sons and daughters.

Based on Rava's explanation, we might think that living in a village is preferable to living in a large city. The answer, of course, is that it depends on a number of factors. If, as Rashi explains, the city in question has a large population, with a heavy traffic of merchants and peddlers constantly passing through, where decadence and promiscuity is rampant, and theft is abundant, the answer is maybe. For we must still ask what kind of village we are talking about. If the village life is clean and simple, if, as Rashi describes, the men and the children can study Torah, even in poverty, then this is a place where the true greatness of Jewish sons and daughters is revealed in all its glory, and the answer is yes.

If, however, the opposite is true — if the city offers protection from unhealthy influences while the village has nothing of value to offer — the answer again is not so simple and depends on other factors, as the following story will illustrate.

A man came to the holy Rabbi Yechezkel of Kuzhmir to ask his advice. Should he establish residence in the city where the conditions are more crowded, and it is more difficult to make a living, or in a village among many non-Jews,

where he could live simply off the land and provide all the needs of his family? What should he do?

The rabbi answered, "It is an explicit verse in the Torah!"

The man didn't quite grasp what he meant. "Where is the answer to my question written in the Torah?"

The rabbi explained. "When Moshe Rabbenu sent the spies forth to search out the land, he instructed thus: 'Head north to the Negev, and then continue north to the hill country. See what kind of land it is. Are the people who live there strong or weak, few or many? Is the inhabited area good or bad? Are the cities where they live open or fortified? Is the soil rich or weak? Does the land have trees or not?' (*Bemidbar* 13:17-20).

"Rashi explained: 'Moshe gave them a sign. If they live in open villages, they are strong, relying on their own prowess. If they live in fortified cities, they are weak.'

"We learn from this," the rabbi concluded, "that a man must know himself. He must know whether he is strong enough to control himself, whether he and his family are capable of standing up under all kinds of pressures, against all kinds of negative influences. If he is, he may live anywhere he wishes, even in such a village. If, on the other hand, he is not sure of himself, he must not endanger himself or his family. He should rather take up residence in the shadow of a strong community which is fortified with a talmud torah, a yeshivah, a beis midrash, Torah classes, a rabbi...."

Nechmad Mi'Zahav, *Shelach*

מִי יִתֶּנְךָ כְּאָח לִי יוֹנֵק שְׁדֵי אִמִּי אֶמְצָאֲךָ בַחוּץ אֶשָּׁקְךָ גַּם לֹא־יָבוּזוּ
לִי׃ אֶנְהָגֲךָ אֲבִיאֲךָ אֶל־בֵּית אִמִּי תְּלַמְּדֵנִי אַשְׁקְךָ מִיַּיִן הָרֶקַח מֵעֲסִיס
רִמֹּנִי׃ שְׂמֹאלוֹ תַּחַת רֹאשִׁי וִימִינוֹ תְּחַבְּקֵנִי׃ הִשְׁבַּעְתִּי אֶתְכֶם בְּנוֹת
יְרוּשָׁלִָם מַה־תָּעִירוּ וּמַה־תְּעֹרְרוּ אֶת־הָאַהֲבָה עַד שֶׁתֶּחְפָּץ׃ מִי זֹאת
עֹלָה מִן־הַמִּדְבָּר מִתְרַפֶּקֶת עַל־דּוֹדָהּ תַּחַת הַתַּפּוּחַ עוֹרַרְתִּיךָ שָׁמָּה
חִבְּלַתְךָ אִמֶּךָ שָׁמָּה חִבְּלָה יְלָדַתְךָ׃ שִׂימֵנִי כַחוֹתָם עַל־לִבֶּךָ כַּחוֹתָם
עַל־זְרוֹעֶךָ כִּי־עַזָּה כַמָּוֶת אַהֲבָה קָשָׁה כִשְׁאוֹל קִנְאָה רְשָׁפֶיהָ רִשְׁפֵּי
אֵשׁ שַׁלְהֶבֶתְיָה׃ מַיִם רַבִּים לֹא יוּכְלוּ לְכַבּוֹת אֶת־הָאַהֲבָה וּנְהָרוֹת לֹא
יִשְׁטְפוּהָ אִם־יִתֵּן אִישׁ אֶת־כָּל־הוֹן בֵּיתוֹ בָּאַהֲבָה בּוֹז יָבוּזוּ לוֹ׃ אָחוֹת
לָנוּ קְטַנָּה וְשָׁדַיִם אֵין לָהּ מַה־נַּעֲשֶׂה לַאֲחֹתֵנוּ בַּיּוֹם שֶׁיְּדֻבַּר־בָּהּ׃ אִם־
חוֹמָה הִיא נִבְנֶה עָלֶיהָ טִירַת כָּסֶף וְאִם־דֶּלֶת הִיא נָצוּר עָלֶיהָ לוּחַ אָרֶז׃
אֲנִי חוֹמָה וְשָׁדַי כַּמִּגְדָּלוֹת אָז הָיִיתִי בְעֵינָיו כְּמוֹצְאֵת שָׁלוֹם׃ כֶּרֶם הָיָה
לִשְׁלֹמֹה בְּבַעַל הָמוֹן נָתַן אֶת־הַכֶּרֶם לַנֹּטְרִים אִישׁ יָבִא בְּפִרְיוֹ אֶלֶף
כָּסֶף׃ כַּרְמִי שֶׁלִּי לְפָנָי הָאֶלֶף לְךָ שְׁלֹמֹה וּמָאתַיִם לְנֹטְרִים אֶת־פִּרְיוֹ׃
הַיּוֹשֶׁבֶת בַּגַּנִּים חֲבֵרִים מַקְשִׁיבִים לְקוֹלֵךְ הַשְׁמִיעִנִי׃ בְּרַח דּוֹדִי וּדְמֵה־
לְךָ לִצְבִי אוֹ לְעֹפֶר הָאַיָּלִים עַל הָרֵי בְשָׂמִים׃

אִם יִתֵּן אִישׁ אֶת כָּל הוֹן בֵּיתוֹ בָּאַהֲבָה, בּוֹז יָבוּזוּ לוֹ

Even when mankind will [wake up to the truth in the World-to-Come, and] offer all its worldly wealth for the sake of this love, they will be sorely ashamed.

The Maggid of Dubno quoted a midrash that explains this verse: In the future, the nations of the world will "wake up to the truth" and declare: "We will give all the wealth of the world for the sake of the Torah!" The Holy One will answer them, however, saying, "Even if you would give Me all the money you own in exchange for the Torah, it would be an embarrassment for you." What is the meaning of this midrash? Another midrash will help to clarify. The Talmud (*Avodah Zarah* 2a-b) records the following

Rabbi Chaninah bar Pappa [and] Rabbi Simlai expounded: In the Ultimate Future, the Holy One will bring a Torah scroll and hold it near His breast. He will say: Let he who occupied himself with this [Torah] come and receive his reward. All of a sudden, all of the idolatrous nations will come and gather together in a great tumult, as it says, "All the nations shall gather together" (*Yeshayahu* 43:9). The Holy One will chastise them, however, saying, "Do not all enter at once before Me in a tumult. Rather, each nation enter separately with its scholars." The verse thus continues: "And all the governments assembled" (ibid.).

Rome will then enter first, for they consider themselves most important of all....The Holy One will ask them, "What were your accomplishments?" They will answer, "We built many marketplaces, we made many bathhouses, we accumulated much gold and silver, and all of this was for Yisrael, so that they could learn Torah!" The Holy One will answer, "Fools, all that you did was for yourselves! You built marketplaces to place prostitutes there, bathhouses to pamper yourselves, and as for gold and silver, that is Mine....Isn't there one among you who occupied himself with this [Torah]?" The Romans will leave shamefaced, and the Persians will enter.... "Isn't there one among you who occupied himself with this [Torah]?"

The Talmud goes on: Other nations will enter. They too will claim to have done everything so that Yisrael could occupy themselves with the Torah. They too will depart embarrassed. Some will attempt to justify themselves by claiming that if they would have been forced to receive the Torah, as Yisrael was, they would have observed it too. This claim is refuted: They did not even keep the minimum of seven commandments that were given to all the children of Noach.

"But," they will retort, "did Yisrael keep the Torah as they should have?" Yes, and witnesses, Yisrael's former enemies and oppressors, will be brought in to the Heavenly Tribunal to testify on their behalf. Nimrod will testify on Avraham's behalf, Lavan on Yaakov's behalf, Potiphar's wife on Yosef's behalf, Nevuchadnetzar on Chananyah, Misha'el, and Azaryah's behalf, and Daryavesh on Daniel's behalf... (*Avodah Zarah* 3a).

Finally, as a last chance, the nations will plead, "Master of the world! Give us a chance to start over. Give us the Torah and we will observe it!" The Holy One's famous answer will be: "Fools, only he who labors on Erev Shabbos partakes on Shabbos! If one did not labor, from where shall he eat?"

This, explained the Maggid of Dubno, is the meaning of our verse, "Even if a man would offer all his worldly wealth for the sake of the love [of this Torah], he would be sorely ashamed" (*Shir Ha-Shirim* 8:7). He illustrated this with a famous parable.

A mighty king had managed to accumulate a tremendous treasure house of diamonds, emeralds, sapphires, rubies, and pearls. His treasurer was an old and wise man who was an authority on precious stones.

Years passed, and the king's treasurer died. The king began searching for someone equally as knowledgeable about gems to take his place. The problem was, how could he be sure of who was really an expert?

The king took one his most expensive and rare diamonds, worth one million gildens, and gave it to his most trusted minister with the following instructions: "Go to the diamond center where dealers from all over the continent gather, and offer this diamond up for sale. The one who recognizes its value will naturally outbid all the rest. This will be your sign that he is the most knowledgeable of them all. Invite him here to the palace, and I will place him in charge of my royal treasures."

That very day, a wealthy aristocrat, who had inherited his father's millions, arrived at the diamond center. To tell the truth, he was an absolute ignoramus about diamonds and gems. His only reason for coming to the center was because people told him he could double his fortune. He had therefore come to "deal in diamonds."

A few of the more cunning — and less scrupulous — diamond dealers immediately spotted him as easy prey. They sold him polished glass for exorbitant prices. The aristocrat rejoiced, however, thinking that he had made a kill, buying such beautiful "diamonds" for next to nothing.

Shortly afterwards, he noticed that some dealers were vying over a particularly beautiful gem. Each buyer offered a little more than the last, and the bidding was hot and serious. Realizing that the merchandise must be worth it if they were not giving up, he outbid all of them, and paid cash on the spot.

Suddenly, there was silence in the center. The king's minister had entered and was holding up the rare diamond in his fingers. Its majestic size and sparkle hypnotized everyone present. The dealers approached the king's minister in order to examine the gem. The atmosphere in the hall was electrifying. Not every day did one see such a diamond!

"One hundred thousand gildens!" the first one bid.

"One hundred and ten!" another voice rang out.

"One hundred and twenty!" another called.

"One hundred and twenty-five!" still another said.

"Fools!" one dealer called out. "This is the rarest diamond ever seen in this hall! I offer two hundred thousand gildens!"

"But it is worth two hundred and fifty thousand, a quarter of a million!" another exclaimed.

"That is nothing compared to the real value of this diamond," the king's minister stated flatly. "Who will add to the price already offered?"

"I will," the ignoramus aristocrat spoke up. "I offer three hundred thousand gildens."

The king's minister looked upon the aristocrat with admiration. This must be the man I am looking for, the greatest expert on gems present in this hall, he thought. He will be the king's treasurer!

The ignoramus aristocrat approached the king's minister to pay for the prized diamond. "I will pay part in cash," he said, "and part in merchandise that I purchased here." The minister agreed.

The aristocrat handed over two hundred thousand gildens and added what he thought was another one hundred thousand worth in polished glass. The minister immediately spotted the fake merchandise and understood what kind of a man he was dealing with.

Shelomo Ha-Melech wrote: "It [the Torah] is more precious than pearls; all that is desirable does not compare to her worth" (*Mishlei* 3:15). In the first half of this verse, Shelomo Ha-Melech concedes that pearls are precious, and merely adds that the Torah is more precious. In the second half, he categorically states that the sum total of all that is desirable, all the gold and silver, diamonds and pearls in the entire world cannot even compare with the Torah. They are not in the same class, and are considered as naught compared to the infinite worth of the Torah.

Shelomo is thus talking about two different types of people. There are those who value the vanities of this world. These he answers according to their own values and point of view. He informs them that the Torah is more important, more valuable, than even their most precious commodity. Then there are those who understand that the entire world and everything in it is inconsequential when compared with just one word of the Torah! To them, he answers straight to the point.

This then is the meaning of the midrash quoted above. Yisrael knows the value of the Torah and cherishes it for its intrinsic worth. They understand that physicality compared to spirituality is like sand compared to diamonds. There are those among the nations of the world, on the other hand, who value only tangible wealth and attach great importance only to that which can yield

material gratification. Of course, when they realize that the reward for keeping the Torah is "more precious than pearls," they will want to sell their worldly possessions in exchange for the spiritual light of Torah. This very act will serve as a proof, however, that they do not understand one iota of the true value of God's light. Like the aristocrat, they fail to distinguish between polished glass and real diamonds. How embarrassed and ashamed they will feel!

Kol Yeshorer 31a

SHIR HASHIRIM
THE SONG OF SONGS

An interpretative translation based on traditional sources (Targum, Midrash, Rashi, Metzudos, Alshich, Gra, Netziv, and Malbim), by Avraham Sutton

I

The Community of Yisrael reminisces:

The Song of Songs, by Shelomo, dedicated to the One to whom all peace and perfection belongs. O' that He would kiss me with the kisses of His mouth [o' that He would reveal the secrets of His Torah to me as He began to do at Sinai]. Your spiritual love is far more precious to me than wine [all the pleasures of this world]. Your fragrant oils are pleasing to the smell; [the fragrance of] Your Name is like precious oil poured forth. Young maidens love You. O' draw me [out of my constricted state]! [Open our bonds and] we will run after You! [I fondly remember when] the King brought me into His chambers. [We await the day when] we will delight and rejoice in You [evermore]! [In the meantime] we recall Your fond love, more pleasant than wine. All who are upright love You! Now, though I seem darkened [by exile], I am comely [for the redemption], o' daughters of Yerushalayim [nations of the world]. [I am darkened without] like the tents of Kedar, [but comely within] as the curtains [of the Temple] of Shelomo. Do not view me with contempt because I am dark, for the sun [of exile] has scorched me. My mother's sons [the children of Esav] were enraged with me, and made me keeper of [their] vineyards [foreign idols]. [As a result] I neglected my own vineyard. Tell me, o' You whom my soul loves, where do You pasture [Your flocks], where do You find shade for them to lie down at midday, [when the sun of exile burns exceedingly hot]? For why should I be left to wander amidst the flocks [of the idolatrous nations] who associate their gods with You?

Hashem answers:

If you do not know yourself [how to restore the intimate closeness we once shared], o' most beautiful of women, follow the footsteps of the flock [your holy ancestors], and pasture your kids beside the tents of the shepherds [patriarchs of My people]. [When you were in Egypt] I likened you to My own horse which Pharaoh had harnessed [and used] for his chariots, o' My beloved. [But then I freed you and brought you to Sinai to give you] My Torah whose words are beautiful bridles for your mouth, and Divine yokes around your necks. I also made [the Tablets] for you, more precious than gold, overlaid with [the Ten Commandments like] silver points.

Yisrael responds:

[But then] just as my King was celebrating [giving the Tablets to Moshe], my evil

odor [the sin of the golden calf] gave forth its scent. [Still, by commanding me to build the Mishkan] my Beloved restored my sweet fragrance to me; He returned to dwell in the Holy of Holies of my heart. Like clusters of sweet-smelling spices in the groves of Ein Gedi, my Beloved has never stopped atoning for my many wrongdoings.

Hashem speaks:

Behold, you are beautiful, My love, you are beautiful, when your eyes are like doves, [looking only to Me].

Yisrael replies:

It is You who are beautiful and pleasant, my Beloved. And our meeting place [in the Holy of Holies of the Temple] is still beloved to me. [Rebuild soon] the beams of our House from strong cedar wood, and our lofts from fir.

II

[When I do Your will, o' Beloved,] I am likened to the rose of Sharon [Garden of Eden], the lily of the valleys [nourished by the waters of Eden].

Hashem says:

[But when you turn away from Me,] My love, you are [torn] like a rose among thorns, [exiled] among the young maidens [nations of the world].

Yisrael replies:

Like an apple tree [Tree of Life] in the heart of the forest, so was my Beloved [praised] in the midst of the youths [angelic hosts] [when He descended unto Sinai]. O' how I longed to dwell under His shadow; to taste the fruit [of His Torah], so sweet to my palate. So He brought me to His banquet hall [Sinai], and spread His canopy of love over me. [Still weak and vulnerable after my long exile,] He sustained me with the cream of the wheat. Because I was lovesick, He surrounded me with fragrant apple blossoms [to restore my soul]. He placed His left hand under my head; His right hand embraces me still.

Hashem speaks:

I caution you, [o' Yisrael, scattered among] the daughters of Yerushalayim [nations of the world], whether by the angelic hosts [of heaven] or by the deer of the field, lest you try to artificially arouse or awaken love [the Final Redemption] until such time as I desire. [When that time does come, however...]

Yisrael will say:

Behold, the call of my Beloved! He is coming [to redeem me before the appointed time]. He is leaping over the mountains [in the merit of the patriarchs]. He is springing over the hills [in the merit of the matriarchs]. [In His haste to redeem me] my Beloved is like a gazelle or a young deer. [I thought He had abandoned me forever, but] behold, He was [near the entire time,] standing behind our wall, supervising from the windows, peering through the lattices. My Beloved will then answer and say to me:

Hashem speaks:
[The time has come for you to] rise up, My love, My beauty, and go forth [from the exile]. For behold the winter [exile] has passed, and the downpour [suffering] is over and gone. The blossoms [righteous souls] are appearing in the world; the season of the zamir [songbird, song of redemption, pruning the wicked] has arrived, and the voice of the tor [turtledove, Torah, Mashiach] is heard in our land. The fig tree is dropping its unripe fruits, while the grapevines in blossom send forth their scent. Arise, My love, My beauty, and go forth [just as you departed from Egypt]. O' My dove, [when you are] caught in the clefts of the rock, concealed in the cliff's terrace, let Me behold your countenance, let Me hear your voice. For your voice is sweet and your appearance is pleasant!
Yisrael says:
We must seize the sly foxes, the little foxes [in our midst], destroyers of vineyards. [They would destroy us from within were not] our vineyards full of blossoms [righteous tzaddikim]. [In their merit] my Beloved is mine and I am His! He continues to shepherd His flock in the merit of the roses [righteous]. O' my Beloved, before the day draws to an end, and the shadows of evening begin to extend, turn [Your face towards me] like a gazelle or a young deer, [and leap] over the mountains that separate us...

III

At night, on my bed, I sought the One my soul loves; I sought Him, but I did not find Him. [I said in my heart:] Let me rise up now and walk through the city [Yerushalayim], in the marketplaces and in the streets. Let me search for the One my soul loves! I sought Him, but I did not find Him. The [righteous] watchmen who roam the city found me. [I asked them:] Have you noticed the One Whom my soul loves? Shortly after leaving them, I found the One my soul loves. I held Him and would not let Him go until I brought Him into my Mother's House [Second Beis Ha-Mikdash], into the chamber [Holy of Holies] of She [Shechinah] Who conceived me. [Then I went into exile again...]
Hashem speaks:
Again I caution you, [o' Yisrael, scattered among] the daughters of Yerushalayim [nations of the world], whether by the angelic hosts [of heaven] or by the deer of the field, lest you try to artificially arouse or awaken love [the Final Redemption] until such time as I desire.
Yisrael pleads:
[True, I am not worthy, but please remember how I followed You in the wilderness for forty years, and then entered the land.] Has there ever been another nation like this that came up from the wilderness like columns of incense, perfumed with sweet myrrh [the merit of Avraham] and frankincense [Yitzchak], more aromatic than all the powders of a merchant [Yaakov]? Behold, [we carried] the couch [Ark] of Shelomo, the One to whom all peace and perfection belongs, surrounded by

sixty [ten thousands] of the valiant warriors of Yisrael. All of them were armed with swords and trained in [the tactics of] war. Each had his sword upon his thigh [to protect] from fears in the night. [In their merit] the One to whom belong all peace and perfection built Himself a Palace from the cedars of Levanon. He ornamented its outer columns with silver, the top of its Ark with gold, its curtain with purple wool, its inner sanctum inlaid with a love more intense than that of all the daughters of Yerushalayim [nations of the world]. Go forth, o' you daughters of Tzion [children of Yisrael], and look upon Shelomo, [gaze upon] the crown with which His mother [the nation of Yisrael] crowned Him on His wedding day [at Sinai], and on the day His heart rejoiced [in building the Temple]!

IV

Hashem speaks:

Behold, you are beautiful, My love, you are beautiful! Your eyes [righteous tzaddikim] are like doves [safeguarded] behind your veil [of modesty]; your locks [simple folk] resemble a flock of goats trailing down from Mount Gilead. Your teeth [soldiers] are like a flock of shorn sheep which have come up from the washing; all of them are paired, and not one is missing. [The prayers of] your lips [have the power to whiten] scarlet threads [sins], and your [Torah] speech is delicate and fine. Your temples [sages] behind your veil are [filled with wisdom] as a slice of pomegranate [is filled with seeds]. Your neck [king] is like the tower of David, built with turrets, upon which hang a thousand shields, the armor of mighty warriors. Your two breasts [ben Yosef and ben David] are like two fawns [Moshe and Aharon], twins of the female roe [Shechinah], grazing among the roses. Before the day draws to an end, and the shadows of evening begin to extend, I will make My way to the Mountain of Myrrh [Moriah] and to the Hill of Frankincense [the Temple Mount]. [There I will find] you entirely beautiful, My love; [there I will declare] you altogether without blemish. Come with Me from Levanon, My bride, come with Me from Levanon; depart from the height of Amanah, from the peaks of Senir and Hermon, from the dens of lions, from the mountain lares of leopards. You have captivated My heart, My sister, My bride; you have captivated My heart with one of your eyes [unquestioning faith], with one link of your necklace [of good deeds]. How precious your love is to Me, My sister, My bride; How much better your love than [the simulated effects of] wine. The scent of your anointing oils [is more enchanting] than any incense spice. My bride, your lips give forth sweet [explanations of My mitzvos]; honey and milk [My secrets] are guarded under your tongue, and the sweet scent of your garments is like the scent of Levanon. You are an enclosed garden, My sister, My bride; you are an enclosed spring, a sealed fountain. Your offshoots are an orchard of pomegranates with [other] rare fruits, henna and nard [atonement for sins]. Nard and saffron, calamus and cinnamon, with many frankincense trees, myrrh and aloes, with all the finest spices. You are a fountain that waters many gardens,

a wellspring of living waters, flowing down from Levanon. Awake, o' north wind, and come, south wind! Blow upon My garden, that its perfumes waft out.
Yisrael asks:
Then will my Beloved come into His garden to partake of His choice fruits?

V

Hashem answers:
Yes, I have come to My garden, My sister, My bride! I have gathered My myrrh and My spice; I have partaken of My honeycomb with My honey; I have drunk My wine with My milk. Partake, loved ones, drink, beloveds, and become intoxicated [with My prophetic spirit].
Yisrael speaks:
[That was long ago; now] I am asleep [in exile], and only my heart is awake. [I dimly hear] the sound of my Beloved knocking: "Open [your heart] to Me, My sister, My love, My dove, My perfect twin, for My head is filled with dew and My locks with the drops of the night!" [But in my sleep, I answer:] I have taken off my robe, how shall I put it on again? [Hashem answered:] "I too have washed My feet, how shall I soil them?" [In one more attempt to awaken me] my Beloved stretched His hand through the portal; my insides longed for Him. I arose to open for my Beloved, and my hands once again dripped with myrrh [good deeds], and my fingers with the finest myrrh [the merit of Avraham], overflowing unto the handles of the door. [But it was already too late, for when] I opened to my Beloved, my Beloved had already withdrawn Himself and was gone. My soul had departed when He spoke [on Sinai]! Now I searched for Him and could not find Him. I called Him, but He would not answer. The watchmen who patrol the city [the nations who destroyed the Temple in Yerushalayim] struck me and wounded me. The guardians of the walls stripped me of my mantle. I therefore caution you, o' daughters of Yerushalayim [nations of the world], if you find my Beloved, tell Him that I am lovesick for Him [and can hardly go on]...
The nations speak:
What distinguishes your Beloved from any other beloved, o' most beautiful of women? What distinguishes your Beloved from any other beloved, that you caution us so?
Yisrael answers:
My Beloved harmonizes pure white [love] and rosy red [strict justice]. He is distinguished among the tens of thousands [of His supernal hosts]. [The crown of] His head is of the purest gold; the locks of His hair flow down in mounds, black as a raven. His eyes are like doves beside flowing streams of water, washed in milky white, well-fitted in their settings. His cheeks are like a bed of balsam spices, producing sweet perfumes; His lips are like roses, flowing with the finest myrrh. His hands are like wheels of gold studded with topaz; His waist is like polished ivory overlaid with sapphires. His legs are like pillars of marble set upon

sockets of fine gold; His appearance is like Levanon, chosen of all cedars. His mouth is sweet; He is altogether desirable. This is my Beloved, this is my Friend, o' daughters of Yerushalayim!

VI

The nations ask:
Where has your Beloved gone, o' most beautiful of women? Where has your Beloved turned, and we shall seek Him with you!
Yisrael answers:
My Beloved has gone down to His garden, to the bed of balsam spices, to graze in [foreign] gardens and to collect roses [precious lost souls]. [Now I know that] I am still my Beloved's and my Beloved is mine; He grazes among the roses.
Hashem speaks:
When your deeds are pleasing, You are as beautiful, My love, as beautiful as in Yerushalayim of old, awesome as when your bannered hosts [marched in the wilderness]. Turn your gaze away from Me, for [your eyes] enchant Me. Your hair resembles a flock of goats trailing down from Mount Gilead. Your teeth are like a flock of sheep which have come up from the washing; all of them are paired, and not one is missing. Your temples are as a slice of pomegranate behind your veil [of modesty]. There are sixty queens [philosophies], eighty concubines [sciences], and maidens [nation states] without number. But My dove, My perfect twin, is unique. She is the only one of her Mother, the chosen of Her that bore her. Maidens behold her and bless her; queens and concubines praise her: Who is this [nation], transparent like the dawn, beautiful as the moon, bright as the sun, awesome as bannered hosts [marching in the wilderness]? I will descend now to the nut garden, to behold the fruits of the river valley, to see whether the vine has blossomed, whether the pomegranates are in flower.
Yisrael says:
[In exile] I completely lost consciousness of myself; [only the exalted source of the souls of] my people made me a chariot for the Generous One.

VII

The prophets speak:
Return [to Hashem], return to your perfection, o' Shulamis! Return, return, so that we may describe to you the great vision concerning your future and the perfection we see in store for you, o' Shulamis! If you will return you will see wonders greater than those experienced by Yisrael when they camped around the Mishkan in the wilderness. How beautiful your footsteps [last generation] when you will ascend to the Beis Ha-Mikdash in pilgrims' sandals, o' daughter of the Generous One. The curves of your thighs [offspring of your loins; students of Torah] are like precious jewels, the work of a master craftsman. Your navel [Sanhedrin] is like a round goblet of wine which never lacks the proper blend of love and justice.

Your belly [oral tradition] is like a mound of tithed wheat surrounded by a hedge of roses [rabbinical ordinances]. Your two breasts [ben Yosef and ben David] are like two fawns [Moshe and Aharon], twins of the female roe [Shechinah]. Your neck [Beis Ha-Mikdash] is like a tower of white ivory [forgiveness]; your eyes [righteous tzaddikim] shed pools of tears when they take a soul-accounting in private, as well as when they correct their people in the public gates. Your nose [panel of judges] is upright when it foresees the eastern border of Yerushalayim extending from the tower of Levanon [Beis Ha-Mikdash] to far-off Damascus. Your head [king] whom you place above you is like Mount Carmel, and the hair [prophetic inspiration] that flows down from your head is like ARGaMaN [Uriel, Rapha'el, Gavriel, Micha'el, and Nuriel]. The Supreme King is bound to you in the merit of your hastening [to serve Him]. How beautiful and how pleasant you are, o' Yisrael, when you attain sublime love [for Your King] even through physical delights! When you reach your full stature, [your priests] will thus stand upright like towering palms to shower blessings upon you, while your breasts [congregations] will bend their faces down to the ground like clusters heavy with dates.

Yisrael says:

Indeed, I yearn to rise up [to my full spiritual stature,] to resemble a towering palm; but what if I can only grasp unto the lower branches?

The prophets respond:

Let your breasts [teachers] be like full clusters of the vine [filled with all the secrets of the Torah]. The spirit of your nostrils [ben Yosef and ben David] will then breathe forth the fragrance of the holy orchard of apples to enliven your souls. Make your tongue [pour out prayer] like the finest old wine; serve my Beloved by following in the footsteps of the upright [prophets] who roused the dead from their sleep with their lips.

Yisrael exclaims:

I am my Beloved's and His desire is for me! Come, my Beloved, let us go out to the field [exile], let us lodge in the villages [of the nations]. Let us arise early to the vineyards [synagogues], let us see if the vine has flowered, if the grape blossoms have opened, if the pomegranates have bloomed. There I will offer my love to You. Behold, the mandrakes [simple folk] have already begun to yield their fragrance; and on our doorsteps are all kinds of rare fruits [exceptional souls], new as well as old, which I have stored up for You, my Beloved.

VIII

Yisrael says to Hashem who calls us His sister:

O' that You would be like a brother to me, nursing from our Mother's breasts! Then even if I would find You outside, I would kiss You [in public] and no one could taunt me. I would then lead You and bring You into our Mother's House [Third Beis Ha-Mikdash] so that You could instruct me in Your ancient ways. I

would serve You from my spiced wine and pomegranate juice [stored away for the righteous]. O' that His left hand [justice] would support my head, and His right hand [unconditional love] embrace me!

Hashem speaks:

I caution you, [o' Yisrael, scattered among] the daughters of Yerushalayim [nations of the world], not to artificially arouse or awaken love [the Final Redemption] until such time as I desire.

Yisrael pleads:

[True, I am not worthy, but please consider:] Is there another nation like this who is ready to ascend from the wilderness [of exile], never having ceased to cleave joyously to her Beloved? Didn't I arouse Your love for me under the apple tree [Sinai]? Wasn't it there that I became Your mother, [so to speak,] to bear Your Name to the world? Wasn't it there that I conceived and bore You? [Therefore, I beg You:] Set me as a seal upon Your heart, as a seal upon Your arm, for love is strong as death, jealousy is cruel as the grave. Love's sparks are fiery coals, a flame of the Divine.

Hashem answers:

Many waters cannot extinguish love [My love for Yisrael], nor can floods drown [their love for Me]. Even when mankind will [wake up to the truth in the World-to-Come, and] offer all its worldly wealth for the sake of this love, they will be sorely ashamed [for it will be too late].

Yisrael's words to Hashem after the redemption concerning those souls who did not awaken in time:

We have a little sister, and she has no breasts. What shall we do for our sister on the day she shall be spoken for?

Hashem answers:

If only she be [found strong in her faith like] a wall, we shall build a castle of true yearning and aspiration upon her. But if she be [vacillating like] a door, we will enclose her [grave] with cedar.

The little sister says:

I am a wall [persevering in my faith], and my breasts are like strong towers. [Since my only desire is to serve Him forever after] may I be found worthy in His eyes of eternal peace!

Yisrael says:

[Yerushalayim is the] orchard of Shelomo, the Perfect One, at the hub of many empires. [While I was in exile from my land] He handed the orchard over to caretakers [foreign kings]. Each one was to pay one thousand pieces of silver for the use of its fruits. [Now that I have returned to Yerushalayim and] my orchard is mine, the one thousand goes directly to You, o' Shelomo, while two hundred goes to the caretakers who guarded its fruit [and defended my right to return home].

Hashem says:
[My beloved] even when you dwell in [foreign] gardens, the companions [angels and righteous tzaddikim in heaven] listen to your voice [speaking Torah and pouring your hearts out to Me in prayer]. Let Me hear you!
Yisrael prays:
[Quickly, let us] flee, my Beloved! [In Your haste to redeem me] be like a gazelle or a young deer on mountains of heavenly incense! [O' how sweet the fragrance of Your Name like precious oil poured forth!]